# Strategic Planning for the New and Small Business

# Strategic Planning for the New and Small Business

Fred L. Fry
and
Charles R. Stoner

UPSTART PUBLISHING COMPANY, INC.
The Small Business Publishing Company
Dover, New Hampshire

Published by Upstart Publishing Company, Inc.
A Division of Dearborn Publishing Group, Inc.
12 Portland Street
Dover, New Hampshire 03820
(800) 235-8866 or (603) 749-5071

Copyright © 1995 by Upstart Publishing Company, Inc.
All rights reserved. No part of this work may be reproduced or transmitted in any form or by any means without express written consent of the publisher.

Neither the author nor the publisher of this book is engaged in rendering, by the sale of this book, legal, accounting or other professional services. The reader is encouraged to employ the services of a competent professional in such matters.

Library of Congress Cataloging-in-Publication Data

Fry, Fred L.
    Strategic planning for the new and small business / Fred L. Fry and Charles R. Stoner.
        p.   cm.
    Includes index.
    ISBN: 0-936894-85-7
    1. Small business--Management. 2. New business enterprises--Management. 3. Small business--Planning. 4. Strategic planning. I. Stoner, Charles R. II. Title.
    HD62.7.F79  1995
    658.4'012--dc20                                                                94-43449
                                                                                                   CIP

Cover design by Pear Graphic Design, Portsmouth, NH.

Printed in the United States of America
10  9  8  7  6  5  4  3  2  1

For a complete catalog of Upstart's small business publications, call (800) 235-8866.

# CONTENTS

**PREFACE** ..................................................................................... xi

**PART I    INTRODUCTION TO STRATEGIC PLANNING** ................................ 1

**CHAPTER 1: THE NATURE OF STRATEGIC PLANNING** ............................. 3
    What Is a Small Business? ........................................................... 5
    Barriers to Planning in Small Business ......................................... 7
    Real Benefits of Strategic Planning .............................................. 8
    Defining Strategic Planning ....................................................... 12
    Determining the Planning Horizon ............................................. 13
    The Need for Vision .................................................................. 14
    The Strategic Planning Process .................................................. 15
    Discussion Questions ................................................................ 18

**PART II    THE ANALYSIS PHASE** .................................................... 21

**CHAPTER 2: ENVIRONMENTAL ANALYSIS** ........................................... 23
    The Value of Environmental Analysis .......................................... 23
    The Proactive Business .............................................................. 24
    What is Environmental Analysis? ................................................ 26
    The Macroenvironment .............................................................. 28
    The Industry Environment .......................................................... 32
    The Immediate Environment ...................................................... 36
    Performing the Environmental Analysis ....................................... 44
    Summary .................................................................................. 48
    Discussion Questions ................................................................ 51
    Case Study: Environmental Analysis for Gaston Ridge Home Health Care, Inc. ...... 53

**CHAPTER 3: INTERNAL ANALYSIS** ................................................... 59
    Value of Internal Analysis .......................................................... 60
    Elements of Internal Analysis ..................................................... 64
    Evaluating Financial Resources .................................................. 66
    Leverage Ratios ........................................................................ 79
    Profitability Ratios .................................................................... 80

Evaluating Marketing Resources........................................................... 82
　　　Evaluting Operational Resources .......................................................... 89
　　　Evaluting Human Resources................................................................. 92
　　　Focus on Strategy................................................................................. 93
　　　Summary................................................................................................ 94
　　　Discussion Questions ........................................................................... 94
　　　Case Study: Internal Analysis of Gaston Ridge Home Health Care, Inc.................. 97

**CHAPTER 4: RECOGNIZING DISTINCTIVE COMPETENCIES AND COMPETITIVE WEAKNESSES**................................................................. 103
　　　Environmental Opportunities vs. Relevent Business Opportunities....... 103
　　　The Role of Distinctive Competency .................................................... 104
　　　Identifying and Developing Areas of Distinctive Competence ............. 107
　　　Relating Distinctive Competencies to Relevant Business Opportunities............... 110
　　　Sustainable Competencies .................................................................. 111
　　　Distinctive Competencies and Strategic Planning ............................... 112
　　　Competitive Weaknesses .................................................................... 114
　　　Summary.............................................................................................. 115
　　　Discussion Questions .......................................................................... 115
　　　Case Study: Distinctive Competencies of Gaston Ridge Home Health Care, Inc.. 117

**PART III  THE ACTION PHASE: DEVELOPING THE PLAN**............................ 119

**CHAPTER 5: DEFINING THE FIRM'S MISSION AND STRATEGIC POSTURE**............... 121
　　　The Mission Statement ........................................................................ 122
　　　The Value of the Mission Statement.................................................... 122
　　　The Parts of a Mission Statement ....................................................... 123
　　　Developing The Firm's Strategic Posture ............................................ 128
　　　The Choice of Strategic Posture .......................................................... 135
　　　Assessing Progress ............................................................................. 139
　　　Summary.............................................................................................. 140
　　　Discussion Questions .......................................................................... 140
　　　Case Study: Mission and Strategic Posture of
　　　　　Gaston Ridge Home Health Care, Inc. .......................................... 143

**CHAPTER 6: SETTING GOALS** ................................................................... 145
　　　Benefits of Specific Goals .................................................................... 145
　　　How Are Goals Created?...................................................................... 147

Conflict Among Goals .................................................................................. 148
Levels and Time Frames ............................................................................. 149
Goal Segmentation Process ........................................................................ 153
Target Action Plans ..................................................................................... 154
The Integrative Goal Model ........................................................................ 158
Summary ..................................................................................................... 160
Discussion Questions .................................................................................. 160
Case Study: Company Goals for Gaston Ridge Home Health Care, Inc. ... 161

## CHAPTER 7: DEVELOPING UNIT STRATEGIES ................................................ 165
The Marketing Strategy .............................................................................. 167
The Operations Strategy ............................................................................. 172
The Human Resource Strategy ................................................................... 176
The Financial Strategy ................................................................................ 178
Summary ..................................................................................................... 182
Discussion Questions .................................................................................. 182
Case Study: Unit Strategies for Gaston Ridge Home Health Care, Inc. .... 183

## CHAPTER 8: WRITING THE PLAN ..................................................................... 185
The Nature of the Business ........................................................................ 187
The Mission Statement ............................................................................... 187
Posture and Goals ....................................................................................... 189
Unit Goals and Strategies ........................................................................... 190
Target Goals and Target Action Plans ....................................................... 197
Sharing the Plan ......................................................................................... 197
Summary ..................................................................................................... 198
A Final Caveat ............................................................................................. 198
Discussion Questions .................................................................................. 198

## APPENDIX A: SAMPLE STRATEGIC PLAN ........................................................ 201

## APPENDIX B: MANAGING THE CONSULTING PROCESS ................................ 207
The Nature of Consulting ........................................................................... 208
The Phases of the Consulting Process ....................................................... 209
Building Rapport ......................................................................................... 209
Defining the Problem ................................................................................. 211
Gathering and Analyzing Data ................................................................... 213
Making Recommendations ......................................................................... 215

**GLOSSARY** .................................................................................................. 219

**RESOURCES** ............................................................................................... 227

**INDEX** ......................................................................................................... 233

**LIST OF FIGURES**

| | | |
|---|---|---|
| Figure 1.1 | Sample SBA Definitions of Small Business | 6 |
| Figure 1.2 | Non-SBA Definitions of Small Business | 7 |
| Figure 1.3 | Small Business Strategic Planning Approach | 16 |
| Figure 1.4 | Strategic Plan Format | 19 |
| Figure 2.1 | Environmental Analysis | 27 |
| Figure 2.2 | Stages in Product Life Cycle | 33 |
| Figure 2.3 | Sources of Capital | 39 |
| Figure 2.4 | Competitive Analysis Profile | 42 |
| Figure 2.5 | Harberkorn Ace Hardware Competitive Analysis Profile | 43 |
| Figure 2.6 | Steps in Environmental Brainstorming | 49 |
| Figure 2.7 | Sources of External Information | 50 |
| Figure A.1 | Competitive Profile Analysis | 58 |
| Figure 3.1 | Internal Analysis Profile | 65 |
| Figure 3.2 | Waverly Custom Jewelers Comparative Balance Sheets | 69 |
| Figure 3.3 | Waverly Custom Jewelers Comparative Income Statements | 70 |
| Figure 3.4 | Comparative Balance Sheet Percentages (Vertical Analysis) | 71 |
| Figure 3.5 | Comparative Income Statement Percentage (Vertical Analysis) | 72 |
| Figure 3.6 | Waverly Custom Jewelers Cash Flow Statement | 73 |
| Figure 3.7 | Comparative Current Ratios | 75 |
| Figure 3.8 | Comparative Quick Ratios | 76 |
| Figure 3.9 | Comparative Inventory Turnover Ratios | 77 |
| Figure 3.10 | Comparative Asset Turnover Ratios | 77 |
| Figure 3.11 | Comparative Accounts Receivable Turnover Ratios | 78 |
| Figure 3.12 | Comparative Average Collection Period | 79 |
| Figure 3.13 | Comparative Debt to Asset Ratios | 79 |
| Figure 3.14 | Comparative Debt to Equity Ratios | 80 |
| Figure 3.15 | Comparative Return on Total Assets Ratios | 81 |
| Figure 3.16 | Location Factors For Retail Businesses | 85 |
| Figure 3.17 | Location Factors For Manufacturing Businesses | 85 |
| Figure B.1 | Internal Profile Analysis | 101 |

| Figure 4.1 | Areas of Distinctive Competence Commonly Recognized By Small Businesses | 109 |
|---|---|---|
| Figure 4.2 | Distinctive Competency Identification Process | 113 |
| Figure 5.1 | Joy's Toy Company Mission Statement | 125 |
| Figure 5.2 | Sample Mission Statements | 126 |
| Figure 5.3 | Variables Affecting Strategic Posture Choice | 136 |
| Figure 6.1 | Characteristics of Good Goals | 147 |
| Figure 6.2 | Levels of Small Business Goals | 150 |
| Figure 6.3 | Examples of Company and Unit-Level Goals | 150 |
| Figure 6.4 | Goal Time Frames | 151 |
| Figure 6.5 | Levels and Time Frames of Goals | 153 |
| Figure 6.6 | Target Action Plan | 155 |
| Figure 6.7 | Target Action Plan for Rabek Manufacturing, Inc. | 156 |
| Figure 6.8 | Integrative Goal Model | 159 |
| Figure 7.1 | Relationship Between Goals and Strategies | 166 |
| Figure 8.1 | Strategic Plan Format | 188 |
| Figure C.1 | Outline of the Final Written Report | 216 |

## LIST OF PROFILES

| Profile 1.1 | Atmosphere Processing, Inc. | 12 |
|---|---|---|
| Profile 2.1 | Peopod, Inc. | 25 |
| Profile 2.2 | Minnetonka, Inc. | 26 |
| Profile 2.3 | New Balance Athletic Shoe, Inc. | 34 |
| Profile 2.4 | Haberkorn Ace Hardware | 41 |
| Profile 3.1 | MMO Music Group | 60 |
| Profile 3.2 | Jacobsen Office Products | 61 |
| Profile 3.3 | Osborne Computer Corporation | 63 |
| Profile 3.4 | Kultur International Films, Ltd. | 84 |
| Profile 4.1 | Courtland Clubs | 105 |
| Profile 4.2 | Son Won Karate Academy | 106 |
| Profile 4.3 | Castille Motors | 107 |
| Profile 4.4 | Columbia Sportswear | 111 |
| Profile 5.1 | Leegin Creative Leather Products | 129 |
| Profile 5.2 | Desktop Channel | 130 |
| Profile 5.3 | The Blue Ribbon Car Wash | 131 |
| Profile 5.4 | Crystal Rug Cleaners | 132 |
| Profile 7.1 | Can Manufacturer's Outlets Beat the Price/ Image Relationship? | 169 |

| | | |
|---|---|---|
| Profile 7.2 | Antiques Unlimited | 171 |
| Profile 7.3 | Business Technology Center | 174 |
| Profile 7.4 | The Yarn and Hoop Shop | 177 |
| Profile 8.1 | Reder Electronics | 186 |
| Profile 8.2 | Haberkorn Ace Hardware | 191 |
| Profile 8.3 | Joy's Toys Company | 193 |

# PREFACE

IN BUSINESS, CAREFULLY developed plans can be the difference between success and failure. The planning process forces owners to consider both external forces and internal capabilities and to use that information to craft successful competitive strategies. Those strategies can then be implemented and evaluated against predetermined goals. Feedback from the results of those strategies influences future plans, creating a circular, ongoing planning process.

We have written this book for three types of readers:

1. Business students in colleges and universities who use the book as part of a small business management or business consulting course. In particular, the book is appropriate for schools that have a Small Business Institute (SBI) program sponsored by the U.S. Small Business Administration. Its information and structure are suitable for SBI teams to use in working with their small business clients. An appendix dealing with the consulting process is especially designed for these students.

2. People whose use the book as part of an education or training program leading to the possible launch of a privately owned business. This book provides thought-provoking material for anyone participating in pre-start-up training.

3. The current business owner. It is especially important for business owners to withdraw from the firefighting demands of operating a business and consider the future. This book is especially directed toward those who are considering formal strategic planning for the first time. We have tried to make the book useful for busy entrepreneurs who want to upgrade their planning skills without being overwhelmed with academic jargon or countless hours spent working through generic checklists of activities. The structure of the book encourages systematic thinking about the planning process, which can then be used to develop viable strategies for the business.

A particularly interesting feature of this book is that we have included an ongoing example throughout. At the end of most chapters, an example based on the same actual company, illustrates how the material discussed in the chapter is applied to a relatively new company. An appendix at the end of the book then pulls together the end-of-chapter information into a written strategic plan for the company, Gaston Ridge Home Health Care, Inc.

We acknowledge the help of a number of people and organizations in the production of this book. First, we thank all the Small Business Institute directors who asked that an earlier version of this book be re-created so that it could be used by SBI teams. We appreciate Upstart Publishing's contacting us about adding this book to their stable of small business-oriented books. In particular, we are grateful for the efforts of Jack Savage, Spencer Smith, and Karen Billipp at Upstart, who worked so well with us in putting the book into production. Thanks to John Bunch at Kansas State University for his helpful review of the earlier book and the suggestions he made to improve it. Special thanks to David Brennan at the University of St. Thomas for his input regarding the market for this book. Lastly, we thank our families for their encouragement.

PART I

# Introduction to Strategic Planning

THIS SECTION INTRODUCES the process of strategic planning and discusses its importance for both new and existing small businesses. Prelaunch strategic planning is critical to the success of a new venture. Indeed, in some cases, the process of developing plans may convince the new entrepreneur that the proposed idea should not be pursued! In most cases, the process will highlight opportunities and suggest ways to capitalize on those opportunities.

Strategic planning is important in order to keep an existing small business on track or move it to a higher plane. The process will also alert the business owner to threats on the horizon—to possible changes in the competitive environment that must receive attention now in order to prevent damage later—thus allowing a proactive operating stance rather than a reactive one. Thus, for both new ventures and existing businesses, strategic planning can be the key difference between success and failure.

# CHAPTER 1

# The Nature of Strategic Planning

OBJECTIVES

In this chapter you should learn:

1. what strategic planning is, and why it is important for new and small businesses.

2. why small business owners often do not plan.

3. how to overcome barriers to planning.

4. the real benefits of planning.

5. the importance of vision.

6. what a planning horizon is.

7. how the strategic planning model works.

PERHAPS NO ACTIVITY more fully symbolizes the American dream than being a small business owner. Taking charge, exercising personal creativity and independence, risking substantial personal funds, working long hours, and planning competitive business strategies are all part of the challenge and excitement that lure one into the world of small business. But the dream of owning and operating a small business can quickly turn into a nightmare of devastating frustrations if the firm's performance lags behind original projections and expectations. Although small firms make up over 95 percent of all United States businesses and employ over 50 percent of the private United States workforce, successful small business ventures are the exception rather than the rule. Of the new small businesses started each year, many will struggle and some will fail within the first five years. These casualties ignite deep and pervasive economic and social consequences. Perhaps more important, however, are the crushed hopes and ravaged fortunes of the strong-willed persons who fought to build their fledgling operations into viable competitive entities—and lost.

Although small businesses encounter difficulties for numerous reasons, certain consistent themes persist. Some companies are victims of unfortunate and largely unpredictable environmental and competitive occurrences. Some simply miss their market completely. However, the vast majority of small firms fall prey to their managers' own lack of foresight. These managers fail because they do not properly analyze and evaluate their relative competitive strengths. They fail because they are out of touch with their market and do not perceive shifting consumer tastes and preferences. They fail because they lack a clear blueprint of necessary goals and support activities and therefore encounter costly duplications, overlaps, and internal inefficiencies. In short, these businesses fail because their owners and managers are unable or unwilling to focus on one of the prime determinants of business success—strategic planning.

Consider the following example. Bill Stern was an intelligent and industrious 28-year-old high school physics teacher. Bill felt particularly restricted and unfulfilled as a teacher and yearned for greater freedom and independence. The logical choice—start his own business. Bill was committed to working hard to make this career change a success. In exploring his entrepreneurial options, he was driven by a strong desire to do hands-on work and not be confined to the rigors and structure of an 8-to-5 job. Because Bill loved and appreciated motorcycles and motorcycle racing and was an accomplished motorcycle mechanic, he decided to open a motorcycle repair shop. Eighteen months later, after exhausting the family's savings and enduring a regular regimen of 70-hour work weeks, Bill recognized that the business was doomed and filed for bankruptcy.

Essentially, Bill's business decisions were spontaneous and unplanned. In the beginning, he reacted to a strong internal need for independent activity without undertaking a meaningful analysis or evaluation of his business prospects. He did not address important questions about the actual demand for the proposed service. Bill relied on personal opinion and feeling and consequently was overly optimistic about market potential.

Further, no competitive analysis was performed. Although Bill knew the names of his major competitors, he had no feel for the size of their businesses, the market niches they attempted to reach, or the degree of success they experienced. His repair shop was geared to the hard-core, serious motorcyclist.

Unfortunately, this was the same segment of the market that his two major competitors (in terms of size and reputation) had targeted. Careful planning and analysis would have revealed that another large segment of the market—the weekend rider who didn't know much about motorcycles—might have been a more viable target for his business. Here, his major competition would have been dealers, who generally have reputations for poor service and high prices. Recognizing this niche and exploiting it through a well-planned advertising program could have attracted numerous customers. (However, a careful analysis of the number of motorcycle riders in the geographic area in relation to the number of competing repair shops would have dissuaded him from moving into this high-risk, low-potential business in the first place.)

Bill's is only one of the many unfortunate stories of good intentions and hard work undermined by a lack of solid, systematic planning. A number of research studies have demonstrated clear and positive associations between planning and organizational performance, and inadequate planning is regularly reported as one of the key causes or predictors of small business failure. Stated simply, thorough and systematic planning can significantly discriminate between successful and unsuccessful small businesses. Accordingly, the purpose of this book is to help small business owners, managers, students, and consultants develop a solid, logical, strategic approach to small business planning.

## What Is a Small Business?

There are a variety of definitions of a "small" business. The Small Business Administration (SBA) has different definitions depending on the industry (see Figure 1.1, p. 6). In some cases, a business can be quite large and still be within the SBA's definition. A precise definition of small is stressed only when government programs are considered. For example, government procurement programs have requirements to ensure that certain percentages of government contracts go to small businesses. Similarly, funding sources that include state or federal involvement are often reserved for small businesses. In these cases, it is important to know when a business is considered small and when it is not. While the formal designation of small business is industry specific, one conclusion is clear: Most businesses in the United States are small businesses.

Longenecker, Moore, and Petty use different definitions in their text, as shown in Figure 1.2, on p. 7. Generally, they include all businesses with fewer than 100 employees. Given this definition, over 95 percent of all businesses in the United States are formally designated as small. However, there are other qualitative requirements a firm must meet in order to be considered small.

In reality, most business owners never give explicit attention to any of these definitions. They simply see themselves as being small-businesspersons. Ultimately, if an owner thinks the business is small, it probably is!

Figure 1.1

### SAMPLE SBA DEFINITIONS OF SMALL BUSINESS

| Industry | Size Standard (number of employees, or revenue in millions) |
| --- | --- |
| Computer Programming Services | $ 7.0 |
| Stationery and Office Supplies | 100 |
| General Contractors | $ 17.0 |
| Dental Equipment and Supplies | 500 |
| Motors and Generators | 1,000 |
| Household Vacuum Cleaners | 750 |
| Flowers and Florist's Supplies | 100 |
| Furniture Stores | $ 3.5 |
| Newspapers | 500 |
| Trucking | $ 12.5 |
| Detective, Guard, and Armored-Car Services | $ 6.0 |
| Physical Fitness Facilities | $ 3.5 |
| Retail Bakeries | $ 3.5 |
| Motorcycles | 500 |
| Motor Vehicle Dealers | $ 11.5 |
| Motion Picture and Video Tape Production | $ 14.5 |
| Heating and Air-Conditioning Equipment and Supplies | 100 |
| Travel Agencies | $ .5 |
| Carpet and Upholstery Cleaning | $ 2.5 |
| Flat Glass | 1,000 |
| Paint, Glass, and Wallpaper Stores | $ 3.5 |

Figure 1.2

**NON-SBA DEFINITIONS OF A
SMALL BUSINESS**

1. Financing of the business is supplied by one individual or a small group. Only in a rare case would the business have more than 15 or 20 owners.

2. Except for its marketing function, the firm's operations are geographically localized.

3. Compared to the biggest firms in the industry, the business is small.

4. The number of employees in the business is usually fewer than 100.

(Source: Longenecker, Moore, and Petty, p. 32)

## Barriers to Planning in Small Business

Even though the planning process is generally considered to be valuable, many small business owners openly resist planning and do not feel the need to involve themselves in the process. Although this resistance has numerous causes and sources, certain common arguments persist. Although these arguments are deeply felt, they are often based on misconception rather than fact.

First, many small business owners contend that while planning may be important for large businesses, it is unnecessary for small businesses. They insist, "I don't need to plan. That's something the big boys do." This notion is an extremely dangerous form of denial. In fact, planning may be more critical for small businesses than for large ones. For example, the small business is likely to be seriously damaged by even minor market or competitive misreadings. Large firms, on the other hand, can more readily absorb the costs of such mistakes. The small business is therefore significantly more vulnerable to the consequences of poor planning.

Second, some entrepreneurs suggest that since the small business is so short-term oriented, planning for the future is only a philosophical exercise. But, planning is necessary to take advantage of opportunities and defend against adverse changes and demands that exist whether the firm's planning horizon is lengthy or compressed. The smaller business is no better able to isolate itself from these forces than the larger firm.

Third, many small business owners feel that formalized planning confines, constrains, and limits their firm's flexibility. Indeed, flexibility, or the capacity to respond quickly and adapt to changing environmental conditions, may be the key competitive edge small businesses have over large firms. However, the assertion that planning restricts this flexibility is based on a misunderstanding of the nature and dynamics of the strategic planning philosophy. Strategic plans are not unyielding parameters, cast in stone, never to be adjusted, modified, or reviewed until the expiration of the operating period to which they apply. Rather, the planning process is a means of gathering information, analyzing the impact of this information on the firm, and refocusing efforts to meet new demands and conditions. As such, strategic planning offers the means to enhance rather than limit the small firm's flexibility.

A fourth frequently held view is that intuitive, unwritten plans are sufficient. A typical small firm owner may say, "I have a plan all worked out in my head, and that's good enough." Unfortunately, it usually isn't. A meaningful plan must analyze the complex interaction of numerous forces and propose a guide for how the firm will deal with these forces. Given the pressures and demands of day-to-day operations, it is folly to believe that even the most insightful owner/manager can track, monitor, analyze, and develop strategies for dealing with these forces on a timely basis without relying on some formal, written, systematic process. In short, it is extremely difficult for entrepreneurs to transfer what is in their minds into sets of objective realities that guide their firms.

## Real Benefits of Strategic Planning

It may be intuitively clear that increases in the level and quality of planning are associated with better overall business performance. However, a more detailed explanation of some of the benefits of strategic planning may be useful.

The overriding benefit is best understood by realizing that strategic planning is a change-oriented process. New and small business owners operate in a dynamic, volatile, and ever-changing environment. They must sift through, understand, and appropriately respond to the complex maze of rapid-fire changes they confront daily. Unless the owner senses the pace and direction of change, environmental shifts can overwhelm a small business operation. Strategic planning encourages a careful and systematic reading of shifts in technology, competitor position, and customer tastes. Further, the strategic planning process involves formulating actions to respond to these critical readings. Accordingly, change becomes a driving force of evolving strength rather than a jarring threat to stability. Consider the following example.

In an industry where similar-sized competitors have recently struggled or gone out of business at an alarming rate, Ross Marketing Services, Inc., has grown and prospered. To a large extent, that success has come because the company recognized that its survival depended on strategically addressing the change within its industry.

In business for 42 years, Ross has resisted the tendency of many small advertising agencies to maintain their traditional, sole focus on the creative side of advertising. Ross reasoned that since graphic arts were rapidly becoming computer-driven, a limited creative focus would be increasingly difficult to maintain competitively. Ross paid particular attention to changing customer needs and made the strategic commitment to transform the business to be able to meet those needs more fully. Accordingly, Ross launched three new business units: Ross Training and Motivation (with services such as events marketing and sales promotion and training), Ross Lead Management (with services such as database management and lead generation programs), and Ross Custom Publishing (with services such as production art and technical writing).

These three new business areas, along with the core Ross Advertising, have enabled Ross to meet an array of customer demands and provide services it previously subcontracted. The focus on change continues, even as Ross Marketing Services, Inc., was recently named Small Business of the Year by its local Chamber of Commerce. Demonstrating true strategic thinking, Ross's leaders reason that looking at new technology and blending that technology to meet evolving customer needs will continue to be the formula for success.

Beyond the broad issue of change, strategic planning offers five specific benefits. First, strategic planning helps focus on the competitive nature of the firm. Externally, the plan encourages the managers to look at the competition, the economy, the community, and other key environmental factors to determine where the firm fits. Internally, the plan forces the managers to assess the firm's strengths and weaknesses. Indeed, this analysis may reveal hidden vulnerabilities or unique strengths. As a result, necessary changes in strategy can be made. It is hoped that initial planning efforts will foster the habit of periodically reassessing the firm's competitive position. In fact, the process of carefully assessing the business and becoming aware of its potential and capacity may be as significant as the plan that is eventually derived from this analysis.

An example illustrates this point. A local businesswoman had been regularly counseled by a business consultant to develop a plan for her growing operation. She was, of course, quite busy and never got around to it. One day, the woman rather excitedly reported, "Guess what, I've started on my plan, even though I haven't finished. But one night while working on it, I suddenly discovered a problem in the business that I corrected the very next day." Because this businesswoman had begun to prepare a plan objectively, she uncovered a correctable weakness she had not seen before.

A second benefit is that the strategic plan sets a formal direction for the business. It helps determine where the business is going. In addition, and perhaps as important, it helps determine where the firm is not going. Thus, the plan helps owners focus on specific objectives and stay there. This planning orientation allows the small business managers to work proactively—to look to the future, anticipate, and plan for change. Managers of proactive firms anticipate opportunities and position themselves to benefit from them. Similarly, these managers recognize impending threats and pursue decisive action to deal with them before disaster strikes. Crisis management is replaced by a more fluid, logical, and systematic approach. The firm's management understands and treats change as a competitive weapon rather than as an uncontrollable nuisance to be ignored as long as economically and competitively possible.

The following example highlights the importance of competitive awareness and focus. An extremely enterprising young man possessed classic entrepreneurial flair. He was involved in three different business ventures and personally headed a firm that operated in such diverse areas as insurance, real estate, and managerial consulting. Not surprising, he was experiencing problems in nearly all phases of his businesses. One might logically assume that the underlying cause of his difficulties was that he was attempting to do too much—spreading himself too thin. While this was true, the condition stemmed from a total disregard for formal planning. He failed to provide a clear view and direction for each business. No attempt was made to prescribe what needed to be accomplished, when, and by whom. He simply reacted and allocated his time and his firm's resources toward the most pressing problem of the day. Consequently, most efforts were temporary fixes that added little to the development of his firm. Additionally, he regularly missed important and potentially rewarding bids and contracts because his focus was on putting out yesterday's fires rather than looking for tomorrow's opportunities. Strategic planning helped this man understand his total business better and develop some concrete moves to enhance his competitive position. Since what needed to be done was now clear, meaningful delegation was possible. He was free to concentrate on making contacts, meeting potential customers, and engaging in the necessary public relations work he was uniquely qualified to perform. Important opportunities were realized and acted on, and internal operations ran more smoothly.

The above example suggests a third benefit of strategic planning. As the firm's direction became clearer, employees were allowed to make decisions. They were allowed to use their skills more fully. They became surer of themselves and more comfortable in their roles, and their jobs were enriched. Most workers have a strong desire to know what's going on and how their efforts contribute to the overall business objectives. Without a clear notion of these objectives, employees are often frustrated and dissatisfied. Planning helps employees become part of the organizational team. As employees know more of what the owner has in mind, they become more motivated, more willing to suggest ideas, and more willing to exert the extra effort needed to give the business an edge over the competition. This is extremely important for the small business. Because a small firm is competitively vulnerable, employee efforts and suggestions often make the difference between success and failure. Indeed, as the business leaders clearly communicate direction, philosophy, and objectives to their workers, the returns are likely to be dramatic.

Fourth, a business plan is useful to the board of directors or the advisory board. These people are not involved with the day-to-day operations of the firm. However, their job is to offer guidance and advice. The plan gives them a basis for their analysis, evaluation, and suggestions for the firm's overall operations.

---

**PROFILE 1.1 ATMOSPHERE PROCESSING INC.**

Alan Hering, owner of Atmosphere Processing, Inc., has this to say about the need for planning: ". . . the company became profitable and found itself doubling in size every three years. But the growth was unplanned; too few people, insufficient plan—a painful experience. . . . We had heard about something called strategic planning and decided there had to be a better way.

"We started talking to some consultants about strategic planning. It made sense. . . . I hope today that we're in a position to take a more disciplined approach. . . . We need it so everyone knows where we are going and how we're going to get there."

---

Finally, the existence of a formal, overall strategic plan makes the creation of special-purpose plans—such as financial business plans—much easier. In fact, the strategic plan contains most of the information used in developing specialized plans. Although a manager may feel that planning is difficult and time-consuming, the impact of the planning process is overwhelmingly positive.

## Defining Strategic Planning

Strategic planning is a powerful management tool designed to help the small business competitively adapt to anticipated environmental changes. Specifically, the strategic planning process provides an overview and analysis of the business and its relevant environment—it describes the firm's current condition and recognizes the key external factors affecting its success. The process then prescribes an outline, or action plan, of how the business will proceed to capitalize on its strengths and minimize its weaknesses and threats.

Although business owners are occasionally asked to write "financial business plans" in order to secure financing, these should not be confused with strategic planning or strategic plans. Financial business plans are single-purpose instruments. As such, they tend to be very specific, reasonably brief, somewhat optimistic overviews of the business, its product line and management, and the proposed use of funds. By contrast, strategic plans require more depth and breadth of coverage. Their focus is the future. They consider internal strengths and weaknesses, since both may affect the strategy selected. They are regularly used and frequently revised to reflect new trends and developments. The strategic plan is both an analytical tool and a working document that guides management action over a specified period of time.

## Determining the Planning Horizon

The noted economist John Maynard Keynes once said, "In the long run we are all dead." We need to be more specific than that in determining the short-, medium-, and long-term goals for a firm! In general (but not always), long-term planning refers to anything beyond the next five years. A three-year period is often the target for medium-term plans. Short-term plans are generally for one year or less. Accountants, on the other hand, often refer to anything over one year as long range.

Actually, the determination of long- versus short-range goals is a function of the industry and the type of product or service. A utility company necessarily looks 15 to 20 years ahead because of how long it takes to build a power plant. A small janitorial service may have no reason to look beyond one year. A small manufacturer is somewhere in between.

The above examples introduce a key factor in planning—that of the firm's planning horizon. The planning horizon is the time required to implement a major strategic change. Beyond that time period, a manager need only do some casual monitoring, because the business can react to any change that might develop.

Suppose, for example, I own a restaurant. I could spend a considerable part of my time studying new housing developments and specific projected growth areas of the city. On the other hand, the total time required to build a new restaurant is probably between six months and one year. Since migration is a relatively slow process, I will have ample time to study site locations once I determine that I do in fact need to expand.

Lest this discussion be seen as encouraging myopia, it should be underscored that the concern is strategic reaction time. The environment must always be monitored to determine developing trends. But serious study need only be done when either a strategic change is desired or when significant changes in the environment dictate. Attempts to react to each minute change will lead to overreaction and/or unnecessary concern with the long run when it cannot be adequately assessed.

The following example illustrates this. An Italian restaurant had an excellent reputation for good, moderately priced food, but its location and size eliminated a major portion of the city's population as potential customers. The owner adroitly decided to add a new location in a growing section of the city, close to a major shopping mall. The move was handled well, and profits flourished because there were few similar restaurants in the area. Less than three years later, the city was plunged into a major recession. In addition, two restaurant chains opened sites within two blocks on either side of the restaurant. At first glance, this would appear to be a classic case of bad planning. Shouldn't the owner have been able to predict three to five years in advance? The answer is no. Even though the restaurant is now in a highly competitive market, there was no way that either the recession or the increased competition could have been projected. The changes were outside the manager's strategic reaction time. His planning horizon was not that distant and should not have been expected to be. The move was a wise move at the time and perhaps would not have been made if concern for what might happen had overridden the decision.

If managers extend the horizon too far, they may lock themselves into a strategy that later becomes inappropriate; if the horizon is too short, opportunities may be missed. A major equipment manufacturer, planning too far into the future, purchased several sites and began construction. If the company's owners had done a better job of analyzing their existing planning horizon, they would have determined that their growth was tapering off as a result of increasing competition from international firms as well as a recessionary economy. They not only did not build on all the sites, but they eventually sold some sites, stopped construction on others, and closed some existing facilities.

Underestimating the planning horizon is the more frequent error. Most firms tend to concentrate on the short term. Managers are so busy fighting fires that they do not take time to consider needed changes within their planning horizon. Managers must consider how long it will take to react to a change in the environment, and plan accordingly.

## The Need for Vision

Many entrepreneurs are visionaries. Sam Walton of Wal-Mart, J. W. Marriott of Marriott Hotels, Paul Galvin of Motorola, John Johnson of Johnson Publications, and Michael Dell of Dell Computers all had a vision for a new product, service, or method of distribution. Here, vision represented a glimpse of some desirable and possible future for the business. These entrepreneurs' vision became the unifying force for their respective organizations.

Some of these entrepreneurs overcame significant hardships to pursue their vision. In addition to possessing drive and a commitment to hard work, they each had the ability to identify a need and fill it. They all had the ability to focus on the market and to marshal resources necessary to launch and expand their venture.

Vision and dedication are necessary ingredients for successful small business owners. As the business environment becomes more and more complex, it is necessary to focus on the future in order to continue to meet the needs of an ever-changing customer. Vision is the precursor to planning. The owner's vision is translated through the strategic planning process into a mission, objectives, and carefully designed strategies.

## The Strategic Planning Process

Dwight D. Eisenhower once said, "Plans are nothing; planning is everything." While it may not be true that the strategic plan, itself, is nothing, it is true that planning is everything. Although it is important to have a written plan, the strategic planning process is critically important for new and small businesses.

Figure 1.3 (p. 16) highlights a small business strategic planning process, made up of two distinct phases. During the analysis phase, the owner develops a clear recognition of the key threats and opportunities in the firm's relevant external environment by concentrating on present environmental forces, projecting trends, and anticipating changes. Managers must not only identify and track changes in key environmental factors, they must carefully assess the impact these forces and changes will have on the firm and its operations. Environmental analysis is therefore future-oriented, seeking to recognize the problems and potential created for the firm by changes in its environment. Chapter 2 presents a thorough overview of the details and specifics of environmental analysis.

Whereas environmental analysis concentrates on forces external to the organization, internal firm analysis evaluates the firm's internal strengths

Figure 1.3

**SMALL BUSINESS
STRATEGIC PLANNING APPROACH**

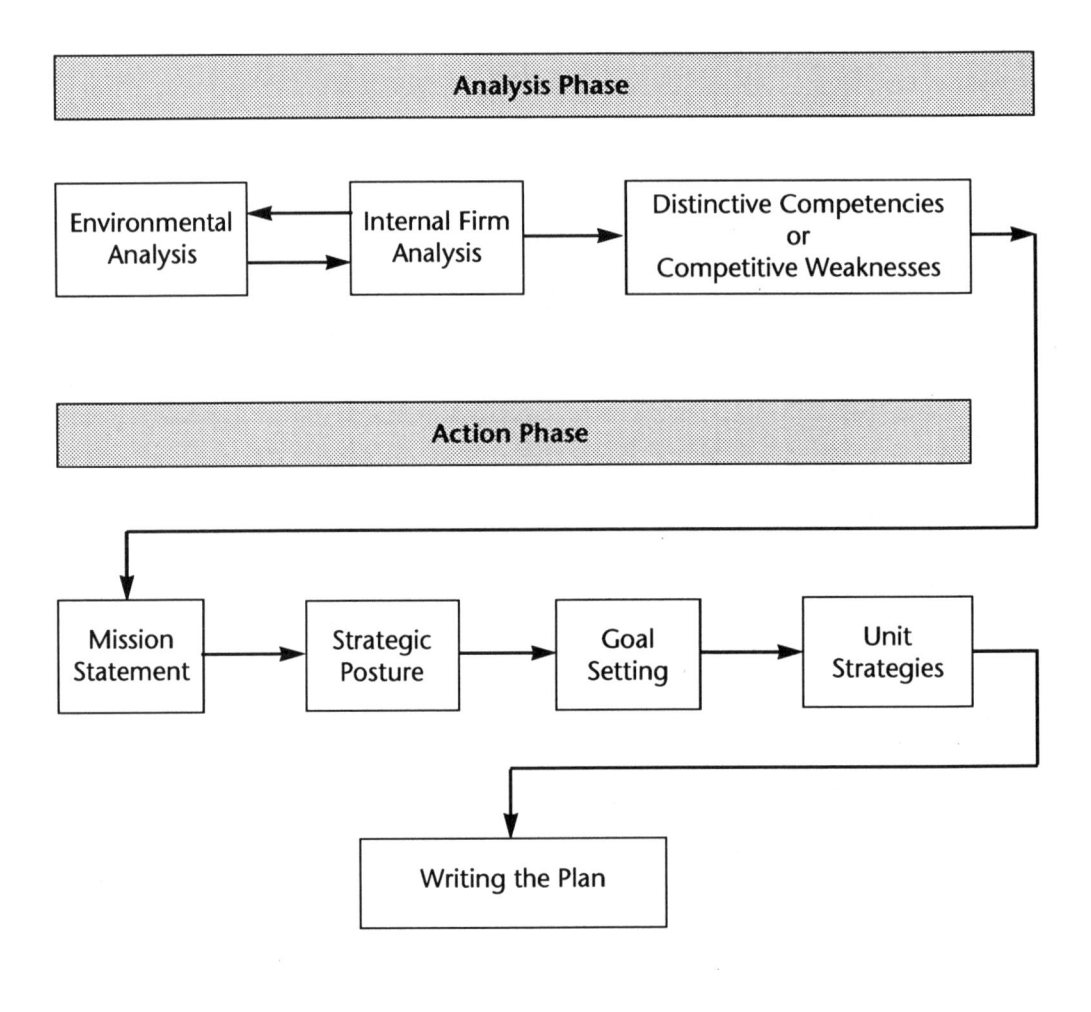

### Analysis Phase

Environmental Analysis ↔ Internal Firm Analysis → Distinctive Competencies or Competitive Weaknesses

### Action Phase

Mission Statement → Strategic Posture → Goal Setting → Unit Strategies → Writing the Plan and weaknesses. A number of important internal considerations must be explored. These will be discussed in Chapter 3.

Environmental and internal analyses enable the firm to portray carefully and objectively both its special competencies and its relative competitive weaknesses. A distinctive competency is any area in which the firm possesses a meaningful edge over its competitors. Similarly, competitive weaknesses represent areas in which the competitors' relative strengths are significant or overwhelming. Armed with this information, the manager can realize and capitalize on evolving competitive opportunities (distinctive competencies) and develop protective measures to minimize the harmful impact of materializing threats and obstacles (competitive weaknesses). Recognizing competencies and weaknesses enables the business owner to choose broad strategies for dealing with these forces. The impact of special competencies and competitive weaknesses is covered in Chapter 4.

After environmental and firm data have been analyzed and evaluated and the firm's special competencies and competitive weaknesses delineated, the manager is ready to embark on the action phase of strategic planning. Here, the manager processes the environmental and firm data and assessments, contemplates their implications, and structures a working plan to guide the firm's activities.

The first steps in this action phase require determining the mission of the business and its strategic posture. It is a logical, functional, and integral process that can guide the firm along the path of success. A discussion of the mission and strategic postures is covered in Chapter 5.

Once a clear understanding of the firm's mission and overall strategic posture is in mind (and written down), the manager may then focus on specific goals for the business. Setting achievable and measurable goals for the company as a whole and for operating units or divisions is an important process. In Chapter 6, the topic of goal setting is covered in depth in order to illustrate both the importance of goal setting and the method of doing it.

Strategies breathe life into goals. Essentially, a goal statement says, "This is what we want to do or what we want to be," while strategies say, "This is how we are going to do it." Decisions to segment the market, change pricing, alter sales policies, acquire additional funds, and change production methods are examples of unit strategies undertaken to move the firm toward the realization of its goals. Unit strategies are presented and discussed in Chapter 7.

The best strategies in the world are of limited value if they are not written down. Chapter 8 presents and discusses a format for the written plan. Appendix A then shows an example of a completed strategic plan based on a real business. This plan can be used as a guideline for developing a plan for any business.

Figure 1.4 is a sneak preview of the strategic plan format. As you move through the rest of the book, you may want to refer back to Figure 1.4 to see how the actions discussed fit into the final strategic planning document.

## Discussion Questions

1. Why is strategic planning perhaps even more important for a small business than it is for a large business?

2. If planning has so many benefits, why don't small business owners do it?

3. Choose a firm with which you are familiar. What specific benefits could arise from doing formal planning in that particular firm?

4. Estimate the appropriate planning horizon for
    a. a utility company.
    b. a bowling alley.
    c. an auto repair shop.
    d. a small manufacturer that is a subcontractor for a large equipment manufacturer.
    e. a dairy.
    f. a university.
    g. a computer software company.

5. How could the major parts of the planning model be used in
    a. national planning for a country?
    b. individual career planning?

6. Give examples of companies whose owners appear to have vision.

## References

Justin G. Longenecker, Carlos W. Moore, and J. William Petty. *Small Business Management: An Entrepreneurial Emphasis.* Cincinnati: South-Western, 1994.

Figure 1.4

**STRATEGIC PLAN FORMAT**

I.  **The nature of the business**
    A. Description of the business
    B. Industry characteristics
    C. Competition
    D. Location description
    E. Distinctive competencies

II. **Mission statement**
    A. Product line or services provided
    B. Philosophy of the business

III. **Posture and goals**
    A. Strategic posture
    B. Company-level goals
        1. Horizon goals
        2. Near-term goals

IV. **Unit-level goals and strategies**
    A. Marketing
        1. Target market
        2. Product-line strategy
        3. Pricing strategy
        4. Distribution strategy
        5. Promotion strategy
        6. Service strategy
    B. Production
        1. Location in distribution channel
        2. Make-or-buy decisions
        3. Lease/purchase of equipment
        4. Sourcing strategy
        5. Production methods
    C. Human resources
        1. Employment strategy
        2. Promote from within versus hiring managers from outside
        3. Wage/salary/benefit strategy
    D. Financial
        1. Debt/equity strategy
        2. Capital sourcing strategy
        3. Growth/stability strategy
        4. Financial projections

V.  **Target goals and target action plan**

# PART II

# THE ANALYSIS PHASE

IN THIS SECTION, we discuss the necessary analysis that precedes the development of a strategic plan. The actions discussed in the next three chapters are the foundation of strategic planning. The time spent on these tasks results in the assessment and understanding of both the internal and external factors affecting the business. After performing these steps, a meaningful strategy can be developed to meet business objectives. Chapter 2 addresses the external environment. Chapter 3 discusses the internal analysis. These analyses are then combined and used to develop distinctive competencies, discussed in Chapter 4.

# CHAPTER 2

# Environmental Analysis

## OBJECTIVES

After reading this chapter you should understand

1. what is meant by external analysis.
2. the major types of external information available.
3. sources of external information.
4. how to determine which information should be monitored carefully and which should be only casually assessed.
5. how to collect and analyze data.
6. the essence of an Environmental Threats and Opportunities Profile.

## The Value of Environmental Analysis

PLANNING IN TODAY'S dynamic environment may be the single most significant factor affecting a company's success or failure. Small businesses must be particularly sensitive to environmental influences for two important reasons.

First, the small firm's responsiveness to environmental issues may be a source of considerable competitive strength. The small business can stay closer to the consumer, holding a monitoring thumb on the pulse of its target customers. By virtue of its smaller size, the firm can move with speed, flexibility, and sensitivity to accommodate shifts in customer preferences. Larger, more structured, and hierarchically bound organizations may be unable to alter their direction or focus quickly. Consequently, the small business may be able to etch out a competitive edge against large firms.

Second, small businesses are particularly vulnerable to environmental influences. They can ill afford to misread the environment. Although one mistake or one misreading of a critical environmental trend may affect a large firm adversely, the error can usually be easily absorbed into the breadth of its total operations. However, a similar mistake may destroy a small business. Rare is the small business whose resources can withstand such mistakes.

Certainly, managers of small businesses wish to realize and capitalize on the opportunities and benefits inherent in their reduced size and to protect themselves from the critical influence of rapidly materializing environmental threats and obstacles. Therefore, a careful and accurate determination of key environmental influences and changes is essential. A thorough environmental analysis is the difference between a proactive and reactive business.

## The Proactive Business

One of the themes noted and built on throughout this book is that planning stems from a proactive perspective. Simply stated, a proactive business looks to the future and anticipates and plans for change. One reason for emphasizing environmental analysis so strongly is that it helps the business develop a proactive rather than reactive style of management. The proactive manager sees opportunities on the horizon and positions the business to benefit from them. Proactive managers also recognize impending threats and take decisive actions to overcome or mitigate these before disaster strikes.

A reactive business, however, is driven by day-to-day demands. Events occur and the firm responds. This business is always undergoing a new, usually unanticipated trauma. Crisis management is the evolving style of operation, and putting out the largest fire is the focus of activities. In all likelihood, the business that fails to recognize and analyze its environment will become the victim of changes and forces within that environment. The literature on small business failures is filled with examples.

An example of proactive thinking is featured in Profile 2.1. Andrew and Thomas Parkinson took advantage of two significant trends. One was the increasing use of home computers featuring on-line services. The second was the decrease in leisure time among contemporary families. They capitalized on both trends to provide a service for those for whom time is perhaps more precious than money.

---

### PROFILE 2.1: PEAPOD, INC.

In selected Jewel Food Stores in Chicago and Safeway, Inc. stores in San Francisco, some of the shoppers do a careful job of shopping even though they are not shopping for themselves. That is because they are employees of Peapod, Inc., a computerized shopping service. Founders Andrew and Thomas Parkinson have made the idea of grocery shopping via computer a reality for over 7,000 customers.

Peapod's customers use their home computers to "shop" for groceries. They are able to select specific brands, compare prices, browse electronic "aisles" such as cereal and breakfast or ethnic foods to get ideas, and even use coupons. The software, which is the key to the operation, also allows customers to maintain grocery lists and indicate acceptable substitutes if the store is out of stock on a particular item. The orders are then transmitted via computer, telephone, or fax to Peapod's professional shoppers. The shoppers gather the groceries, which are delivered within a 90-minute window. Customers can pay by check, credit card, or computer account. Customers subscribe to the service either on a flat-rate basis or on a per-usage basis.

Projected sales for Peapod are $15 million, and plans include expanding to Boston. All this is possible because two entrepreneurs found a way to combine technology with one of the most mundane of all tasks—shopping for groceries.

(Source: Marsh, p. B2)

---

Another example of the impact of environmental analysis and the importance of proactivity is the former Minnetonka, Inc. (see Profile 2.2, p. 26). Taylor's success, at least in part, came from carefully assessing his environment, analyzing unmet consumer needs, capitalizing on these opportunities, and constantly being poised to modify and change direction in light of environmental (competitive) influences. Taylor was proacting and, as such, succeeded in industries dominated by giant international firms.

---

### PROFILE 2.2: MINNETONKA, INC.

Minnetonka, Inc. is a classic story of entrepreneurial zeal and astute environmental awareness. Robert Taylor sought to enter the highly lucrative yet competitively saturated soap-manufacturing business. His prospects seemed highly unlikely given the size, experience, and public awareness of his competitors—names like Proctor & Gamble, Armour-Dial, Lever Brothers, and Colgate-Palmolive. Taylor recognized an untapped niche within the industry, however, by sensing that liquid soap dispensed from a plastic container by a pump possessed significant advantages over traditional bar soap. Minnetonka's Softsoap was born.

The success of Softsoap was fantastic. In its introductory year (1980), Softsoap's sales soared to $35 million. Major competitors, who initially dismissed Softsoap as a short-lived fad, soon recognized the potential to be gleaned from this innovation. To his credit, Taylor was not blinded by success. In fact, his foresight was as strong as ever. Rather then rest on his laurels, Taylor reasoned that his success placed him in a most precarious position. His business had grown by carefully positioning Softsoap to appeal to consumer needs and to avoid head-on, direct competition with the soap-industry giants. Yet he knew that eventually his admirable profit picture would lure larger firms into the liquid soap market, thereby establishing direct competition. He reasoned that Minnetonka could not withstand such competition. Taylor was already planning his next move—Showermate, a new product aimed at a new niche. He realized that if this proved successful, he would again be inundated by competition—so he returned to the drawing board. The result—Minnetonka presented another new product, a plaque-fighting toothpaste in a pump, called Check-Up. Again, Taylor was positioning himself in a major industry but avoiding direct competitive threats. An indication of Taylor's success was his sale of Minnetonka in 1989 to Unilever for $376.2 million.

(Source: Business Week)

---

## What Is Environmental Analysis?

A business's environment establishes the context within which the firm functions. A business's environment comprises a set of factors (conditions and forces) that affect the business and impact its performance but that are external to and largely beyond its control. When managers perform an external or environmental analysis, they identify and examine key external factors and assess and evaluate the impact these factors will likely have on the firm's operations and success. Managers analyze present forces and also attempt to project trends and anticipate changes. Environmental analysis is future-oriented. The business owner seeks to determine what problems and opportunities will likely be created by changes in the environment.

The process of analyzing the environment is illustrated schematically by the inverted triangle shown in Figure 2.1. The broadest set of variables comprises those economic, technological, social, and political variables that may affect the business in only a general way. These variables make up the **macroenvironment**. A somewhat narrower set of variables that may have a more significant impact make up the **industry environment**. These factors tell us something about the dynamics of the industry and the players within it. A third category of variables, much closer to the business and much more dramatic in their impact, makes up the immediate environment. The **immediate environment** comprises specific competitors, suppliers, the cost of capital, the labor force, and the ambiance of the community.

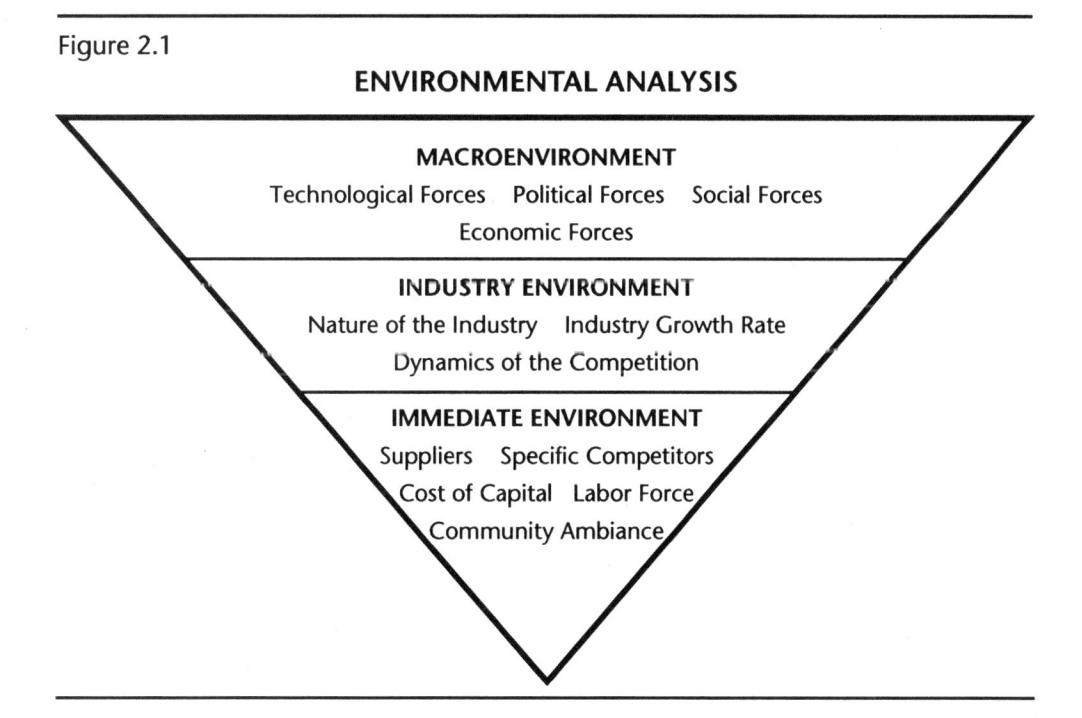

Figure 2.1

**ENVIRONMENTAL ANALYSIS**

**MACROENVIRONMENT**
Technological Forces   Political Forces   Social Forces
Economic Forces

**INDUSTRY ENVIRONMENT**
Nature of the Industry   Industry Growth Rate
Dynamics of the Competition

**IMMEDIATE ENVIRONMENT**
Suppliers   Specific Competitors
Cost of Capital   Labor Force
Community Ambiance

## The Macroenvironment

The macroenvironment comprises variables that are not company or industry specific. These variables apply to and affect all firms, although their impacts may be felt differently by each firm. Four areas of macroenvironmental variables need to be considered: technological changes, political and legal changes, social and demographic changes, and economic changes.

### TECHNOLOGICAL CHANGES

Clearly, we live in a time of exciting technical innovation. The presence and continued proliferation of computerized information is revolutionizing organizational procedures, activities, and communication. For example, hardly a day passes without some reference in the media to the "information highway." Clichés abound about getting lost on the information highway, missing the on ramp to the information highway, or even hitting potholes on the information highway.

New technical processes are rapidly emerging and changing the nature and focus of organizational action. Key technological changes affecting the business and its industry should always be tracked. By following developments reported in trade literature and following reports of advances noted by suppliers or sales representatives, owners may be reasonably aware of these key changes. Failure to monitor and address major technological innovations may adversely affect the firm's competitive position—particularly if competing firms avail themselves of technical improvements.

This does not, of course, mean that every fad or innovation must be accepted. Rather, it requires a careful analysis and systematic consideration of each advance to determine its potential effect on the firm. In so doing, the best and most relevant changes may be exploited. Further, the manager avoids being caught in a position where customers perceive the business as being technologically backward or inferior to its competitors. If this occurs, a significant number of customers may be lost, and the business may be forced to incur substantial expense to bring its technology up-to-date and on-line.

For example, an insightful middle-aged man recently started his own graphic design business. He possessed extensive experience in the industry, having been employed by his largest competitor for fourteen years. Through his experience and exposure to the industry and his careful analysis of evolving trends, he concluded that all six firms in his selected target market were using equipment and approaches that were outdated. He felt that his business, by availing itself of the latest technological advances, could offer customers better quality at lower prices—thus attaining a competitive edge.

## POLITICAL AND LEGAL CHANGES

Factors such as changes in government policy and regulations, legal developments, and changes in political philosophy may all impact the business. For example, the stock market reacted significantly in late 1992 when it became apparent that Bill Clinton would be elected president. The passage of the North American Free Trade Agreement (NAFTA) provides a potential bonanza for those small companies that can take advantage of more favorable export/import conditions with Canada and Mexico. Even before its passage, many small business owners were keenly aware of the provisions of NAFTA and recognized its potential effects. In many cases, these owners were planning the development and restructuring of their firms to avail themselves of the trade opportunities that NAFTA offered.

It is not unusual for social pressures to prompt legislative action that creates guidelines and demands that affect small business operations. For example, recent attempts to change health-care policy may have a dramatic effect both on small companies' opportunities and their ability to compete.

From time to time, tax laws change, with resulting effects on the structure and reporting practices of small business. Political pressures within a particular community or trade area may affect not only the general business climate, but also philosophies toward the promotion of small business. These and any number of other political/legal concerns must be addressed.

Local newspapers, Chamber of Commerce reports, trade publications, and general business publications (such as *Business Week* and the *Wall Street Journal*) are important informational sources. Even more current information can be found through the many sources available on Internet. Some computer users make a habit of checking the latest developments each morning. By reading and staying up-to-date on current and impending developments, the small businessperson can maintain a reasonably accurate appraisal of political

## SOCIAL AND DEMOGRAPHIC CHANGES

Social and demographic factors such as age and gender distribution are important, particularly if they indicate developing trends. Consider the following example. A local Italian restaurant has experienced marked shifts in its business over the past 20 years. The owners have always provided good food in a friendly atmosphere, with a fairly broad and diverse menu of Italian food. The business is noted for personalized service by friendly waiters and waitresses. Most important, the owners stress "home cooking." When an order is placed, the cooks (who are also the owners) prepare each entrée with that "special touch." The business has existed on the same corner for over 20 years. After a few rocky years when survival was questionable, business is again brisk and the future looks promising.

Although many factors may help explain the performance of this firm through the years, demographics and social factors should be considered. During the 1970s and 1980s, the United States experienced a critical shift in the dining-out experience. Much of this shift could be explained by social and demographic changes. First, there were more two-career families, which explained the desire for eating out. However, the attitude toward and function of dining out had also changed. Time was critical, and families seemed to want to eat more quickly. They desired less of a "dining experience" than a functional activity. Quickly filled orders were seen as reasonable trade-offs for limited menus with few or no frills. The Italian restaurant did not respond to these needs and therefore lost ground to more "in-touch" competitors.

Today, however, maturing baby boomers are increasingly looking for upscale, casual dining. Restaurants with quality menus are reaping the benefits as many consumers reject fast food. In particular, specialty niches, such as Italian food, appear quite popular. The restaurant is capitalizing on this popularity as its specialities are again consistent with consumer desires.

As another example, consider the spectacular growth of services aimed at responding to the needs of dual-career families. The number of dual-income households with children under 18 and annual incomes in excess of $50,000 has risen from just over 7 million households in 1989 to over 8.6 million households in 1994. As work-family conflicts have surfaced and moved to the social forefront, approaches for addressing and reducing those conflicts are begging for attention. In many cases, well-attuned small business owners are etching out new competitive niches. For example, KangaKab, started in 1992 by Judith London and David Parkin, transports preschoolers to and from daycare centers, filling in for parents whose hectic schedules prohibit the more traditional mom or dad shuttle.

As a final example, consider a store catering to runners. Fifteen years ago the business carried only running shoes and appealed to a target of hard-core, serious runners. However, changing social values have twice forced the store to change. Beginning in the mid 1980s, large numbers of people turned to running. It became an activity that refused to be bound by sex or age. As running has gained in popularity, the consumer demand has expanded beyond shoes to include running gear, books, and accessories. In the 1990s, some runners, and many others who had never exercised at all, took up walking, thus providing an additional market for the store. By tracking these changes and anticipating their effects, the store owners were able to continue to expand the business.

One may argue that logically any business would do this. Any store concentrating only on top-of-the-line shoes would be forced to change because of consumer demand. That may be true, but it is not the key point. If the store's owners are blind to evolving changes in this industry and maintain their strict reliance on one kind of shoes alone, other entrepreneurs will soon enter the market and fill the gap. On the other hand, if the owners monitor the environment, they can anticipate these changes and modify and expand their offerings. Here, the business reduces the threat of potential competition and capitalizes on an opportunity for expanding its product line and increasing sales volume.

**ECONOMIC CHANGES**

Economic projections or forecasts are important because of the lag time between economic changes and their effect on business forces and consumer decisions.

Generally, macroeconomic information (perhaps at the national or state level) is readily available. However, this data may be of little real value to the small business dealing in more isolated and unique markets. Therefore, awareness of economic factors within the relevant target market becomes critical. For example, small business owners are concerned about factors such as movements or trends in local interest rates, unemployment levels, total sales within the community, tax rates, and availability of capital. Of course, the influence of these factors will vary considerably across firms and industries.

## The Industry Environment

Once the macroenvironment has been sufficiently examined, analysis should turn to the industry. Three factors should be addressed: the nature of the industry, its growth rate, and the dynamics of the competition.

### NATURE OF THE INDUSTRY

The owner must consider whether the industry is dynamic regarding such things as technological change, product quality, distribution channels, and product obsolescence. The medical diagnostics industry differs greatly from the printing industry. The food-processing industry differs from the automobile-manufacturing industry. Restaurants differ from bicycle shops. Is the industry constantly updating and using state-of-the-art equipment, or does it rely on existing equipment? Do customers in the industry demand high-quality products and service, or are they willing to accept whatever is produced? Is the industry in a product market or a service market? Is the industry part of the consumer market or does it sell its products to intermediary firms? Are products manufactured totally within a single company or do subcontractors make components? Understanding the nature of the industry gives the business owner a feel for how successful particular strategies may be.

### INDUSTRY GROWTH RATE

A firm competing in a high-growth market has far different opportunities and constraints than one that competes in a slow-growth or declining market. In a growth environment, errors and inefficiencies can be tolerated. In a low-growth market with limited profits, errors can be fatal.

Here, the concept of product life cycle may be a useful analytical tool. Typically, as noted in Figure 2.2, products are seen as passing through four distinct developmental stages. Knowing where a product falls in this continuum may critically

Figure 2.2

**STAGES IN PRODUCT LIFE CYCLE**

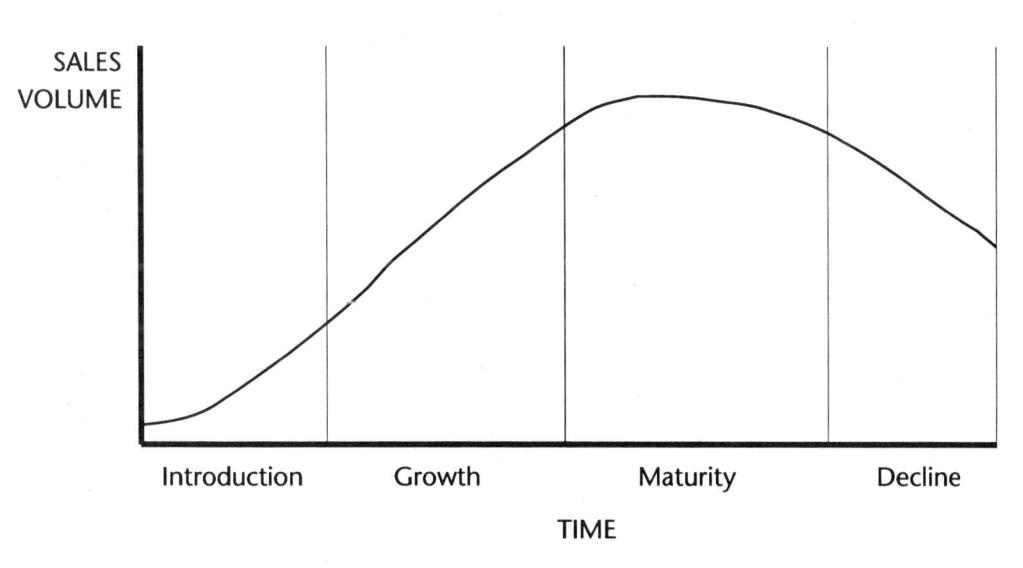

[Graph showing sales volume over time, with curve rising through Introduction and Growth stages, peaking at Maturity, and falling through Decline. Y-axis: SALES VOLUME. X-axis: TIME, divided into Introduction, Growth, Maturity, Decline.]

affect the business, since each stage is accompanied by a unique series of opportunities and difficulties. For example, if a company's products are in the latter stages of the cycle (late maturity or decline), significant future problems may arise. This is particularly true if attractive alternative products are being offered by competitors and the business does not possess a strong market share. Managers may need to search for new products or reposition the business to deal with this threat.

One must also understand how long it will take to move through the stages of the life cycle. Products may be approaching maturity, but if this stage is seen as lasting for a lengthy period, the impetus for immediate action is lessened. Similarly, relying too heavily on a product caught for too long in the introduction stage may adversely affect sales. Many factors, including the availability of substitutes and shifts in consumer tastes and preferences, will affect the rapidity of movement through the product stages. Failing to understand the level and extent of demand can produce harsh consequences. Reading the life-cycle position correctly and enacting a strategy consistent with these readings can be important factors of success.

The strategic impact of shifting life-cycle stages is demonstrated in Profile 2.3, p. 34. Fitness, as a social trend, certainly was a theme that captured the

1980s and fueled the growth of related industries. But, the obsession with fitness reached its peak by the latter part of the 1980s and began to wane. In fact, recent statistics indicate that overall participation in exercise and strenuous activity is declining (Robinson and Godbey). The decline seems to be across all age groups and therefore does not appear to be the result of an aging population. Americans seem to be turning toward moderation in their exercise programs and are focusing on leisure activities like walking. Players in fitness and related industries must realize they are likely to experience rapid life cycles. Typically, these product areas experience accelerated growth, early maturity, and speedy declines as fickle consumers change attitudes, interests, and leisure lifestyles at a dizzying pace. Rowing machines, aerobic videos, and perhaps even jogging accessories have felt the consequences of these movements.

---

### PROFILE 2.3: NEW BALANCE ATHLETIC SHOE, INC.

In 1972, Jim Davis paid $100,000 to buy New Balance Athletic Shoe, Inc. This small, sleepy shoe manufacturer had been in existence for over 60 years and had been making athletic shoes for about 10. Davis's purchase coincided perfectly with market demands, as the fitness and running movements were poised to explode on the American scene. As physical fitness became a national obsession during the 1980s, the athletic footwear business experienced annual growth rates as high as 20 percent. Typical of an industry with rocketing growth, new manufacturers emerged to meet the demand.

With the market soaring, Davis's strategy during the early years was quite basic—manufacture a quality product and get it into the hands of anxious buyers. New Balance, like many small businesses in this industry, pursued a follower strategy. Industry leaders Nike and Reebok dictated product movements and New Balance mirrored their actions. Unfortunately, New Balance followed the leaders as they expanded into an ever-growing range of product areas. This splintering of manufacturing focus consistently left New Balance with insufficient levels of product in their traditionally strong running shoe market. In addition, the company suffered from low brand awareness, and few advertising dollars were available to enhance that awareness. Not surprisingly, from 1986 to 1989, the company saw growth leveling off, despite continued surges in the industry.

By the early 1990s, the athletic footwear industry began to contract as sales dipped industrywide. Analysts posited a number of possible explanations. Perhaps the impact of the domestic economy's recession was being felt. Perhaps the market was saturated. Perhaps consumer interests and preferences were shifting. Whatever explanation was accepted, one outcome seemed apparent: An industry shakeout was likely, and survival of all existing brand name manufacturers appeared doubtful.

Clearly, New Balance's existence depended on some very careful strategic thinking. Davis's response was to build on the business's traditional strengths and focus on a few tactical approaches that could be competitive advantages. He termed his strategy Operation Quick Strike. While Operation Quick Strike contained many planks, certain themes were central. First, New Balance etched a niche in this intensively competitive industry by focusing on width sizing. While other running shoe manufactures offered few widths, New Balance offered ranges on some shoes from AA to EEE. Although width sizing was difficult and expensive, it enabled New Balance to develop an image as a customized manufacturer. Its focus on customized quality was supported by strong production control and just-in-time retailing. In addition, New Balance expanded its line with great care. Reading demographic and social trends carefully, New Balance surmised that baby boomers were in the process of switching from running to exercise walking. Accordingly, a line of walking shoes became an attractive addition to the business. Operation Quick Strike strategy also focused on increased advertising aimed at carefully selected targets who were most consistent with the themes the company wished to stress. With a growing reputation for producing quality shoes that fit better than the competition's and by selectively gearing efforts toward emerging hot segments of the market, New Balance seems positioned to be one of the more successful niche players in the highly competitive athletic footware industry. Today, New Balance's sales have reached the $100 million mark. With Operation Quick Strike firmly in place, Davis has set a $200 million sales goal.

*(Source: Finegan)*

---

The nature of industry supply must also be addressed. If demand is strong and supply is limited, businesses can take risks and exercise considerable flexibility. However, as supply increases relative to demand, operational efficiency and cost control become critical, and weaker firms are likely to be driven out of markets. Management must consider the entry and impact of new competition in the industry. Who are these competitors? How will they affect or modify the existing structure and balance of the industry? What happens when an industry dominated by small independents must react to the entry of large, national chains or franchises? In that situation, the independents must recognize that the entire composition of the industry has been radically affected and must make necessary adjustments.

**DYNAMICS OF THE COMPETITION**

Here, we are interested in the type and magnitude of competition. For example, do the firms in the industry compete only indirectly and coexist peacefully, or do they compete aggressively and attempt to drive each other from the marketplace? Is the competition price-based, quality-based, service-based, or a combination of all three?

Included in the dynamics of the competition is the relative size and market share. Some industries may be dominated by two or three major competitors. Competing in these markets is extremely difficult for small companies. Other industries are highly fragmented, with no dominant players. Still others may have one or two national firms along with a number of small niche firms. Restaurants typify this arrangement, in that national chains compete along with locally owned restaurants. What is the role of franchises in the industry being considered? Independent businesses often have a difficult time competing with franchised units because of the substantial name recognition and support provided by a national firm.

# The Immediate Environment

The immediate environment comprises those external areas with which the business has the most direct and regular contact. For the new or small business, five components of the immediate environment should be addressed: customer target market, suppliers, sources and cost of capital, specific competitors, and the ambiance of the community. For new and small businesses, changes in the immediate environment can mean instant death, major success, or simply frustration.

## CUSTOMER TARGET MARKET

A starting point in understanding the customer is to carefully recognize the trade area. The trade area represents the geographic area or boundaries from which customers are drawn. It is limited by the size of the business and management's capabilities. A business owner should regularly assess the scope and nature of the trade area. For example, changes in population size and composition, distribution of wealth, shifts in competition within the area, and changes (increases or decreases) in the business's capacity may necessitate a restructuring of the trade area.

Within the trade area, the key focus of concern is on the target market. The target market is that specific set of individuals within the trade area that the business chooses to attract as its primary consumers. A clear recognition of the needs, concerns, and makeup of this group is critical, since marketing, promotion, and general sales efforts are designed to appeal to and address the special concerns of this group. Products and services are not ends in and of themselves. Many small business owners forget this and become so enamored with their products or services that they fail to understand or see the customer's perspective. Products or services, no matter how brilliantly conceived and developed, will only be successful if they provide satisfaction or meet some consumer need. Shifts in consumer tastes and preferences must be constantly monitored. Understanding the demographic and social makeup of the target market, specifically the sex, age, marital status, income, occupation, and lifestyle of the target market, helps identify its needs and concerns. Shifts in target markets often offer new opportunities for the business.

## SUPPLIERS

It is important to keep abreast of suppliers and the factors affecting their success. A manager must consider the firm's relationship to suppliers in light of two factors—dependency and vulnerability. Each business will differ, often considerably, in terms of these two factors.

Dependency refers to the extent to which a business depends on or requires extensive raw materials or subassemblies provided by suppliers. Some businesses are fairly self-contained and self-supporting, thereby exhibiting little dependency, while others are almost totally dependent on their suppliers.

Vulnerability refers to the extent to which the business would be affected by breakdowns in the supply network. Typically, business vulnerability is determined by the number of competing suppliers who could provide items for the business and the track record of these suppliers. In general, the fewer sources of supply, the more vulnerable the business is to the arbitrary actions of the existing suppliers.

Sometimes the dependency and vulnerability issues surface over key customers rather then key suppliers. If, for example, a business is a captive supplier of a larger firm—that is, it sells nearly all of its products or services to one customer—then the small business is extremely vulnerable when the larger firm encounters a strike or significant downturn. In most cases the larger firm survives the trauma, but the smaller, dependent firm may not.

In considering high dependency and/or vulnerability, it is critical to be aware of forces that may affect the availability of raw materials or other components as well as their price and delivery. For example, a small company sold fine chocolate candies. Through astute marketing to local businesses, restaurants, and hotels, they had established an extensive demand for the candies. The profitability of the firm, and indeed its survival, was threatened, however, because it had entered into an exclusive contract with a single supplier. This supplier was a small, fledgling operation located nearly 500 miles from the store. Unfortunately, as the candy store's reputation grew and demand expanded, its supplier was unable to provide the needed candies. Extensive backlogs existed and customers, quite understandably, became frustrated. Before the candy store's owners were able to sever their relationship with their supplier and search out larger, more consistent sources, customer confidence had eroded to the point that the business was doomed. Again, a careful analysis of the supplier and its capacity and ability to deliver, coupled with the firm's own projections of demand, should have enabled the candy store owners to recognize this threat early enough to circumvent and overcome these disastrous implications. Again, proacting rather than reacting is the key.

## SOURCES AND COST OF CAPITAL

A key issue every small business faces is financing. Questions of where and how the business will secure the funds necessary for its operations are often perplexing, and the answers may spell the difference between success and failure. Rare is the small-businessperson who possesses sufficient financial resources to fund personally the range of needs the business will encounter. Therefore, outside sources must be used. Two fundamental concerns should be addressed.

First, it is important to identify the sources of capital available to the business. These may be fairly informal contacts, such as loans from friends or family. They may also be more formally established institutional bases, such as commercial banks, the Small Business Administration, venture capitalists, or suppliers' credit. This, of course, is by no means an exhaustive list. Figure 2.3 offers some additional sources that may be considered.

Recognizing sources of capital is only the first step. It is also necessary to identify and clearly understand the cost of capital. The small business owner has to decide whether the financial cost of securing the capital is worth the gains that will accrue from applying the capital. Cost of capital is not limited to purely financial terms. Some of the sources of capital noted in Figure 2.3 impose definite restrictions on the business, affect the business's flexibility, and alter the owner's degree of control. These costs must be realized and balanced as one considers each source of funds.

---

Figure 2.3

### SOURCES OF CAPITAL

1. Personal savings

2. Friends and family

3. Commercial banks

4. Small Business Administration

5. Partnerships

6. Venture capital

7. Sale of stock

8. Trade credit

---

## COMPETITION

One of the most critical parts of the environmental analysis deals with competitive assessment. In many regards, the competition is the most visible, commonly perceived threat the firm faces. Recognizing and identifying competitors is no simple task, however. Competitors may take new forms as markets evolve and change. Customer needs shift and are always being met in new and unique ways. Traditional businesses may encounter new types of competition that were not even considered in the past. Clearly, a successful small business must be attuned to the changing face of competition. For example, consider the case of Edwards Service Station.

Edwards Service Station was a full-service gas station started in 1970 by Curt Edwards. A superb mechanic, Curt, along with his brother and one part-time worker, transformed the single-bay, neighborhood station from a fledgling start-up to a financially thriving and well-respected operation in its first decade of existence. When Curt's son Mike joined the business in 1980, full-service stations were still dominant.

Over the next decade, however, the complexion of the industry changed dramatically. The American quest for speed and specialized service began to appear in new competitive forms. Specialized muffler and brake franchises began to drain business by offering a price structure that Curt could not match. Similarly, specialty oil-change and lube franchises offered speed, price, and convenience options that Curt was unable to duplicate. Curt largely discounted the impact of this new competition. He knew what a service station was supposed to be, and he was sure his customers would remain loyal because of the personal attention to detail that he had always provided.

But by the early 1990s Curt was fighting a losing battle. Nationally, full-service stations were in rapid decline and accounted for only about 35 percent of the total stations in the country. Mike encouraged Curt to convert to a one-stop convenience center, emphasizing convenience store items and self-service gasoline. Not surprisingly, Curt rebelled. With true professional pride, Curt argued that there would always be a place for the traditional service station. By mid-1992, Edwards Service Station was losing money, and Curt was dipping into the savings he had set aside for his retirement. In late 1994, as Edwards closed, many observers commented that its owners had been driven out of business by a new set of competitive threats.

Initially, managers should determine the number and market share of competing firms in the trade area. Although precise determination of market share may not be possible, some general understanding of relative market share is likely. It is important to assess the strengths, weaknesses, and unique competencies of competitors in addition to strategies they seem likely to use in the future. One of the best ways to assess competitors and relate their strengths and weaknesses to one's own firm is to use a competitive analysis profile. This analysis indicates the key factors that affect the firm's success and compares competing firms' status with regard to each of the factors. The factors chosen for consideration may vary, but the 15 factors listed in Figure 2.4 (p. 42) are typical. The comparison or rating does not need to be extensive or particularly sophisticated. This analysis profile provides a clear snapshot of where each firm stands in terms of the 15 factors. Such awareness allows managers to recognize threats and opportunities and pursue actions to deal with them. For example, consider the case of Haberkorn Ace Hardware in Profile 2.4.

---

### PROFILE 2.4: HABERKORN ACE HARDWARE

Haberkorn Ace Hardware was founded by Paul Haberkorn in 1955. It is a full-service hardware with 15 employees in nine departments and is known for its friendliness. In exploring its external situation, consultants for Haberkorn Ace Hardware relied heavily on existing data sources. For example, recent secondary data from the U.S. Census Bureau, Survey of Buying Power, Standard and Poor's Industry Surveys, *Hardware Age* magazine, and the National Retail Hardware Association provided a wealth of information pertinent to Haberkorn Ace Hardware. Locally, each key competitor was identified, analyzed, and compared on a series of competitive factors.

There are many competitors in Haberkorn's trade area. However, seven of these competitors are dominant and pose the strongest competitive threat to Haberkorn. A detailed competitive profile is offered for each of these competitors, and their strengths and weaknesses shown, in Figure 2.5, p. 43. The table gives each competitor an overall performance index, a measure of how strong each competitor is perceived to be based on a total point index of 125. The characteristics chosen by Haberkorn were specific to their particular competitive situation.

---

Figure 2.4

## **COMPETITIVE ANALYSIS PROFILE**

| Business | Company A | Company B | Company C | Your Company |
|---|---|---|---|---|
| Competitive Factor | | | | |
| Product Uniqueness | | | | |
| Relative Product Quality | | | | |
| Price | | | | |
| Service | | | | |
| Availability/Convenience | | | | |
| Reputation/Image | | | | |
| Location | | | | |
| Advertising & Promotional Policies/Effectiveness | | | | |
| Product Design | | | | |
| Caliber of Personnel | | | | |
| Raw Material Cost | | | | |
| Financial Condition | | | | |
| Production Capabilities | | | | |
| R & D Position | | | | |
| Variety/Selection | | | | |

Figure 2.5
## HABERKORN ACE HARDWARE COMPETITIVE ANALYSIS PROFILE
(Scale from 1-5; 1 (very poor), 2 (below average), 3 (average),
4 (above average), 5 (outstanding))

| Competitive Factor | Helper's World | Lesters | Donners | Build Rite | Pilgram Pride | Garrods | Kennelly |
|---|---|---|---|---|---|---|---|
| **General Characteristics** | | | | | | | |
| - Reputation | 3 | 5 | 2 | 3 | 5 | 4 | 4 |
| - Store Hours | 5 | 3 | 4 | 4 | 3 | 3 | 3 |
| - Speed of Checkout | 4 | 3 | 3 | 4 | 3 | 3 | 3 |
| **Merchandise Offering** | | | | | | | |
| - Variety/Selection | 4 | 4 | 3 | 3 | 3 | 2 | 4 |
| - Quality of Mdse | 4 | 4 | 4 | 3 | 3 | 3 | 3 |
| **Environment** | | | | | | | |
| - Store Layout | 4 | 5 | 4 | 3 | 3 | 3 | 2 |
| - Displays | 4 | 4 | 4 | 3 | 3 | 4 | 2 |
| - Merchandising | 5 | 5 | 5 | 4 | 3 | 3 | 2 |
| - Clutter | 4 | 4 | 4 | 4 | 2 | 4 | 2 |
| - Cleanliness | 5 | 4 | 5 | 4 | 3 | 4 | 2 |
| - Lighting | 4 | 4 | 5 | 2 | 3 | 4 | 1 |
| - Inside Decor | 5 | 5 | 3 | 3 | 2 | 4 | 1 |
| - Exterior | 4 | 3 | 3 | 4 | 2 | 3 | 2 |
| **Prices** | | | | | | | |
| - Values | 4 | 3 | 3 | 3 | 3 | 3 | 2 |
| - Specials | 4 | 4 | 4 | 3 | 3 | 3 | 3 |
| **Personnel** | | | | | | | |
| - Friendly/Courteous | 3 | 3 | 4 | 2 | 5 | 3 | 4 |
| - Knowledgeable | 3 | 3 | 4 | 3 | 4 | 4 | 3 |
| - Service Level | 3 | 4 | 4 | 3 | 4 | 3 | 3 |
| **Site** | | | | | | | |
| - Accessibility | 4 | 4 | 4 | 5 | 5 | 3 | 3 |
| - Parking Facilities | 4 | 4 | 4 | 5 | 3 | 2 | 3 |
| - Visibility | 5 | 4 | 3 | 4 | 4 | 2 | 2 |
| -Shopping Pull | 4 | 3 | 2 | 4 | 4 | 3 | 2 |
| - Walk-In Traffic | 4 | 2 | 2 | 4 | 3 | 2 | 2 |
| **Advertising** | | | | | | | |
| - Expenditure | 5 | 4 | 3 | 3 | 2 | 2 | 2 |
| - In-Store/P.O.P. | 4 | 3 | 3 | 3 | 1 | 2 | 2 |
| **Overall Performance** | | | | | | | |
| Index | 102 | 94 | 87 | 85 | 79 | 76 | 62 |

## AMBIANCE OF THE COMMUNITY

The community in which a firm operates can have a significant impact on the firm's strategies. A firm operating in a distinctively blue-collar area may have difficulty selling upscale products or services. On the other hand, a luxury service or product may be readily salable in an affluent community. As an example, a recent college graduate decided to open a day spa. Many of her former classmates felt that a day spa was a luxury that few customers could afford. However, the entrepreneur lived in an exclusive suburb of Chicago. It was not unusual, when driving through the suburb, to see BMWs, Mercedes, Lincolns, and Acuras. The typical runabout car was a Volvo stationwagon instead of an old Chevrolet Caprice. In this community, a day spa would be readily accepted if sufficient services were provided to the clientele.

Community ambiance also determines how readily accepted a new product may be. Some communities are known to market researchers as very conservative cities that are slow to change. Others are more progressive and open to new products or services. Community ambiance may also determine the distribution strategy used.

# Performing the Environmental Analysis

Previous sections have discussed factors that should be included in the firm's external analysis. Attention now turns to the actual analysis.

## ENVIRONMENTAL THREATS AND OPPORTUNITIES PROFILE

The Environmental Threats and Opportunities Profile (ETOP) can be an easily used and quite beneficial tool for the small business owner. The owner looks at the firm's environment in order to identify significant threats and opportunities. As used here, a "threat" is any factor that may limit, restrict, or impede the business in the pursuit of its goals. A range of factors may need to be considered. The presence of strong competition, changing public attitudes toward the firm's products, an adverse economic climate, or the bankruptcy of a key supplier are all examples of environmental factors that may pose threats for the business.

On the other hand, an "opportunity" is any factor that offers promise or potential for moving closer or more quickly toward the firm's goals. New high-growth markets, unmet or changing customer demands, the development of new products to complement existing lines, or a general upsurge in the local economy may all produce genuine opportunities for the business. More will be added on the use of ETOP in a subsequent portion of this section.

## DECIDING WHAT TO CONSIDER

First, an owner must decide which environmental factors to track. For most small businesses, it is totally unrealistic to believe that all the external factors that may have some influence on the firm can be constantly studied. There is neither the time nor the resources to do so. Moreover, much environmental information is extraneous to a particular situation and therefore has negligible effects on the business. Managers must select the specific environmental factors that have the most critical impact on their firms. These become the factors to track, study, and analyze. Although certain general matters may be commonly felt by all firms, each company's managers will concentrate on a few key environmental factors peculiar to its situation.

Consider the following example. All small firms are affected by the economic situation of their particular community or trade area. However, the need to track and monitor specific economic changes differs greatly from business to business.

A local variety store may see their business as being affected by interest rates and unemployment. However, because the bulk of their sales come from low-price, high-turnover items, interest rates and unemployment do not visibly impact the store's sales. In comparison, a small woodworking business that specializes in the crafting and building of kitchen cabinets is in a much different situation. Its sales represent investments by consumers in their homes. Kitchen cabinets are expensive, a luxury that consumers might postpone if economic times are tough. The firm's management knows that as interest rates and unemployment climb, consumers are less likely to consider purchasing new kitchen cabinets. Therefore, in developing their environmental analysis, these managers closely monitor interest rates and unemployment shifts as indicators of their level of business activity.

## HISTORICAL APPROACH

One way to be sure which external factors are most important to the business, both today and in the near future, is to rely on historical trends. A careful examination of the past may reveal the environmental factors that have most critically affected the business and that are relevant for future consideration. There is considerable merit and value to this approach.

However, two problems exist with the use of and dependence on historical evidence. First, these historical data may not be available because the variables may not have been monitored carefully in the past. Secondly, historical evidence may not be relevant to the firm's future needs because contemporary business exists in a rapidly changing, volatile environment.

It may be unrealistic and even dangerous to assume that past trends are indicative of future business conditions. Therefore, forward-looking, insightful, proactive thinking may be lost if one adheres totally to historical trends. This does not imply that past records and trends don't provide meaningful and interesting input that should be considered. It does imply that the firm needs to consider more than just historical records—to extend beyond the domain of these records. To the extent that it is available and relevant, historical information is valuable, but it is the beginning rather than the end of the analysis.

## ENVIRONMENTAL BRAINSTORMING

In order to identify the key environmental concerns most relevant to a business, managers may periodically engage in a creative exercise of environmental brainstorming. Environmental brainstorming is an open, freewheeling discussion that zeroes in on the dynamics of a firm's particular environment. These sessions not only solicit important contributions from employees, but are also an excellent vehicle for communication. Discussing the needs and direction of the business can foster understanding by and commitment from key employees.

Questions about how often such meetings should be held, who should attend, and how long they should last are difficult to answer. However, here are some guidelines. The timing of these brainstorming sessions is dictated by the rate of change presently taking place in the industry. A business that exists in a fairly stable industry with few contemplated changes can afford to meet less often. A business in a growing or evolving industry that is inundated with new forces, demands, technology, and competition will be forced to have more frequent sessions. At a minimum, these sessions should occur annually, with more volatile industries convening perhaps every six months.

Three to four hours should be allotted for such sessions. Once the program is in place, the necessary pre-meeting preparation can be done by employees on their own time, thereby shortening the meeting time. Initially, however, it's important to allow enough time for good, creative points to surface. Participants should include all employees who have key contacts with the environment. For example, top salespeople or marketing people, financial people, those who contact or deal with customers and suppliers, and the board of directors (if there is one) would be reasonable persons to invite to share their comments.

Procedurally, environmental brainstorming can follow a number of directions. However, a fairly structured format is preferred (at least for the initial iteration). It may be started by asking participants to prepare an ETOP. This approach to ETOP is slightly modified from traditional parlance so that it is more relevant to the needs of the smaller business. First, ask participants to list (independently) the key environmental threats and opportunities that they see for the business both today and for the next year.

Reaching conclusions is not important at this stage. The object is to bring ideas and points for thought to the surface. It is probably best to accept everyone's suggestions without comment, waiting until later to reflect, analyze, and pare down the list.

Once everyone has listed their threats and opportunities, they should rate each factor in terms of its impact or significance to the firm. It probably isn't necessary to prescribe a detailed rating scheme—try asking participants to rate each factor as extremely significant, significant buy not of the highest priority, or only midly significant.

After all items have been rated, participants then present their ratings along with their justification or reasoning. Concentrate on commonalities—these will require little discussion. If everyone lists new competition as a key threat and assigns it the highest priority, then this factor most clearly becomes an area of needed focus. If differences exist, participants should discuss them: Why does one participant recognize suppliers as being a critical threat when no one else even lists this factor, for example. Maybe this person knows something no one else does, or perhaps he or she is off base. Nevertheless, this input and ensuing discussion is critical.

This process takes time, but it forces key personnel to become involved in the planning process and provides good notions that may be unavailable or insufficiently detailed in historical analysis. The composite listing/rating that evolves, in conjunction with insights gained from historical data, identifies the environmental factors the firm will attempt to track, and information on these factors needs to be constantly gathered and monitored. It is important that the business realize environmental analysis is an ongoing task. Figure 2.6 provides an overview of the steps in environmental brainstorming.

### SOURCES OF EXTERNAL INFORMATION

The small-businessperson may secure information necessary for environmental analysis from a number of sources. These may be secondary sources as shown in Figure 2.7, p. 50 or primary sources such as conducting market research, interviewing customers, or studying competitor's products. The approach used to gather either primary or secondary information may be either structured and formal or informal and judgmental. Whichever approach or combination of approaches is used, constant awareness, monitoring, and openness to environmental shifts and fluctuations are critical.

## Summary

Environmental analysis must be ongoing. Just as a firm's environment is continually in a state of flux and evolution, the firm's analysis efforts must be similarly dynamic. When times get tough and the business is troubled, many small business owners turn their backs on environmental analysis. They argue that they are confronted by too many pressing problems to spend the time and energy necessary to deal with environmental concerns. Such reasoning is dangerous and may serve to exacerbate an already difficult situation. How can the business make the necessary decisions to reorient its business and adjust its strategic outlook without a keen awareness of its key environmental concerns? Environmental assessment and analysis form the basis for overcoming the firm's problems. Rather than being a time-consuming barrier, environmental analysis is a tool for corrective action.

Figure 2.6

## STEPS IN ENVIRONMENTAL BRAINSTORMING

| Area of Consideration | Explanation |
| --- | --- |
| —How often to meet? | —Depends largely on industry <br> —At least annually <br> —More often for rapidly changing, more dynamic industries |
| —Who should attend? | —Top salespeople <br> —Top marketing people <br> —Top finance people <br> —Those in direct contact with customers <br> —Those in direct contact with suppliers <br> —Board of directors |
| —Preplanning? | —All participants bring to the session any data relevant to their areas of expertise |
| —Meeting dynamics? | —Each participant shares information <br> —Participants prepare and rate ETOPs <br> —FTOPs and rating are shared and discussed <br> —Commonalities are noted <br> —Priorities are established |

Figure 2.7

## SOURCES OF EXTERNAL INFORMATION

*Census Data*
The Bureau of the Census provides statistics on population, housing, and various industries for a variety of geographical sites ranging from the entire United States to cities to census tracts and neighborhoods.

*County and City Data Book*
Issued annually by the Bureau of the Census, this offers a variety of state and local information.

*Statistical Abstract of the United States*
General summary of a number of factors, issued annually.

*Survey of Buying Power* (**Sales and Marketing Management Magazine**)
Provides more specifics relating to the local area.

*Chambers of Commerce*
Often have quite valuable information and insights into local situations.

*Trade Association Reports & Trade Magazines*
Most associations prepare regular reports that can be useful for external analysis.

*General-Purpose Business Publications*
Publications such as *Business Week* and *Wall Street Journal* provide important insights into general environmental and industry movements.

*Magazines for Small Business such as* **Inc.** *and* **Entrepreneur**
These are often useful as sources for new ideas/approaches. Helps one keep abreast of new developments.

---

We also caution that organizational success may foster an attitude of invincibility and also prompt the small business owner to refrain from devoting the necessary energy to environmental analysis. A firm's past success can be a formidable barrier to planning and change. An argument often heard is: "We've done it this way for 20 years and we've been successful. Why should we change now?" Businesses with such an outlook are forced to change when the bottom line suddenly shows declining results. This does not mean that the business has always to be in a state of flux. Indeed, one may determine that there is no need for change. But, the decision must be based on careful analysis and evaluation, not the result of complacency. If a manager continually assesses, analyzes, and interprets key environmental cues, the basis for decisions is grounded in thoughtful reason.

The case study at the end of this chapter is an external analysis done for a home health-care company. It illustrates the information that is available for this type of analysis, as well as the results of the analysis.

## Discussion Questions

1. Why is an ETOP important?

2. How do you determine if a piece of information is relevant?

3. Which general environment information is most relevant for a
   a. shoe repair store?
   b. car dealer?
   c. liquor store?
   d. computer software company?
   e. manufacturer of tool and die equipment?

4. For a retail store, what are the best sources of information on the local economy and general conditions?

5. How can I find information about my competitors' prices, services, profits, and strategies if
   a. they are a publicly held company?
   b. they are a privately held company?

## References

Barbara Marsh. "Peapod's On-Line Grocery Service Checks Out Service." *Wall Street Journal*, June 30, 1994, p. B2.

"Is the Bar of Soap Washed Up: Minnetonka, Inc. Marketing of Liquid Soap," *Business Week*, January 12, 1981, p. 109+.

Michael Selz. "Enterprise: From School to the Doctor's Office to Home; Ride Service Does the Driving for Parents," *Wall Street Journal*, May 6, 1994, p. B1.

John P. Robinson and Geoffrey Godbey. "Has Fitness Peaked?" *American Demographics*, vol. 15, no. 9, September 1993, pp. 36–42.

Jay Finegan. "Surviving in the Nike/Reebok Jungle (New Balance Athletic Shoe, Inc.)." *Inc.*, May 1993, V15 #5, pp. 98-102.

# CASE STUDY

# Environmental Analysis for Gaston Ridge Home Health Care, Inc.

## Introduction

Gaston Ridge Home Health Care, Inc., owned and operated by four experienced registered nurses, began operations in 1993. The agency provides home health care services to patients in small communities and rural sections of an eight-county area of southern Illinois. Most of the current clients are homebound by advanced age or disability.

Many factors, both in the environment and within the industry, affect the growth and development of the home health care field. To assess these factors and provide a thorough environmental analysis, consultants for Gaston Ridge relied on both primary and secondary data sources. For example, existing data sources, such as the U.S. Census of Population and chambers of commerce and business assistance centers in the market area, were used. Additionally, interviews were conducted with experts in the field, and surveys of potential clients and physicians in the target market were conducted.

As should always be the case, this analysis focuses on those elements of the macroenvironment that are most relevant to the firm. Accordingly, some areas are given significant coverage, while others are accorded more limited attention. In this regard, the frameworks provided in this chapter are guides that should be tailored to the situation at hand.

## The Macroenvironment

### POLITICAL AND LEGAL CHANGES

Both the American Federation of Home Health Agencies and the National Association for Home Care will work to increase awareness of the industry and lobby for legislation that targets home health care as a cost-saving alternative to institutional care for the elderly and as a reasonable response to the government's desire to cover health care needs of more people at a lower cost. These efforts should benefit agencies like Gaston Ridge. Further, managed care is being touted as part of the government's program of health care reforms. Managed care deemphasizes hospital-based care and encourages less costly alternatives such as outpatient and home-based care. Further, care for the elderly is expected to shift from nursing homes to home health agencies, providing firms like Gaston Ridge with an expanded client base.

Federal and state laws and accreditation organizations require licensing, employee orientation programs, and thorough documentation and review of patient care policies and procedures. While these requirements help reduce liability risks, compliance is expensive. Therefore, the effects on Gaston Ridge will be both positive and negative.

The number of malpractice and malfunctioning-equipment lawsuits filed against home health care agencies is expected to increase. Similarly, legal concerns surrounding AIDS will increase. Consequently, the importance of careful documentation will continue to increase as well. While essential, this increase will carry significant added expense.

## SOCIAL AND DEMOGRAPHIC CHANGES

One important factor that affects home health care is the changing demographic structure of society. Nationally, there is a projected increase in people aged 65 and over who will require care. Consistent with this trend, the eight-county area served by Gaston Ridge will see a growing percentage of the population in the 65-and-over age bracket. This provides an obvious benefit for Gaston Ridge, since the majority of patients served by home health care agencies are within this age bracket.

Experts suggest that Americans are becoming increasingly health conscious and will increasingly take actions to foster better health. The impact of this social movement is uncertain and must be followed with care. On the one hand, increased health consciousness may lead to a decreased need for health care. On the other hand, as health-conscious consumers become more aware of the range of services provided through home health care and the relative cost advantages of these services, the demand for home care may increase.

## TECHNOLOGICAL CHANGES

Advances in technology allow complex procedures such as dialysis, cancer chemotherapy, drug infusion for congestive heart failure, and intravenous blood transfusion (to name only a few) to take place in patients' homes. Further, the recent mobilization of the EKG and X-ray machines is expected to foster further technological advances in the field. In order to be competitive in the home health care field, firms such as Gaston Ridge must have access to these equipment innovations. These purchases will be costly.

Increasingly, home health care agencies will be expected to provide products as well as services. Physicians and other referral sources seem more inclined to use an agency that can handle most of a discharged patient's needs with a single phone call from them. Thus, agencies will have to be a central source for all facets of patient care.

Further, as home health care service expands, more sophisticated systems for patient tracking, scheduling, and control will be necessary. Although the cost for remaining current with these technological advances will be high, firms that fail to meet these technological demands will have greater difficulty keeping up with competitor agencies.

## ECONOMIC CHANGES

Perhaps the major economic variable affecting home health care is the United States system of health insurance. Currently, the foundation of our insurance-based health care system is Medicare and Medicaid. Certain parts of home health care services are covered by these programs. For example, Medicare covers part-time or intermittent nursing care if the individual meets the criteria for benefits. Medicare pays 100 percent of the approved amount for home health care and 80 percent of the approved amount for durable medical equipment. However, Medicare does not cover custodial services, drugs, or full-time nursing care.

Economic data suggests stability and slow, incremental growth in the economy. For example, unemployment rates are rather low and interests rates are forecast to remain low. Economic data in the eight counties that make up Gaston Ridge's market area are consistent with national trends and suggest favorable interest and unemployment rates.

## Nature of the Industry

Home care is the fastest-growing segment of health care. As a result of the interaction of political issues, social and demographic changes, and technological advances noted previously, the home health care industry should incur significant growth over the next decade. Further, the home health care industry will remain in the growth stage of the product life cycle for some time. Indeed, much of this sustained growth is due to the fact that the costs of traditional health care will continue to increase, prompting alternative considerations such as home care. Further, growth is enabled by the relatively low entry barriers firms face in this industry.

A variety of options are available for those in need of intermittent health care. Most notable are hospitals, nursing homes, and retirement communities. Of these, home health care will continue to be the most convenient and cost-effective.

Perhaps the major factor affecting this industry is the strong likelihood that new firms will enter the industry. Most notable are hospitals and nursing homes that currently do not have home health care divisions. These institutions possess considerable resources that could be transferred to the home health care setting. Further, hospitals have the distinct advantage of being able to refer discharged patients directly to their internal home health care facility. While some of the hospitals in Gaston Ridge's market area are involved in home care, none has made home care a major area of focus at this time. However, there are indications that these hospitals will enhance their involvement in home health care in the future. Since Gaston Ridge lacks any hospital affiliation, this looms as a key environmental threat.

Currently, the industry is experiencing strong demand for physical therapists. This suggests that firms that include physical therapy services will experience benefits. However, the lean supply of qualified therapists suggests that firms will incur significant expenses in recruiting therapists. For these reasons, many firms contract out physical therapy services rather than hire internal staff.

# The Immediate Environment

### SERVICE AREA AND TARGET MARKET

Gaston Ridge serves an eight-county, 490-mile area of Southern Illinois. Over 60 percent of Gaston Ridge's market resides in rural areas, with most of the remainder being in small communities. The geographic dispersion of the target market leads to long travel times and scheduling difficulties. Marketing is also difficult and potentially costly since there are few opportunities to share advertising media across the area.

The target market is primarily aged or disabled people who are homebound. However, as noted earlier, social changes and the availability of new technologies may lead to an expansion of this target market.

### COMPETITION

Gaston Ridge has 16 competitors that operate in at least one of the counties within its service area. However, some of these agencies command a minor presence. Six major competitor agencies are key players in the area and thus pose the strongest competitive threat to Gaston Ridge. The competitive analysis profile for these agencies is offered in Figure A.1, p. 58. The assessment is based on both specific factual information (such as the availability of services and price) and perceptions of relative strengths. The profile has been modified to fit the unique competitive situation faced by Gaston Ridge.

The profile provides a snapshot of relative competitive effects. Some stand out. For example, both Illini and Capital possess strong services in physical and occupational therapy relative to the competition. However, these services are costly, so their prices are above average. The profile suggests that services such as meals, sitters, and homemakers are relatively unexploited and may be areas of growth. Further, no competitor possesses strong consumer familiarity. No doubt because of their hospital affiliations, Illini and Capital possess strong physician and discharge planner referral bases relative to other competitors.

Figure A.1

## COMPETITIVE PROFILE ANALYSIS

(Availability and Perception of Quality, 1 = Below Average; 2 = Average; 3 = Above Average)

| | Gaston Ridge | Mid Central Home Health Association | Pioneer Homecare | Cashing Home Health Care | Illini Home Health Care Affiliate of Illini Medical Center | Capital Center Hospital | Senior Dimension Home Care |
|---|---|---|---|---|---|---|---|
| **Services** | | | | | | | |
| Skilled Nursing | 3 | 3 | 2 | 1 | 3 | 3 | 2 |
| Home Health Aides | 2 | 3 | 2 | 3 | 3 | 3 | 2 |
| Physical Therapy | 2 | 2 | 2 | 1 | 3 | 3 | 2 |
| Occupational Therapy | 2 | 2 | 2 | 1 | 2 | 3 | 2 |
| Speech Therapy | 2 | 2 | 2 | 1 | 2 | 3 | 2 |
| Overnight Sitters | 2 | — | 2 | 3 | — | — | 3 |
| Meals | — | 1 | — | — | 3 | 3 | — |
| Homemakers | 2 | — | 3 | 4 | — | — | — |
| Others—Flexible as Needed | 2 | 2 | 1 | 1 | 2 | 1 | 1 |
| **Prices** | 2 | 2 | 2 | 3 | 3 | 3 | 1 |
| **Marketing** (1 = weak; 2 = fair; 3 = strong) | | | | | | | |
| Physician Referral Base | 2 | 1 | 1 | 1 | 3 | 3 | 1 |
| Discharge Planner Referral Base | 2 | 1 | 1 | 1 | 3 | 3 | 1 |
| Advertising | 2 | 2 | 1 | 1 | 2 | 2 | 2 |
| Consumer Familiarity | 2 | 2 | 1 | 2 | 2 | 2 | 2 |

# CHAPTER 3

# Internal Analysis

---

OBJECTIVES

After reading this chapter, you should be able to

1. understand the complexities of an internal analysis.
2. determine which areas of a business should be analyzed.
3. measure strengths and weaknesses in a business.
4. create a company profile for a business.

THE ENVIRONMENTAL ANALYSIS has provided a series of insights into the firm's external situation that should help you view the business more clearly in its competitive environment. Further, this analysis should make you aware of key environmental threats and opportunities. In this chapter we extend the analysis phase of the strategic planning model by examining the firm's internal condition. The internal analysis offers a profile of the company's operations and is geared toward pinpointing and assessing the key internal strengths and weaknesses of the firm.

## Value of Internal Analysis

Objective internal analysis is essential for at least two reasons. First, many managers of small businesses have totally inaccurate conceptions of the firm's internal state of affairs. Often, they rely on personal opinion or "feel" to assess their firm's internal condition. This biased view may result in an unrealistic perspective of the company's capacity, potential, and areas of concern. Only through a careful and systematic internal analysis can a reasonable and meaningful profile be attained.

The second reason is even more important. Essentially, internal analysis reveals whether the business has available the means for dealing with the environmental opportunities and threats. This revelation is critical. It can change the focus of a company's activities and strategies and, in many situations, save the business from disaster. Yet, for many companies and managers, it is a forgotten step in the logical planning sequence. Business owners tend to look at opportunities and move strategically to capture an opportunity without carefully considering their ability to do so successfully.

Consider the example of MMO Music in Profile 3.1. Here, environmental analysis was performed successfully and effectively. Indeed, the process revealed a significant market opportunity in the international arena. The owners seemed to understand the potential of this market and included it as a new avenue for business growth. However, the business lacked the internal capacity (both resources and personnel) to effectively capitalize on this apparent opportunity. Accordingly, the potential of this emerging market was not fully realized until internal capacity was addressed. A careful internal analysis would have revealed personnel and time commitments as problems before a commitment to action was made. If these problems would have been addressed sooner, the company could have benefited earlier from a promising market opportunity.

### PROFILE 3.1: MMO MUSIC GROUP

MMO Music Group produces sing-along tapes for karaoke machines. MMO, like many astute small businesses, saw burgeoning market opportunities in Asia and Europe. In fact, as trade shows and federal and state export initiatives grew, foreign clients actively sought the services of

MMO. However, MMO faced a problem common among small firms. With the domestic side of the business growing rapidly, management time and expertise to cultivate foreign business was in short supply. Thus, although MMO had been "involved" in overseas sales for more than 15 years, the export side of the business was frequently ignored while domestic operations boomed. Although a realistic and formidable market opportunity existed, that opportunity was not fully seized because the business lacked the resources (both staff and time) necessary to work with foreign clients. Finally, in 1993, MMO hired an international sales director and began to tap the sales potential of the lucrative foreign market.

*(Source: Mehta, p. B2)*

---

Now consider the example of Jacobsen Office Products in Profile 3.2. Again, environmental analysis was performed successfully and effectively. And again, the process revealed a significant market opportunity. The owner was excited about this newfound avenue for business growth. However, the shop lacked the trained sales and repair personnel to capitalize on this apparent opportunity effectively. Accordingly, the promising computer opportunity could not be realized. In addition, the present business was adversely affected. A careful, objective internal analysis would have revealed the personnel problems before a commitment to action was made. Such an effort would have enabled Jacobsen either to correct the personnel problems and thus strengthen the probability of realizing the opportunity or to look for other avenues for growth. In either case, the lesson is clear. Internal analysis is extremely important. It seeks to determine if the firm is able to effectively pursue a particular strategic or competitive thrust.

---

### PROFILE 3.2: JACOBSEN OFFICE PRODUCTS

Jason Jacobsen opened Jacobsen Office Products in 1985. He sold a line of office furniture, office supplies, and office equipment such as copiers, shredders, and telephones. His business grew steadily through 1991 and then tapered off to slow but acceptable growth.

In 1992, Jacobsen decided to move into the office computer business. Since there were already dealers for IBM, Compaq, and Apple products, Jacobsen reasoned that he could enter the low end of the computer business and sell either imported units such as Gold Star or generic units ordered from suppliers using the lowest-cost components from individual suppliers of keyboards, monitors, and CPUs. He added a line of low-end printers as well. He felt that his computers could be sold by the same staff that sold the other office equipment.

Jacobsen had correctly assessed that a number of customers were as willing to purchase the low-end computers from him as they were from Best Buy or other retail stores. The image that Jacobsen had created for quality office furniture and supplies was successfully transferred to the computer area. The company's sales grew rather quickly because of well-done promotional campaigns that tied the computers with the copiers and other goods into a one-stop shopping concept.

Jacobsen felt that service would not be an issue. Computers no longer require much minor service. Any problems that did occur would be handled by an exchange program in which Jacobsen would exchange the unit for a temporary one and send the defective unit back to the manufacturer or assembler for repair. This would usually take two weeks.

Unfortunately, Jacobsen did not accurately assess his own capabilities in the service area. The staff that had sold and serviced copiers could not work on the computers at all except for extremely minor problems. Customers often knew more than his staff did about what was wrong with the machine. Jacobsen often did an exchange when it was not really necessary. And it was inconvenient to have to transfer files from the old computer to the temporary one and then transfer them back when the old one was returned.

Jacobsen finally advertised for a computer service person, but the person he hired was not professionally trained. As a result, problems were often diagnosed incorrectly. By late 1994, Jacobsen realized that the computer business was draining his profitability and causing concern for his overall image. He decided that eliminating the computer business completely was the only way to save the rest of the business. Jacobsen Office Products is still surviving, but not without a substantial loss in clientele and customer respect.

The business must mesh its environmental awareness and insight with a corresponding understanding of internal demands. Moving aggressively in the external environment without commensurate internal support will, in most cases, lead to serious difficulties. These points are reinforced quite dramatically in the now-classic example of Osborne Computers, noted in Profile 3.3.

### PROFILE 3.3: OSBORNE COMPUTER CORPORATION

In the early 1980s, Adam Osborne revolutionized the personal computer industry. By carefully assessing consumer needs and using astute marketing, Osborne built his empire to one that by 1983 was selling 10,000 machines a month and earning annual revenue of more than $100 million.

His approach was basic. He delivered a technologically sound machine (Osborne I), sold it at two-thirds the price of its closest competitor, offered over $1,500 worth of brand name software at no additional cost, and packaged it in a portable, 26-pound easy-to-carry unit.

When the Osborne I proved successful, competitors recognized the viability of this new segment of the computer business and aggressively entered the market with their own products. To counter, Osborne developed a new portable computer, the Osborne Executive. This machine improved on the original Osborne I by providing more memory storage and a larger screen, yet still sold for a relatively attractive $2,495. Further, the Executive was to be IBM compatible.

Mr. Osborne began publicizing the machine in electronics journals and publications well in advance of its expected delivery date. Because of the notable improvements over the Osborne I, dealers were impressed. In fact, they were so impressed that they stopped orders of the Osborne I to wait for the arrival of the Executive.

However, production delays plagued the Executive. Publicity was out, dealers were ready to order, but the machine was not yet available. At the same time, sales of Osborne I were falling. Osborne had so effectively convinced dealers of the power of his new machine that they abandoned the original one. Unfortunately, the Executive couldn't be delivered. A two-and-a-half-month period of dwindling sales brought on a debilitating cash squeeze.

This was one of the key factors that pushed Osborne Computer Corporation into bankruptcy.

## Elements of Internal Analysis

Internal analysis is somewhat time-consuming and requires meaningful effort. The rewards for conducting the analysis, however, are many. The task of completing internal analysis is made easier by first considering the various elements of the analysis.

### INTERNAL STRENGTHS AND WEAKNESSES

One of the most basic, yet insightful, approaches to internal analysis focuses on the identification of internal strengths and weaknesses. As the term is used here, a strength is any resource or occurrence that helps the business realize its objectives and strategies, capitalize on its opportunities, or defend against its threats. Conversely, a weakness is any factor that hinders the business from realizing its objectives and strategies, capitalizing on its opportunities, or defending against its threats.

All small businesses possess both strengths and weaknesses. Jacobsen Office Products, for example, had fostered a favorable company image over its seven years of operation—a specific and important strength. However, the number of employees and the range of their skills were inappropriate for computer repair—a powerful weakness. Given their dual presence, it is important that both elements be identified so that strengths can be developed and used and weaknesses can be recognized and handled.

To make the analysis of internal strengths and weaknesses more workable divide them into four categories: financial resources, marketing resources, operational resources (organizational and technical), and human resources. The relevant subcomponents are included in the profile in Figure 3.1.

### RATING INTERNAL STRENGTHS AND WEAKNESSES

In developing a meaningful internal analysis or profile, some sort of evaluation or rating scheme must be used to identify strengths and weaknesses. Such a scheme should be easy to use yet comprehensive and complete. The Internal Analysis Profile in Figure 3.1 fulfills these objectives. Each internal factor or resource examined is given one of five ratings: slight weakness, strong weakness, neutral, slight strength, or strong strength. Clearly, degrees of strength and weakness exist. A given factor or resource must be

Figure 3.1

**INTERNAL ANALYSIS PROFILE**

| Internal Resource | Strong Weakness | Slight Weakness | Neutral | Slight Strength | Strong Strength |
|---|---|---|---|---|---|
| **FINANCIAL RESOURCES** | | | | | |
| Overall Performance | | | | | |
| Ability to Raise Capital | | | | | |
| Cash Position | | | | | |
| **MARKETING RESOURCES** | | | | | |
| Market Performance | | | | | |
| Knowledge of Markets | | | | | |
| Location | | | | | |
| Product | | | | | |
| Advertising & Promotion | | | | | |
| Price | | | | | |
| Image | | | | | |
| Distribution | | | | | |
| **OPERATIONAL RESOURCES** | | | | | |
| Production Facilities | | | | | |
| Access to Suppliers | | | | | |
| Inventory Control | | | | | |
| Quality Control | | | | | |
| Organizational Structure | | | | | |
| **HUMAN RESOURCES** | | | | | |
| Number of Employees | | | | | |
| Relevancy of Skills | | | | | |
| Morale | | | | | |
| Compensation | | | | | |

assessed and weighted as either being slight, neutral, or strong. Further, some factors may not be relevant at this time, but may still be noted in the analysis if it is anticipated that they will become relevant in the near future.

Evidence such as financial ratios, defective-product rates, or labor turnover data may provide an objective basis for choosing a particular rating category. However, such evidence is often unavailable. For example, a store owner may want to know the rate of advertising effectiveness, but no figures relating sales to advertising efforts have been gathered. Therefore, judgmental approaches are often used. Of course, steps can be taken to build confidence and objectivity into these judgments. The following section addresses some of those steps.

Many variables are available for analysis. Within the financial area alone, over two dozen ratios could be considered. Many of these, however, may not be relevant for some businesses and may be unavailable for others. You should select those variables that meet three requirements. First they must be relevant. Second, they must be assessed with at least a reasonable degree of accuracy. Third, they must be within the owner's range of influence. Only if the variables meet all three tests are they useful for analyzing and improving the firm's condition.

We recommend four categories of variables to analyze. You may want to select different categories or different items within the categories.

## Evaluating Financial Resources

The internal factor that most visibly affects the small firm's efforts is its financial resources. Excellent environmental opportunities may be identified along with reasonable strategies for capitalizing on them. But without adequate financial resources, these plans may lay dormant for years, never to be implemented. Even more disturbing, a business may be forced to halt a viable project or program in midstream after its financial capacity has been exhausted. Analyzing financial resources can help identify such problems and prevent such disappointing occurrences.

Problems uncovered in the financial analysis command the owner's attention. The problems may be in marketing, inventory control, purchasing, pricing, or perhaps even human resources. But the problems eventually show up in financial performance, and the financial analysis therefore becomes the most obvious starting point.

As you begin to examine and rate the relative strength of the firm's financial resources, keep certain caveats in mind. First, existing financial statements are used as tools in the evaluation process. These statements rely on historical data and thus are pictures of past behavior. It is reasonable to assume that past behavior can indicate present capacity and future expectations. Yet, particularly for small businesses, these figures may not capture the firm's vitality or future prospects.

For example, the business may have endured some extremely lean years but be poised to capitalize on new market opportunities. The financial statements reflect a weak and questionable position, even though the business is progressive and healthy. Therefore, remember that financial analysis is only one of many tools employed to determine the state of the business's internal condition.

Additionally, financial analysis is only as powerful as the extent and quality of the information on which it is based. If the firm's owners have gathered little meaningful data or have prepared scant and limited statements, it becomes much more difficult to draw worthwhile financial conclusions. In these cases, the statements are supplemented with personal opinion and interpretation. Although possibly misleading, such interpretations may lead to more logical conclusions than relying only on limited numerical data.

Many business owners find it useful to compare their financial picture against some general standard. Understandably, they want to know how they stack up against industry performance norms. Such comparisons can be useful barometers or checkpoints for the business but must be approached with some degree of caution. Financial ratios, for example, may be significantly higher or lower than comparative standards yet have perfectly plausible explanations. Therefore, comparisons are only one way to assess the company's financial condition.

Comparative financial information may come from a variety of sources. Dun and Bradstreet publishes *Industry Norms and Key Business Ratios*. Robert Morris Associates publishes *Annual Statement Studies*. Leo Troy publishes the *Almanac of Business and Industrial Financial Ratios*. Each covers a vast number of industries, typically further broken down by company asset size and by sales. The Robert Morris Associates volume seems especially useful for smaller companies. Additional comparative information may be obtained from trade associations, trade magazines, annual reports of publicly held competitors, and other sources specifically related to particular industries.

## COMPARATIVE FINANCIAL SUMMARIES

The balance sheet and income statement are important first steps in analyzing the financial health of a company. They are especially useful when presented both in dollars and in percentages and compared over a period of several years. Although changes are never easy to assess, the comparative statements can be quite useful when studied specifically to determine the causes of change.

Consider the balance sheet (Figure 3.2) and income statement (Figure 3.3, p. 70) for Waverly Custom Jewelers, a small corporation that has been in business for several years. These statements show Waverly's financial summaries for each of the last four years. This historical view can offer some interesting insights regarding key changes or trends. For example, there has been considerable growth in total assets for this firm over the four years.

It is also interesting to look at the year-to-year changes in each category. For example, cash grew slowly in 1992, substantially in 1993, and remained almost constant in 1994. As shown in Figure 3.3, sales increased, decreased, and then increased again. Net income fell when sales increased, rose when sales decreased, and then increased as sales went to the high level of 1994. This information gives Waverly's owners hints as to problems that may need further study.

Identifying the causes of the reported changes can be quite difficult. Generally, you must know the business and the various conditions and occurrences that may account for the pattern of changes in order to offer reasonable explanations and evaluations.

## COMPARATIVE PERCENTAGE SUMMARIES

It is often useful to present the items on the balance sheet as percentages of total assets (see Figure 3.4, p. 71). Similarly, income statement items can be presented as percentages of total sales (see Figure 3.5, p. 72). This procedure provides a clearer basis for year-to-year comparisons and enables fluctuations and deviations to be readily noticed. Operating results (Figure 3.5) suffered in 1992, as compared to 1991, when cost of goods sold increased as a percentage of sales revenue. The picture changed in 1993. Waverly was able to raise its prices considerably with a much lower decrease in sales. This gave a much

Figure 3.2

**WAVERLY CUSTOM JEWELERS**
**COMPARATIVE BALANCE SHEETS**

|  | 1991 | 1992 | 1993 | 1994 |
|---|---|---|---|---|
| **CURRENT ASSETS** | | | | |
| Cash | $ 11,100 | $ 13,500 | $ 20,500 | $ 20,200 |
| Accounts Receivable | 13,500 | 16,900 | 24,700 | 27,500 |
| Inventory | 110,400 | 147,900 | 157,000 | 165,800 |
| Prepaid Expenses | 9,000 | 8,000 | 7,000 | 8,000 |
| Total Current | $144,000 | $186,300 | $209,200 | $221,500 |
| | | | | |
| **FIXED ASSETS** | | | | |
| Equipment | 46,400 | 46,400 | 76,400 | 96,400 |
| Less Depreciation | (11,600) | (23,200) | (37,800) | (57,400) |
| TOTAL ASSETS | $178,800 | $209,500 | $247,800 | $260,500 |
| | | | | |
| **CURRENT LIABILITIES** | | | | |
| Accounts Payable | $ 21,600 | $ 31,000 | $ 19,000 | $ 20,000 |
| Expenses Payable | 16,200 | 18,800 | 14,400 | 15,500 |
| Interest Payable | 900 | 1,000 | 1,600 | 1,000 |
| Tax Payable | 3,000 | 2,000 | 12,000 | 3,000 |
| Note Payable | 52,000 | 32,000 | 20,000 | 10,000 |
| TOTAL CURRENT LIABILITIES | $ 93,700 | $ 84,800 | $ 67,000 | $ 49,000 |
| | | | | |
| **LONG-TERM LIABILITIES** | | | | |
| Long-Term Loan | 0 | 27,000 | 47,000 | 40,000 |
| TOTAL LIABILITIES | $ 93,700 | $111,800 | $114,000 | $ 89,000 |
| | | | | |
| **OWNER'S EQUITY** | | | | |
| Stock | $ 70,100 | $ 70,100 | $ 70,100 | $ 70,100 |
| Retained Earnings | 15,000 | 27,600 | 63,700 | 101,400 |
| TOTAL LIABILITIES & OWNER'S EQUITY | $178,800 | $209,500 | $247,800 | $260,500 |

Figure 3.3

**WAVERLY CUSTOM JEWELERS**
**COMPARATIVE INCOME STATEMENTS**

|  | 1991 | 1992 | 1993 | 1994 |
|---|---|---|---|---|
| Net Sales | $421,200 | $489,000 | $464,000 | $493,000 |
| Cost of Goods Sold | 280,800 | 342,300 | 278,400 | 295,200 |
| Gross Profit on Sales | $140,400 | $146,700 | $185,600 | $196,800 |
| Expenses: | | | | |
| Operating Expenses | 93,600 | 104,000 | 92,100 | 97,800 |
| Depreciation Expense | 11,600 | 11,600 | 14,600 | 19,600 |
| Net Income from Operations | $ 35,200 | $ 31,100 | $ 78,900 | $ 79,400 |
| Less Interest Expense | 5,200 | 5,900 | 6,700 | 5,000 |
| Net Income Before Tax | $ 30,000 | $ 25,200 | $ 72,200 | $ 74,400 |
| Less Income Tax Expense | 15,000 | 12,600 | 36,100 | 37,700 |
| **NET INCOME** | $ 15,000 | $ 12,600 | $ 36,100 | $ 37,700 |

better gross profit percentage in 1993. With the lower level of activity, operating expense decreased as a percentage of sales revenue. Growth in sales in 1994 led to a small increase in net income after tax over 1993, with almost no changes in percentages.

Figures 3.2 and 3.4 indicate the firm became less dependent on short-term borrowed funds as they moved from 1991 to 1994. Long-term debt was added in 1992 and 1993, which was used partially to increase inventory and partially to decrease short-term debt.

Figure 3.4

## COMPARATIVE BALANCE SHEET PERCENTAGES
(Vertical Analysis)

|  | Industry Average | 1991 % | 1992 % | 1993 % | 1994 % |
|---|---|---|---|---|---|
| **Current assets:** | | | | | |
| Cash | 7 | 6 | 7 | 10 | 9 |
| Accounts receivable (net) | 9 | 7 | 8 | 10 | 13 |
| Inventory | 69 | 62 | 70 | 63 | 63 |
| Prepaid expenses | n/a | 5 | 4 | 3 | 3 |
| Total current assets | 86 | 80 | 89 | 85 | 85 |
| **Long-term assets:** | | | | | |
| Equipment, furniture & fixtures | 10 | 20 | 11 | 15 | 15 |
| **TOTAL ASSETS** | **100** | **100** | **100** | **100** | **100** |
| **LIABILITIES:** | | | | | |
| **Current liabilities:** | | | | | |
| Merchandise payable | 18 | 12 | 15 | 8 | 8 |
| Operating expenses payable | n/a | 9 | 9 | 6 | 6 |
| Interest payable | n/a | 1 | 1 | 1 | 1 |
| Income tax payable | n/a | 2 | 1 | 5 | 1 |
| Short-term notes payable | 13 | 29 | 15 | 8 | 4 |
| Total current liabilities | 43 | 53 | 41 | 28 | 20 |
| **Long-term liabilities:** | | | | | |
| Notes payable | 14 | 0 | 13 | 19 | 15 |
| **Owner's equity:** | | | | | |
| Common stock | 38 | 39 | 33 | 28 | 26 |
| Retained earnings | * | 8 | 13 | 25 | 39 |
| **TOTAL LIABILITIES & OWNER'S EQUITY** | **100**** | **100** | **100** | **100** | **100** |

\* Stock & Retained earnings combined = 38%
\*\* Does not add to 100% because of differences in reporting
n/a = not available in Robert Morris Associates

Figure 3.5

**COMPARATIVE INCOME STATEMENT PERCENTAGE**

(Vertical Analysis)

|  | Industry Average | 1991 % | 1992 % | 1993 % | 1994 % |
|---|---|---|---|---|---|
| Net Sales | 100 | 100 | 100 | 100 | 100 |
| Cost of Goods Sold | 53 | 67 | 70 | 60 | 60 |
| Gross profit on sales | 47 | 33 | 30 | 40 | 40 |
| Expenses: | | | | | |
| Operating expenses | 42 | 22 | 22 | 20 | 20 |
| Depreciation expense | n/a | 3 | 2 | 3 | 4 |
| Net income from operations | 5.8 | 8 | 6 | 17 | 16 |
| Less interest expense | n/a | 1 | 1 | 1 | 1 |
| Net income before tax | 4.2 | 7 | 5 | 16 | 15 |
| Less income tax expense | n/a | 3.5 | 2.5 | 8 | 7.5 |
| **NET INCOME** | n/a | 3.5 | 2.5 | 8 | 7.5 |

## CASH FLOW STATEMENT

In spite of the importance of the income statement as a financial analysis tool, the success of small businesses may hinge more on cash flow than on net income—cash is the lifeblood of the business. A firm may show a profit on paper and still not have sufficient cash to operate.

There are at least three reasons for this. First, if sales are made on credit, the registering of a sale does not mean that cash is tendered. The firm may not receive the actual cash for 60 to 90 days. Second, payments for inventory may be required at the time of ordering or receiving the product, but the actual products may not be sold for several months. Third, some expenses may be recorded on a uniform monthly basis when the payment for the expense is either quarterly or annually. Cash outflows therefore seldom match cash inflows, and a business can be cash poor in spite of making money on every sale.

This can be illustrated using the Waverly Custom Jewelers case. Figure 3.6 shows the cash flow for each month of 1994. Total sales for the year are the same as in Figure 3.3, but Waverly experiences a significant seasonality in

Figure 3.6

## WAVERLY CUSTOM JEWELERS
## CASH FLOW STATEMENT
## 1994

|  | Jan | Feb | Mar | Apr | May | Jun | Jul | Aug | Sep | Oct | Nov | Dec | TOTAL |
|---|---|---|---|---|---|---|---|---|---|---|---|---|---|
| **CASH INFLOWS** | | | | | | | | | | | | | |
| Cash Sales | 9500 | 28500 | 9700 | 10500 | 25200 | 10200 | 7500 | 6800 | 7800 | 7550 | 50500 | 72750 | 246500 |
| A/R Receipts | 71250 | 9500 | 28500 | 9700 | 10500 | 25200 | 10200 | 7500 | 6800 | 7800 | 7550 | 50500 | 245250 |
| **CASH OUTFLOWS** | | | | | | | | | | | | | |
| Inventory | 34200 | 11640 | 12600 | 30240 | 12240 | 9000 | 8160 | 9360 | 9060 | 60600 | 87300 | 10200 | 294600 |
| Rent | 2000 | 2000 | 2000 | 2000 | 2000 | 2000 | 2000 | 2000 | 2000 | 2000 | 2000 | 2000 | 24000 |
| Advertising |  |  |  | 500 | 1000 |  |  |  |  | 500 | 2000 | 2000 | 6000 |
| Salaries | 2000 | 2000 | 2000 | 2000 | 2000 | 2000 | 2000 | 2000 | 2000 | 2000 | 2000 | 24000 |  |
| Wages | 2775 | 2775 | 2775 | 2775 | 2775 | 2775 | 2775 | 2775 | 2775 | 2775 | 4000 | 4000 | 35750 |
| Loan Payments | 750 | 750 | 750 | 750 | 750 | 750 | 750 | 750 | 750 | 750 | 750 | 750 | 9000 |
| Taxes |  | 9425 |  |  | 9425 |  |  | 9425 |  |  | 9425 |  | 37700 |
| Miscellaneous | 1200 | 975 | 825 | 1100 | 400 | 800 | 1050 | 875 | 900 | 1100 | 850 | 1100 | 10275 |
| **NET CASH FLOW** | 37825 | 8435 | 17250 | -19165 | 5110 | 18075 | 965 | -12885 | -2885 | -54375 | -50275 | 101200 | 49275 |

CHAPTER 3: INTERNAL ANALYSIS / 73

their sales. A high percentage of sales occurs in November and December, when customers purchase Christmas presents. Another relatively high peak is in May and June, because of graduations, weddings, Mother's Day, and Father's Day. February experiences a brief surge just before Valentine's Day. Sales are also not all in cash. Some sales are on credit cards and some are on store credit. Assume for this example that half the sales are cash and the remainder are paid in the following month. It is also important to note that jewelry is purchased by the store two months before the jewelry is actually sold to customers. Waverly has a good credit rating and makes its purchases on credit, typically making payment the month afterward. Thus, for Waverly, cash payments precede the sales by one month. Miscellaneous operating expenses are not broken down into specific expenses, but items such as insurance, attorney fees, and utilities vary over the year. Although both the inflow and the outflow of cash vary over the year, they do not vary in concert.

The importance of analyzing cash flow can be seen by even a cursory look at Waverly's financial statements. The income statement shows total income for 1994 of $37,700. The cash flow statement shows a net cash flow for the year of $49,275, or approximately $12,000 higher than net income. However, monthly net cash flows varied from a + $101,200 in December to a -$54,375 in October. This is primarily because Waverly's owners were purchasing inventory in October that was sold in November and December. If a business similar to Waverly Custom Jewelers was low in cash and then experienced a month like October or November, they would have severe cash flow problems.

## FINANCIAL RATIOS

Analyzing the three financial statements—balance sheet, income statement, and cash flow statement—provides a wealth of information with which to assess the financial health of a business. Even more information can be gleaned by tracking ratios of variables taken from the financial statements. The dozens of ratios that can be computed fall in four categories: **liquidity ratios, activity ratios, leverage ratios,** and **profitability ratios.** We suggest selecting a few ratios from within the four categories that can be tracked and computed easily.

## LIQUIDITY RATIOS

These ratios indicate the firm's capacity for meeting its short-run or near-term obligations. In other words, these ratios help in determining whether the business has enough working capital to get by, pay its bills, invest in the future, take advantage of immediate opportunities, and fight off unforeseen short-term crises. The two most important of these are the **current ratio** and the acid-test or **quick ratio**.

The **current ratio** is derived by dividing current assets by current liabilities. Waverly Custom Jewelers' current ratios are shown in Figure 3.7. Generally, most experts feel that the current ratio should be 2 to 1. This is only a rough rule of thumb, however, and varies considerably from industry to industry. For example, if the industry is one in which the bulk of sales are made on credit, a larger current ratio may be needed in order to feel comfortable. A business like Waverly, which has a high amount of expensive inventory, would be expected to have high current assets. The size of the current ratio is a function of how the inventory is financed. If short-term debt is used, the ratio will be lower than if long-term debt or equity is used. The desirability of a high ratio also depends on the conservativeness of the owner. A very conservative owner may want high inventories, high amounts of cash, and high accounts receivable to feel secure. However, inventory uses up cash that could be used for other purposes, and a liberal accounts receivable policy means that we are underwriting our customers' debt at no interest. Further, keeping excess cash or short-term investments on hand means that those funds are not being invested to their maximum potential.

---

Figure 3.7

### COMPARATIVE CURRENT RATIOS

Current Ratio = Current Assets / Current Liabilities

| Year | Calculation | |
|---|---|---|
| 1991 | 144,000 / 93,700 = 1.5 | |
| 1992 | 186,300 / 84,800 = 2.2 | Industry Average – 1.8 |
| 1993 | 209,200 / 67,000 = 3.1 | |
| 1994 | 221,500 / 49,000 = 4.5 | |

---

It is important to see how a firm compares with the industry and also how it compares with itself in previous periods. In the Waverly example, it is useful to note the changes that have occurred in the current ratio over the years. At the end of 1991, the ratio was below the rough rule of thumb of 2 to 1. It improved in 1992, largely because long-term debt was substituted for short-term payables. By 1994, the ratio was very strong. In fact, the current ratio suggests that the firm should now consider some more productive use of cash. This is particularly significant given that the industry average for jewelry companies of this size is only 1.8.

The **quick ratio** (sometimes called the acid-test ratio) is computed by dividing current assets less inventories by current liabilities. Since inventories may not be easily converted to cash, this ratio gives a more accurate picture of a firm's capacity for short-run response to opportunities and crises by subtracting the value of these inventories. Although considerable variability is possible, a quick ratio of 1 to 1 is typically sought. Figure 3.8 shows the quick ratios for Waverly Custom Jewelers. The retail jewelry industry has an extremely low quick ratio because of the value of inventory. Waverly's ratio exceeds the industry in each of the last four years and is quite high in 1994.

---

Figure 3.8

### COMPARATIVE QUICK RATIOS

| | | |
|---|---|---|
| 1991 | 33,600 / 93,700 = .36 | |
| 1992 | 38,400 / 84,800 = .45 | Industry Average = .30 |
| 1993 | 52,200 / 67,000 = .78 | |
| 1994 | 55,700 / 49,000 = 1.14 | |

---

## ACTIVITY RATIOS

These ratios offer insight into how effectively the firm is using its resources.

The **inventory turnover** ratio is computed by dividing cost of goods sold by average inventory. Again, rules of thumb vary depending on the industry. Therefore, it is valuable to compare to the industry as well as to a company's historical trends. The inventory turnover ratio for Waverly (see Figure 3.9) has consistently exceeded the industry average, but the ratios in 1993 and 1994 were lower even though profits were higher. Waverly may have purchased more inventory than it needed when it changed its pricing strategy in 1993, and the store's inventory management probably requires additional study.

---

Figure 3.9

**COMPARATIVE INVENTORY TURNOVER RATIOS**

| | | |
|---|---|---|
| 1991 | 280,800 / (110,400 + 98,600)/2* = 2.82 | |
| 1992 | 342,300 / (147,900 + 110,400)/2 = 2.65 | Industry Average = 1.2 |
| 1993 | 278,400 / (157,000 + 147,900)/2 = 1.10 | |
| 1994 | 295,200 / (165,800 + 157,000)/2 = 1.83 | |

*Beginning inventory plus ending inventory divided by 2.*

---

The **asset turnover** ratio is computed by dividing sales by total assets. The asset turnover ratios for Waverly Custom Jewelers shown in Figure 3.10 show a drop in 1993 that correlates with the drop in the inventory turnover ratio, suggesting the need to study asset management.

---

Figure 3.10

**COMPARATIVE ASSET TURNOVER RATIOS**

| | | |
|---|---|---|
| 1991 | 421,200 / 178,800 = 2.37 | |
| 1992 | 489,000 / 209,500 = 2.33 | Industry Average = 1.5 |
| 1993 | 464,000 / 247,800 = 1.87 | |
| 1994 | 493,000 / 260,500 = 1.89 | |

---

The **accounts receivable turnover** ratio is computed by dividing annual credit sales by average accounts receivable. Accounts receivable turnover is the time it takes to collect credit sales. This ratio should be monitored carefully and compared to industry standards; it is most frequently used to check the receivables collection rate. Approximately half of Waverly's sales are on credit. The store's accounts receivable turnover ratios are shown in Figure 3.11.

---

Figure 3.11

### COMPARATIVE ACCOUNTS RECEIVABLE TURNOVER RATIOS

1991    210,600 / (13,500 + 11,500)/2* = 16.9

1992    244,500 / (16,900 + 13,500)/2 = 16.1    Industry Average = 32.5

1993    232,000 / (24,700 + 16,900)/2 = 11.2

1994    246,500 / (27,500 + 24,700)/2 = 9.4

*Beginning accounts receivable plus ending accounts receivable divided by 2.*

---

The **average collection period** is calculated by dividing 365 by the accounts receivable turnover ratio. This variable is important in cash flow analysis. It indicates the average length of time a business must wait to collect its **credit** sales. This is especially important when you also consider the **average inventory holding period** (365 days divided by the inventory turnover ratio). If an owner pays cash for inventory purchases, then that cash is not returned until both the inventory turnover period plus the average collection period have passed. For example, if inventory is held an average of 35 days and the average collection period is another 25 days, the owner is waiting a total of 60 days for the return of the cash. If this figure is greater than industry norms or is increasing over time, it may mean that the business either is too liberal with its credit policy or has unusual difficulty in collections.

It is important to determine the average collection period over the past few years. Significant shifts should be examined to determine if they are caused by deliberate changes in company policies or changing customer behavior. The collection period for Waverly Custom Jewelers has lengthened considerably (see Figure 3.12). This may be a danger signal, even though the store's liquidity ratios are high.

Figure 3.12

**COMPARATIVE AVERAGE COLLECTION PERIOD
(IN DAYS)**

| | | |
|---|---|---|
| 1991 | 365 / 16.9 = 21.6 | |
| 1992 | 365 / 17.5 = 20.9 | Industry Average = 11.2 |
| 1993 | 365 / 11.2 = 32.6 | |
| 1994 | 365 / 9.4 = 38.8 | |

## Leverage Ratios

**Leverage ratios** indicate the extent to which the business's capital is secured through equity or debt. These figures are quite critical for the new or growing firm, because its ability to raise additional capital may be affected by the present leverage position.

The **debt to assets ratio** indicates the percentage of assets that are funded through debt and is measured by dividing total liabilities by total assets. A ratio that is too high may be risky. Too much debt may restrict growth and the ability to raise additional funds externally. Conversely, a low debt to asset ratio may indicate inefficient use of capital. Waverly shows a healthy decrease in its debt to asset ratio (see Figure 3.13). The store may be in a position to pay out cash or to enlarge its investment in noncurrent assets.

Figure 3.13

**COMPARATIVE DEBT TO ASSETS RATIOS**

| | | |
|---|---|---|
| 1991 | 93,700 / 178,000 = 52% | |
| 1992 | 111,800 / 209,500 = 53% | Industry Average not available |
| 1993 | 114,000 / 247,800 = 46% | |
| 1994 | 89,000 / 260,500 = 34% | |

The **debt to equity ratio** is computed by dividing total debt by total owner's equity. This ratio indicates the extent to which operating funds have been generated by the owner(s). The debt to equity ratio for Waverly Custom Jewelers (see Figure 3.14) shows a significant decrease in reliance on debt.

---

Figure 3.14

**COMPARATIVE DEBT TO EQUITY RATIOS**

| | | |
|---|---|---|
| 1991 | 93,700 / 85,100 = 110% | |
| 1992 | 111,800 / 97,700 = 114% | Industry Average = 150% |
| 1993 | 114,000 / 133,800 = 85% | |
| 1994 | 89,000 / 171,500 = 52% | |

---

## Profitability Ratios

Profitability ratios measure a firm's financial performance and financial returns. These ratios are important both on their own, as they pertain to a particular company, and as they compare to industry averages. Significant deviations from industry standards or strong negative movements internally may signal that the economic viability of the business is in serious question. In short, these ratios give a quick, bottom-line picture of the firm's current financial results.

The **gross profit margin** is computed by subtracting cost of goods sold from sales and dividing the result by sales. This ratio indicates how the selling activity provides the margin to cover operating costs and leave a profit balance. This ratio is also reported directly on the comparative percentage statements in Figure 3.15.

The **return on total assets ratio** is calculated by dividing net income from operations by average total assets. This ratio measures the firm's operating performance. In other words, it is the rate of return on the total investment made by creditors and owners. Waverly Custom Jewelers, as should be expected, shows improvement in years 3 and 4 as compared to years 1 and 2 (see Figure 3.15). While total assets have grown, net income has increased at a faster rate. Additional funds from incurring long-term debt seemed to do much to improve ratios and performance for this company.

---

Figure 3.15

## COMPARATIVE RETURN ON TOTAL ASSETS RATIOS

1991    35,200 / (178,800 + 158,200)/2* = 20.9%

1992    31,100 / (209,500 + 178,800)/2 = 16%

1993    78,900 / (247,800 + 209,500)/2 = 34.5%

1994    79,400 / (260,500 + 247,800)/2 = 31.2%

*Average total assets = beginning assets plus ending assets divided by 2.*

---

## DRAWING STRATEGIC CONCLUSIONS

As noted frequently above, conclusions are more difficult to draw than financial ratios are to compute. Indeed, in assessing the firm's financial state, ratios and statement comparisons must be used as tools to guide planners in their decisions.

But these measures are only one of the possible information sources that should be considered. The owner's knowledge and awareness of the business may be necessary either to temper or to augment what the financial information projects. Good sense and perspective must be used in conjunction with the objective figures and computations.

Strategic thinking should pervade the entire financial analysis. For example, a low current ratio suggests that the firm has trouble paying its bills. However, the strategic significance is that any substantial change in the net use of funds may cause the firm's liquidity position to worsen. Long-term capital may need to be secured to underwrite the strategy and clean up the current liquidity problem.

Similarly, the leverage ratios may suggest strong or weak positions in regard to debt versus capital, but they may also dictate a financial strategy prior to planned expansion.

Interpretations of ratio analyses and financial statement information are the basis for three financial resource evaluations. First, what is the **overall financial performance** of the business? A number of items may need to be considered in reaching this conclusion. Next, is the firm **able to raise needed capital**? Cash flows, availability of internal funds, and the firm's debt position may all be important considerations. Finally, what is the firm's **cash flow position**?

It may appear overly simplistic to reduce the evaluation of financial resources to these three questions, but they are typically the three most critical the business owner must ask before committing to the pursuit of any objective, strategy, or environmental opportunity.

## Evaluating Marketing Resources

Most small business owners and analysts readily agree that marketing is a critical concern and can powerfully influence the overall success of the business. Despite this realization, marketing resources are rarely subjected to close analysis or scrutiny. Often, the business has no valid measure of the relative effectiveness of its marketing efforts. Likewise, owners often fail to understand the capacity and limitations of the existing marketing system. It is therefore necessary to evaluate the marketing function very carefully.

In analyzing the internal strengths and weaknesses of the marketing system, you should consider eight general categories of marketing resources: market performance, knowledge of markets, location, product, advertising and promotion, price, image, and distribution.

### MARKET PERFORMANCE

A logical starting point is to evaluate or rate actual market performance. The most reasonable and tangible factor to consider is the firm's relative market share. One may occasionally have enough information about the industry, market area, and competitors to calculate an objective and accurate statement of market share. More often, one arrives at a reasonable estimate based on sketchy or piecemeal data.

For example, a small hardware store's owners may know that they face competition from six other stores in the basic market area. Furthermore, they know that three of the stores command the bulk of the business. Even without any specific data, these business owners clearly understand that their firm's market share rating is relatively weak. Usually there will be some objective information available, which, when complemented by sound subjective judgments, allows you to arrive at a pretty accurate picture of relative market share.

Market share is a rather limited indicator of a company's performance, addressing only past performance and indicating nothing about future potential. However, quite useful inferences may be drawn from this assessment. For example, if the market is competitively saturated and industry growth prospects are limited, the strength or weakness of the present market share is probably a key indicator of whether or not the business will be able to withstand and survive the industry shakeout that is likely to occur.

**KNOWLEDGE OF MARKETS**

Owners first must know their target markets. Who are the firm's customers? What is the demographic makeup of the target market and how is it changing? Perhaps most important, what are the customer preferences and needs and how will these be changing in the future?

Owners must also know their market area. What changes or developments are occurring that may reflect on or affect the business? Is the demographic composition of the market area changing? Are important new competitors entering the market area? Owners must be aware of important market changes and directions. True, knowledge and awareness are intangible concepts are susceptible to a wide range of interpretations. Yet this knowledge may be most critical in helping position the business to deal with future obstacles and opportunities.

Consider the case of Kultur International Films in Profile 3.4, p. 84. Dennis Hedlund initially misread the target market for the performing arts tapes. He attempted to market them to the general public rather than to the specific clientele interested in them. A more careful understanding of the appropriate target market enabled him to achieve his firm's potential.

---

PROFILE 3.4: KULTUR INTERNATIONAL FILMS, LTD.

In the early 1980s, Dennis Hedlund conceived the idea of selling performing arts videos—operas, symphonies, ballets, and other highbrow material—through video stores. It was not easy finding videos of such material, and getting the rights to them was even harder. But neither of these tasks proved as difficult as selling the videos to video stores.

Hedlund and his wife worked long hours trying to get video stores to buy the tapes. Mr. Hedlund even signed on as a sales representative for other video companies in order to gain access to the video stores. Still, video stores would not purchase his tapes. Store managers preferred to buy tapes of popular movies rather than stock even a few of the performing arts videos.

Finally accepting that there simply was not a demand for the tapes in normal video stores, Hedlund began marketing the tapes through museums, dance studios, and art galleries. He also bought mailing lists and made special deals with fan clubs of the performers. He placed ads in specialty magazines catering to his particular target market.

By 1994, Kultur International Films, Ltd. had 450 different videos for sale with sales reaching nearly $5 million, an increase of 25 percent over the previous year.

(Source: Tannenbaum, p. B2)

---

## LOCATION

Although sometimes preestablished and unalterable, location dynamics can exert a significant impact on the business. In fact, poor location is generally listed as one of the primary reasons for small business failure. Rating the relative strength of a location involves examining some rather obvious issues. Location may be a source of considerable strength if it provides visibility to the target market or clientele. On the other hand, a superb product or service may never be accepted if the business is in a bad location.

Location involves more than visibility. Other key factors include ease of access, availability of parking, traffic patterns, demographics, the complementary nature of neighboring businesses, and the location's image. Location image can often determine customers' reactions to and perceptions of the business. For example an upscale boutique located in a deteriorated section of the community will probably not attract the desired clientele. Similarly, a family restaurant will be seriously and negatively affected if it is located in a high-crime area and buffered by bars on either side. The image of the location should support the desired image of the business.

Figure 3.16 lists a number of location factors to consider when starting a new retail business. Figure 3.17, p. 86, lists location factors that are important for a manufacturing business. Many of the factors that are critically important for retail businesses are of no concern to manufacturing businesses. For businesses such as service businesses, in which the business representative goes to customers' homes, the specific location is immaterial.

Figure 3.16

## LOCATION FACTORS FOR RETAIL BUSINESSES

| Factor | Excellent | Good | Fair | Poor |
| --- | --- | --- | --- | --- |
| General location | | | | |
| Proximity to customers | | | | |
| Proximity to competitors | | | | |
| Demographics of target market | | | | |
| Size of building | | | | |
| Size of parking lot | | | | |
| Number of cars passing location | | | | |
| Speed of cars passing location | | | | |
| Distance from traffic signal | | | | |
| Distance from corner | | | | |
| Entrance/exit | | | | |
| Visibility distance | | | | |
| Setback from street | | | | |
| Placement of utilities, drainage, etc. | | | | |
| Distance to nearest commercial neighbor | | | | |
| Compatibility of commercial neighbors | | | | |

Figure 3.17

**LOCATION FACTORS FOR MANUFACTURING BUSINESS**

| Factor | Outstanding | Good | Fair | Poor |
|---|---|---|---|---|
| General region | | | | |
| Proximity to raw materials | | | | |
| Proximity to transportation | | | | |
| Types of available transportation | | | | |
| Condition of available structures | | | | |
| Zoning restrictions | | | | |
| Tax rates | | | | |
| Inducements from city | | | | |
| Availability of utilities | | | | |
| Availability of labor | | | | |

**PRODUCT**

A firm's owner must evaluate the strength of the products sold. Products can be evaluated in absolute terms. However, the rating should also reflect the relative strength of products from a competitive perspective. Three aspects of the product should be considered.

First, you need to evaluate the firm's product line. Product line refers to the variety of products the firm offers. Consider both the breadth and depth of the product line. A broad or complete line enables the business to meet a wider range of consumer needs. Depth refers to the choices available within a product category. For example, one shoe store may offer a very narrow product line, limiting its business exclusively to shoes, but offering a great number of styles and sizes. A competing store, presenting a broader product line, offers not only shoes but an array of complementary or supportive products, such as polishes, socks, purses, and leather goods. Frequently, the store with the narrow line can still compete because of the depth of styles and sizes. The evaluation of product line must consider not only competitive influences, but also the strategic approach the business is trying to promote. If the owner visualizes the business as a specialty shop, its product line should reflect this strategy.

A second product-rating decision relates to the attractiveness of the firm's products. Here, you need to view both product image and product quality from a consumer or market perspective. Purchases are made on the basis of perceived image and quality, even though the perceptions may be inconsistent with reality. If these perceptions are inaccurate, remedial action, perhaps in the form of advertising or promotion, can be used to help correct the misperceptions. Strive to obtain an objective and unbiased evaluation of these factors. Often, outsiders may have to be consulted (small business owners are sometimes too close to their products to make an objective assessment).

Finally, you need to consider product service. Product service relates to the firm's assurances that consumer and product concerns will be effectively and fully addressed once sales have begun. Here, product warranties and guarantees are important, as is the number, availability, and quality of service representatives and service technicians.

**ADVERTISING AND PROMOTION**

The strength of the company's advertising and promotion efforts need to be evaluated. In some situations, there may be objective evidence of the effectiveness of these efforts. For example, a business may note sales growth following certain advertising or promotional campaigns. Often, however, such information is not available, making advertising and promotion one of the most difficult areas to assess. Although most small business owners realize the significance of reaching consumers, informing them of the company's products, and encouraging them to make purchases, the overall advertising and promotional emphasis is rarely analyzed from an objective and competitive perspective. This may be one reason managers often feel that advertising and promotion is one of the most expendable resources: When the business encounters financial strains, the advertising and promotion budget is one of the first to be reduced or eliminated.

In order to evaluate advertising and promotion, you must have a feel for how important these factors are to the industry in which the business operates. For example, if competitors in the industry rely heavily on advertising to generate sales, then meager and ineffective advertising and promotion may be a significant and meaningful weakness. However, if the industry sales are driven by a few established and regular contract sales, large investments in advertising and promotion may be unnecessary. In this regard, it may be useful to compare advertising and promotion expenditures to those typical of the industry. Consider, too, the actions of immediate competitors. If they are investing heavily in advertising, a similar response may be necessary to keep or gain market share.

## PRICE

A business owner should carefully evaluate the firm's pricing strategy. Price can be a difficult and complex factor to rate and must be approached carefully. First, price should reflect the strategy or image the business desires to project. For example, a discount store makes a statement with its low prices. However, a business stressing quality, service, or exclusivity sets high prices to reflect this image.

The strength or weakness of a pricing strategy is strongly affected by the competition. For example, an owner may set prices based on costs (for raw materials, assembly, sales, etc.) and be unable to lower them and still receive an acceptable return. But, if a key competitor lowers its prices, the firm's inability to respond accordingly may be viewed as a price weakness. Size of operations, economies of scale, and production efficiency may enable a business to offer products at consistently lower prices than the competition. Here, price may be rated as a definite strength.

## IMAGE

Image has both internal and external ramifications. That is, the image of the business is reflected through its internal culture or climate and in that way affects the employees. In addition, the image is also perceived by those outside the business and affects their attitudes toward the business. The image should be consistent with the strategies of the business. If this is the case, image emerges as an important strength. If not, image can be a restrictive weakness. For example, if a business wishes to stress personal service as a competitive factor, then it should present an image reflecting openness, concern for workers, communication, and trust. If quality is being stressed, an image of high skill, training, and attention to detail is valuable.

Image evolves as the firm operates. The public's perception of image is based on their historical exposure to the business. Past mistakes, missed deadlines, and arrogant prior owners may all be to blame. Clearly these perceptions may not be the fault of present owners, and present conditions may suggest an image drastically different from the common public view. If this is the case, the present owners need to recognize image as a problem area and create changes in the public's perception of it. Changes tend to be incremental. Remember that image definitely affects customer attitudes toward the business and, in turn, their consumption patterns.

### DISTRIBUTION

Are the channels of distribution accessible and acceptable? Does the product flow from the business to consumers in a reasonable and cost-effective way? In many cases, the firm's product reaches the ultimate consumer only after passing through a set of intermediaries. For example, the small manufacturer may distribute directly to retailers, or to a wholesaler who in turn sells to a number of retailers, or to both retailers and wholesalers. Each stage of the distribution process may need to be evaluated to gain a clear notion of the relative strength of the entire system.

For many small businesses, no intermediaries are involved. The business sells directly to the consumer. Although simpler to evaluate, the effectiveness of the sales and delivery activities must still be considered.

## Evaluating Operational Resources

Operational resources are those that are involved with or support the production of a product or service. Operational resources may relate to the physical elements of the job or to relationships within the business and with key contacts outside the business. Clearly, resources relevant to these categories are numerous. However, there are five key areas: production facilities, access to supplies, inventory control, structure, and quality control.

### PRODUCTION FACILITIES

Production facilities should be viewed rather broadly, and a number of issues should be considered when developing this rating. First, examine the firm's existing plant and equipment. Is the physical plant large enough to handle the desired scope of business operations? Has the business made the technical advances in plant and equipment necessary to remain competitive? Is the equipment used by the business technically and operationally sound and efficient?

Part of this analysis should address the issue of capacity. Is the business operating near capacity or significantly below capacity? Either condition could be viewed as a potential weakness, depending on the growth projections of the business. Further, explore the physical layout and work flow. Do the production facilities permit work to be arranged in the most efficient and productive manner?

## ACCESS TO SUPPLIERS

Two basic questions emerge here. The first concerns basic availability. Does the business have ready access to the necessary raw materials and suppliers? Availability must be tempered by cost considerations. How much do these materials and supplies cost? A promising opportunity may be negated by either costly or inconsistent sources of supply.

Consider this example. An entrepreneur wanted to sell sports buttons and pins to area schools. She convinced the school's administrators that having these items available for students would enhance school spirit and pride. Her marketing efforts were successful and orders were far above initial expectations. Unfortunately, she had lined up only one very small supplier located many miles away. Not only was the supplier unable to meet the required demand, but he refused any shipments until the price was renegotiated. Glumly, the entrepreneur was forced to cancel orders and, in the process, see her credibility and image shattered.

## INVENTORY CONTROL

In examining inventory, the manager evaluates the strength of the system for stocking, ordering, and reordering materials (raw or finished products). Success in this area may be the key to meeting the customer's needs on time. Does the owner know what materials are on hand? Can they be located and accessed? Are there clear, established procedures for initiating reorders? Is there typically an acceptable level of materials in stock, or is the business regularly plagued with inventory backlogs and outages? The inventory control system need not be computerized nor highly sophisticated, but it should prompt action that will ensure steady, desired inventory flows.

## STRUCTURE

The structure of an organization is the formal flow of information and authority within it. It indicates the jobs that people do and their accompanying areas of responsibility. The organizational structure should be consistent with and support the strategies and objectives of the business. If the business desires operational flexibility, an informal or open structural system may be preferable. For example, in a business geared toward completing highly visible projects, activities can be structured around those projects. The key to evaluating the structure is to note if the business and its personnel are restricted by the demands of the structure or if the structure is logical and helps employees fulfill their responsibilities.

## QUALITY CONTROL

Evaluate the policies and procedures that the organization uses to assure the quality of its products and services. We live in an era when business is held to ever-rising quality standards. In fact, quality is one of the strongest reasons behind the long-term success of a business in today's competitive environment. Although quality may be assessed from many perspectives, users of a business's goods and services often offer the most important signals.

Customers and clients provide excellent evidence of their satisfaction with quality by their reactions to the products and services they receive. For example, if your small business provides components for a large industrial manufacturer, quality specifications are normally designated contractually. Fail to meet these standards, and you lose the contract. On the other hand, if your small business serves a retail or service market, customer returns or client complaints may signal quality deficiencies.

However, you should not assume that quality is acceptable simply because customer complaints are not being heard. A slip in quality is often difficult to detect, and quality comparisons between competitors are often quite subjective and subtle. Therefore, specific procedures must be enacted to detect quality concerns. For example, some businesses rely on customer surveys to note potential quality problems. Others conduct regular internal audits to spot problem areas. Whatever set of procedures are used, the quality assessment is a critical factor in the internal analysis.

## Evaluating Human Resources

The final category of internal factors to be analyzed relate to the firm's personnel, or human resources. Although this component is often overlooked, the firm's personnel are its most critical assets. We view human resources broadly to include all personnel of the firm, along with their unique skills and abilities.

A key initial concern is to examine the number of employees and the relevancy of their skills. If the business is considering a strategic realignment or expansion, you need to determine how many employees are needed and what specific skills are required and then compare these requirements to the existing human resource supply. If there are discrepancies, corrective action must be taken before the strategy is enacted. If the required skills are missing, the firm must either train existing employees or hire additional workers who have these skills. Human resource planning need not be excessively complex, but small businesses must objectively consider these issues.

A second human resource consideration is to assess employee morale and management/labor relations. Morale is a key factor, yet fairly difficult to measure accurately. In most situations, the small firm need not take the time and effort to conduct a formal morale survey: A set of more informal indicators should suffice. Employee turnover, absenteeism, tardiness, and a general assessment of the workday climate should provide a notion of morale. Frequent grumblings, complaints, arguments, and conflicts may indicate weakened morale. Again, the attempt here should be to get a general feeling about morale as it affects business action.

For example, if the business is considering a new expansion program, with its attendant turmoil and stress, morale becomes critical. A business with weak morale may expect a series of problems (perhaps significant enough to undermine the expansion efforts) that a firm with stronger worker commitment and morale can avoid. Similarly, for unionized firms, the quality of labor relations is important. A history of adversarial relationships with bitter disagreements and an underlying tone of mistrust may be considered a key obstacle to expansion.

A third factor to examine is the compensation system of the organization. Compensation refers to wages and salary plus any fringe benefits. Compensation is worthy of detailed consideration. However, for our purposes, the essential determinations are whether the present compensation system is (1) adequate and (2) consistent with the strategic direction of the firm.

The adequacy of the firm's compensation is determined by both internal and external comparisons. Internally, most workers will feel compensation is adequate if it is distributed equitably. That is, better performers earn more than lesser performers. However, if considerable work is being done in teams, team members must feel their compensation is fair in relation to one another. Indeed, an internal perception that compensation is equitable is key to employee motivation and the credibility of the compensation system. Externally, adequacy is largely a function of competition. Are workers receiving compensation that is reasonably consistent with that of workers in similar firms and industries?

Workers may be willing to accept a lower salary if other factors make up for it. For example, two businesses are competing for the same labor market. One provides a slightly higher compensation package. The second, however, offers a more challenging, interesting, and pleasant work environment. Some workers may feel that the opportunities available at the second business outweigh the compensation difference. But managers should not deceive themselves. In general, workers expect compensation that is similar to or better than that of competitors.

The adequacy of the firm's compensation system affects many areas, including employee motivation and the firm's ability to attract and keep quality workers.

The compensation system must also be consistent with the strategic thrust of the firm. If the firm is moving aggressively into new markets and is depending on the efforts of its sales force to attract new customers, the compensation system must reflect this. Quotas, bonuses, or a commission system may be needed to entice workers to attract new contacts and businesses. The firm's hourly wage may have worked fine in the past, but the new demands require new motivational efforts.

If the business is attempting to build a unified, loyal work force with a strong commitment to the business, companywide performance incentives may be appropriate. A properly designed system can help the manager achieve desired results.

## Focus on Strategy

This chapter is good reading for any student or manager interested in assessing the current position of a firm. The focus of this book, however, is strategic planning. More important than the firm's current position, therefore, is the firm's position related to its future ability to compete and its ability to achieve long-term corporate goals.

We are interested in the firm's current financial position, but we are more interested in its capability to embark on a new strategy given the current position. We may determine that the distribution system is adequate. But when we consider that we may be expanding next year, then the distribution system may not be adequate. The morale in the manufacturing plant may be acceptable, but will it still be after we make major changes in the manufacturing process? The focus must be on the future.

## Summary

In this chapter we have divided internal analysis into four resource categories, each with a number of focus areas. Our list of internal areas or factors is by no means all-inclusive. It is intended to provide a general framework for those beginning the process of internal analysis. Managers of small businesses must select those items that are most relevant to their particular situation, perhaps evaluating areas other than those noted here. Or the list can be a condensed version of what was presented here. As the strategic planning process becomes more comfortable, the internal analysis will become more focused and specific to the needs and demands of the business. You will soon learn which factors are key indicators for your business and analyze these factors in greater depth.

## Discussion Questions

1. Should the external analysis be done before the internal analysis? Why or why not?
2. Why is collecting accurate data about the "people" part of the business difficult?
3. How do you decide which areas to analyze first and in how much depth?
4. For a company that you are familiar with, do as complete an internal analysis as time allows.

5. What would likely be key internal factors for the following businesses? Will your answer be the same for each of them?
   1. A motorcycle dealer
   2. A producer of computer printers
   3. A food wholesaler
   4. A grocery store
   5. A manufacturer of equipment for the space program

## References

Stephanie A. Mehta. "Small Companies Look to Cultivate Foreign Business." *Wall Street Journal*, July 7, 1994, p. B2.

Jeffrey A. Tannenbaum. "Video Distributor Thrives at Last in Offering Culture." *Wall Street Journal*, May 4, 1994, p. B2.

# CASE STUDY

# Internal Analysis of Gaston Ridge Home Health Care, Inc.

AUTHORS' NOTE: The following is a description and assessment of Gaston Ridge Home Health Care, Inc. The analysis includes information regarding Gaston Ridge's strengths and weaknesses in marketing, human resources, structure and culture, financial resources, and technology and equipment.

## Marketing

Gaston Ridge operates in an eight-county area of Southern Illinois. It directs its marketing toward smaller communities and rural areas, thus avoiding direct competition with larger and more powerful agencies that operate in and serve larger communities. Gaston Ridge is located in Perryville, a small community centrally located in the eight-county region, and is housed in a medical building. The site is used primarily for administrative purposes, although some consultation with families of patients and prospective patients is conducted at this location. The site is acceptable and its central location is critical, because employees need to travel to patients' homes. The target market is primarily aged and disabled patients homebound by their physical conditions.

Gaston Ridge Home Health Care, Inc., offers services in 15 areas: diabetic counseling, venipuncture, intramuscular injections, intravenous therapy, medication instruction, hypertension management, diet instruction, home catheter insertion and maintenance, feeding tubes, postoperative care, wound care, hot/cold applications, physical therapy, occupational therapy, and speech therapy. These service offerings are similar to those of competing firms. Although there is a strong demand among the patient population for meal service, Gaston Ridge does not currently offer it. The quality of services, overall, ranks at average levels relative to the competition. However, the skill of the nurses and the quality of skilled nursing care are excellent. Physical therapy, occupational therapy, and speech therapy services are contracted through outside sources, thereby limiting the degree of direct control Gaston Ridge has over the manner of delivery in these areas. However, patient complaints have been limited and the overall feeling is that these services are provided in an acceptable manner.

With the demand for home health care growing significantly, the specific determination of market share is difficult. Clearly, Gaston Ridge is not the dominant agency in the service area. This is probably because the agency has only been in business for a year and because two of its competitors have a strong physician and discharge planner referral base. Overall, Gaston Ridge is the third-strongest competitor in terms of market position.

Minimal advertising is currently done to increase awareness and obtain new patients. Current promotional efforts include free blood pressure and glucose screenings at various community events. These events have enhanced awareness of Gaston Ridge and have provided potential patients the opportunity to meet Gaston Ridge's nurses. Physician referrals strongly affect home health care service choice, and Gaston Ridge does not have a strong physician referral base.

Consumers are quite price-sensitive. A recent survey indicated that nearly 80 percent of the consumers in the service area comparison shop for home health care services after being released from the hospital. Overall, Gaston Ridge's pricing structure is average relative to competitors in the service area.

## Human Resources

Rene Price, RN, is the administrator and president of Gaston Ridge. She had experience developing a home health care unit before she started Gaston Ridge. She is responsible for payroll, insurance, benefits, and scheduling. Jane Heske, RN, is the director of nursing services. Her responsibilities include Medicare filing, operating the computer, and billing. Michelle Lewis, RN, and Tami Skinner, RN, are case managers in charge of all patients. These four principals each draw a salary from the business.

Gaston Ridge employs one full-time health care aid and three part-time time health care aids. These women are paid an hourly wage competitive for the industry and area. Physical therapy, occupational therapy, and speech therapy are handled, as needed, on a contractual basis through outside sources. These therapists are also paid an hourly wage. As noted earlier, the contractual relationship makes quality assurance more difficult for these services.

The morale among agency employees is generally high. There are times when the case load is very heavy and travel becomes hectic and stressful. This seems most prevalent during the winter months, when the demand for services increases and the weather conditions make travel difficult and slow.

## Structure and Culture

The agency is structured very loosely. The owners operate the business in a team-oriented manner, with open communication and group consensus guiding major decisions. All employees are encouraged to contribute ideas and suggestions.

Gaston Ridge spends considerable time and energy building strong relationships with patients and their families. They are extraordinarily sensitive to the unique needs of patients and their loved ones. Employees are encouraged to build rapport, confidence, and trust as they attend to their patients. Clearly, this cultural approach distinguishes Gaston Ridge from the somewhat more businesslike approach of somecompetitors.

## Financial Resources

Since Gaston Ridge has been in existence for only one year, the income statement reflects only that year. Gaston Ridge has received strong community support in the Perryville area and has been able to obtain funds as needed. The county has provided a low-interest loan of $17,000 at 5 percent interest. Further, Legion Bank, located in Perryville, has offered a $20,000 line of credit at 10 percent. Accordingly, Gaston Ridge has sufficient capital available to conduct daily operations. Gaston Ridge owners have built strong relations with community and banking leaders, which should prove beneficial if support is needed for additional funds.

Clients are billed on an accounts receivable basis. The average accounts receivable collection period is three months after the date of billing.

## Technology and Equipment

Currently, Gaston Ridge has standard technology and equipment consistent with most of its competitors. However, it does not possess, nor does it have ready access to, some of the newer equipment and machines such as mobile EKG and X-ray machines. Further, the agency does not have the technology to perform some of the more complex procedures being heralded in the industry. Capital Center, due to its affiliation with a large hospital, is the only competitor in the area to offer the more advanced procedures. Even here, their offerings are limited. Therefore, although further equipment and technology will eventually be needed, little competitive impact is felt at this time. Gaston Ridge's computer and software applications can handle the necessary patient tracking, scheduling, and control. Figure B.1 shows the completed Internal Profile Analysis for Gaston Ridge.

Figure B.1

## INTERNAL PROFILE ANALYSIS

| Internal Resource | Strong Weakness | Slight Weakness | Neutral | Slight Strength | Strong Strength |
|---|---|---|---|---|---|
| **Financial:** | | | | | |
|    Ability to Raise Capital | | | | | X |
|    Cash Flow Position | | | X | | |
|    Overall Performance | | | | X | |
| | | | | | |
| **Marketing:** | | | | | |
|    Quality of Services | | | | X | |
|    Range of Services | | X | | | |
|    Advertising | X | | | | |
|    Promotion | | | X | | |
|    Referral System | X | | | | |
|    Price | | | X | | |
|    Location | | | | | X |
|    Delivery System | | | X | | |
| | | | | | |
| **Human:** | | | | | |
|    Sufficient Number of Employees | | X | | | |
|    Skill of Employees | | | | X | |
|    Morale | | | X | | |
|    Compensation Package | | | X | | |
| | | | | | |
| **Operational:** | | | | | |
|    Structure | | | | X | |
|    Quality Assurance | | X | | | |
|    Image | | | X | | |
| | | | | | |
| Technology & Equipment | | | X | | |
| | | | | | |
| Culture and Image | | | | | X |

# CHAPTER 4

# Recognizing Distinctive Competencies and Competitive Weaknesses

OBJECTIVES

After studying this chapter, you should know

1. what is meant by "distinctive competencies."
2. how to exploit distinctive competencies.
3. how to develop a strength into a distinctive competency.
4. the importance of a "sustainable" competency.
5. the difference between a weakness and a significant competitive weakness.

CHAPTERS 2 AND 3 detailed the process of analyzing the external environment and internal strengths and weaknesses of the firm, discussing the importance and relevance of careful analysis efforts. This chapter considers the final step in the analysis phase of our model—recognizing distinctive competencies and competitive weaknesses.

## Environmental Opportunities Versus Relevant Business Opportunities

Analyzing the relevant external environment will likely reveal a number of possible areas of opportunity. Perhaps competitors have become so big they no longer provide the "personal touch" that consumers have come to desire and expect. Perhaps new segments or niches in the market are appearing but have not been targeted. Perhaps consumer needs and preferences are shifting so that adding complementary products or services will significantly increase sales and profits.

Merely identifying opportunities, however, does not mean that the firm is either willing or able to take advantage of these opportunities. This determination is made after carefully considering the internal analysis. For example, changing demographic and social factors within a given community may suggest that a restaurant–dinner theater combination is an attractive opportunity. Suppose there is no dinner theater in the community and the increasing population base of young, upscale consumers seems likely to support one. A particular restaurant in the community may accurately recognize this as an environmental opportunity. But internal analysis clearly reveals that the restaurant has neither the personnel nor the financial resources to commit to such a project. To this restaurant, the environmental opportunity can not be translated into a relevant business opportunity. Environmental opportunities only become relevant business opportunities when the internal analysis reveals that the business is able to capitalize on these opportunities.

A business may be able to identify a number of environmental opportunities. In general, the more dynamic and growth-oriented the industry, the greater the number of environmental opportunities. Similarly, the more open, responsive, flexible, and sound the business, the greater the number of relevant business opportunities it is likely to identify.

The distinction between environmental opportunities and relevant business opportunities may be somewhat arbitrary or subjective, yet it is critical to the strategic planning process. The business must be concerned with acting on those opportunities that have survived the scrutiny of internal analysis and become relevant business opportunities.

## The Role of Distinctive Competency

A distinctive competency is any area, factor, or consideration that gives a business a meaningful competitive edge. Distinctive competencies positively distinguish a firm from its competitors. They are activities that a firm not only does well, but does better than everyone else. Courtland Clubs (Profile 4.1) has such a distinctive competency.

## PROFILE 4.1: COURTLAND CLUBS

Courtland Clubs was an established tennis club in a medium-sized metropolitan location. Courtland had been in business for more than 25 years and had prided itself on the quality and aesthetics of both its indoor and outdoor courts. Although its prices were high, the club had attracted a prosperous, upscale clientele and had experienced steady growth. Courtland Clubs had developed a reputation as the "in" club among the business and professional community. In the late 1980s, Courtland's management team became aware that physical fitness was becoming more significant to its target market than the socialization factor had been in the past. They feared that membership might start to dip, since many members viewed the club from a social perspective.

In analyzing its environment, Courtland recognized numerous growth opportunities—becoming a health club, complete with weight machines and general workout equipment; adding racquetball facilities; installing an indoor running track; and offering year-round aerobic workouts. Courtland possessed the staff, land, and physical and financial resources to capitalize on any or all of these possibilities. However, other clubs were already providing these features, and it appeared that the last thing the community needed or could support was another health and exercise club. Courtland's owners felt they had responded too slowly to environmental shifts and new consumer needs and were thus stuck in a losing situation.

Courtland's management team assembled to discuss the problem. One of them asked, "Is there any way we can compete in the health club, racquetball, and running club areas given the present level of competitive saturation?" The answer was perhaps, if the Courtland design was unique or special enough to attract users from existing clubs to its facilities. But how were they to build such a club?

The answer lay in the distinctive competency that Courtland had so carefully nurtured over its 25-year existence—quality facilities, luxuries, and a competent and helpful staff that catered to the wishes of its unique (and growing) target market. With this competency in mind, the owners were able to devise a strategic plan and direction and enlarge its offerings.

Often distinctive competencies emerge and grow as the business owner positions the firm to enhance its competitive position. Basically, this was the case with Courtland Clubs. It is also the approach taken by Son Won Karate Academy (see Profile 4.2).

---

### PROFILE 4.2: SON WON KARATE ACADEMY

Son Won started the Son Won Karate Academy in 1980, partly because of his interest in karate and tae kwan do (Won was a third-degree black belt) and partly to capitalize on the growing market opportunity he observed in the midsized American city where he lived. Won's first students were tough, aggressive, macho types, like those who patronized the four competing academies in his market area. Nearly all his students were adults.

By the early 1990s, the karate industry was booming and the market area boasted eight competing academies. Son Won analyzed the industry and discovered certain clear changes. The sport was increasingly receiving a self-defense focus. Further, nearly two thirds of those taking karate classes were now children, about a quarter of them girls. As he explored further, Son realized that relatively affluent, dual-income parents were encouraging their children to take karate lessons, not only for self-defense but also for the exercise and discipline. The sport was particularly attractive because it required no specific skills or equipment.

Won began to promote his academy as a center for building discipline and fitness in young minds and bodies. His newspaper advertisements pictured a young boy and girl and included a message on building self-discipline. He regularly conducted demonstrations at local primary schools, and he enthusiastically courted parents with talk of the self-assurance and discipline their child would develop by studying the sport. He encouraged parents to observe while their child took a free trial lesson, stressing the carryover benefits of better social adjustment and better school performance. Won geared his approach and his advertising and promotional policies to the demographic trends he observed in the industry. In the process, he created a distinctive competency among the affluent parents in his market area and a clear competitive edge over his rivals.

---

## Identifying and Developing Areas of Distinctive Competence

Distinctive competencies may appear in either of two ways. First, the competency may be present as part of the firm's operations. As the business exists over time, it operates in such a manner that clear and important customer areas of competence are stressed. These competencies may have initially arisen out of the firm's mission or managerial orientation. Over time, they become an integral part of the business. Courtland Clubs is an example of this approach. In its competitive situation, Courtland needed to recognize its areas of competence, determine whether they were still viable, and then proceed to use them as the focus for evaluating environmental opportunities and strategic direction.

However, in some situations, distinctive competencies may need to be developed or nurtured—particularly if none currently exist. Here, the owner analyzes the competitive environment, scrutinizes internal resources, and carefully and objectively decides which areas are most fruitful for development. In this approach, the owner attempts to build areas of competence. To a large extent, this is the approach Son Won took in his karate academy.

Such a building or development process can be quite trying for small business owners. Essentially, managers should investigate areas where they can create a meaningful competence, realizing that competencies are dictated by the competitive environment, the firm's internal capacities, and the firm's reactions within its competitive environment. Consider the case of Castille Motors (Profile 4.3). Castille Motors purposely identified an area of competitive uniqueness and committed energy and resources to develop it. This area became a truly distinctive competency because it was important to the market, meeting the needs of and becoming a buying criterion for certain customer segments.

---

PROFILE 4.3: CASTILLE MOTORS

Castille Motors, alarmed at the general public's distrust of car dealerships, recently decided to alter its customer orientation and company image. The company learned that historically many customers and potential customers believed they would be victimized by the negotiation process involved in buying a new car. The company was concerned that this fear kept some potential customers from even coming onto the lot! Clearly, many customers felt they were the object of deceitful and less-than-open-price deliberations. These perceptions were not unique to Castille; to a large extent, they seemed to plague the industry.

Castille management vowed to become more customer-oriented by promoting open and frank communications, honesty, and a friendly, pressure-free customer environment. The hallmark of this approach was their nonnegotiable, bottom-line sticker price. Salespersons were forbidden to negotiate price by even a dollar. Salespersons were encouraged to get to know customer needs and to build relationships with customers. Price was discussed in clear terms, with all charges and additional costs disclosed. At first, customers were leery of the approach, particularly given the competitive climate of other dealers. However, over a number of months, Castille built a reputation for honest and friendly dealings with customers. The company saw a marked jump in sales. Its image was special and touched a responsive chord in its customers.

---

It is difficult to generalize an exhaustive set of competencies. However, Figure 4.1 notes nine of the more common areas of distinctive competence likely to be recognized by small business.

*Quality* is a key area of competence and one that is of growing importance to consumers. Here, the business offers the consumer a product or service that is of discernibly higher quality then can be secured from the competition. Accordingly, consumers come to associate a quality image with the business.

*Service* often moves hand in hand with quality. Here, the business is concerned with aiding the consumer in their dealings with the business and its products. This may occur as service prior to the sale or as repairs and follow-up after the sale.

*Location* is a factor that often dictates the firm's success. It can be an area of considerable competence when recognized and exploited. Location may affect the firm's visibility, its likelihood of attracting the target market, and its competitive edge over businesses offering similar products or services.

*Filling a special niche* is a particularly important competence and one that can be developed after careful analysis of the competitive situation. The business may choose to enter an untapped market, provide unique services or products (and thus limit direct competition), or add aspects of novelty or originality to existing products. Such extensions and variations must be focused on real needs of some segment of the market, however. Providing a unique product that no one cares about or wants to purchase is counterproductive.

*Flexibility and adaptability* may be particular strengths a small business can focus on that offer it a competitive edge over larger, more formalized and rigid operations. For example, a small business may do custom work and thereby attract customers from larger firms who don't offer custom services.

---

Figure 4.1

**AREAS OF DISTINCTIVE COMPETENCE
COMMONLY RECOGNIZED BY SMALL BUSINESSES**

| | |
|---|---|
| Quality | Strong consumer orientation |
| Service | Reputation and image |
| Location | Personnel |
| Filling a special niche | Price |
| Flexibility and adaptability | |

---

A *strong consumer orientation* is often promoted by the smaller business. Smaller firms, perhaps because of a less formalized, bureaucratic process, are able to stay in closer touch with shifting consumer needs and demands and respond more quickly to these preferences. Consumers are likely to feel that the company's employees know them and are willing to adapt and modify their methods and operations to accommodate their customers' individuality.

*Reputation and image* are often quite important. These competencies may be a function of a number of other areas, yet consumers often see the cumulative effect in a general or encompassing way.

*Personnel* can be an area of competence. If management and workers have extensive experience or knowledge, these factors are business strengths. When customers recognize these strengths and believe they are superior, a distinctive competency exists. For example, two hardware stores both have experienced, knowledgeable workers. One store, however, is primarily self-service. The second emphasizes personal interaction and help. Both stores possess personnel strengths, but only the second has transferred that strength into a distinctive competency.

Finally, *price* is often stressed. Price is a tenuous competency—powerful yet remarkably fragile. Its potential as a competency may be significant if competitors are conservative and new entrants into the market are unlikely. However, if a competitor is willing or able to alter its existing price structure in return, this competency can be stripped of its value very quickly. Price is therefore often viewed as a rather short-term competency.

Remember that these nine areas are competencies only if they are perceived as such by the firm's customers. Perception is often more important than reality. For example, a business owner may correctly feel that the firm's customer service is superior to that of the immediate competition. However, if customers are unaware that this service is different from and better than that of competitors, it is not a distinctive competency. It is at best an unexploited strength. A strength must be built or developed into a true area of distinctive competence. Effectively marketing the strength may be the bridge to creating a distinctive competency.

## Relating Distinctive Competencies to Relevant Business Opportunities

As noted earlier, not all environmental opportunities are relevant business opportunities, and not all business opportunities should be exploited. Which of a given series of relevant business opportunities should the business owner choose to pursue? In general, management will select those business opportunities in areas where they possess some unique or special advantage over competitors. In other words, the business should focus on those opportunities for which it has distinctive competencies.

The significance of this point is often overlooked or misunderstood. Often, owners believe that if a relevant business opportunity is present, they should try to capitalize on it even though it may be a poor use of the firm's resources. For example, a number of competitors may be about to respond to the same opportunity, and some of these competitors may be better able to do so. To commit to an area where a firm is, from the outset, at a definite competitive disadvantage is poor business sense. Areas where the business possesses a meaningful competitive edge over its competitors are the areas that should be emphasized.

## Sustainable Competencies

It is one thing to have or develop a distinctive competency. It is quite another to maintain it. The more successful a company is because of a competency, the more competitors will attempt to copy or improve on it. Anything an owner can do to sustain a competency and prevent competitors from encroaching on the territory will go far in ensuring success for the business. Actions that can sustain a competency include patenting a product or process, keeping formulas for products secret, advertising the product heavily in order to develop brand loyalty, and developing unique containers and catchy slogans or product names that encourage customers to identify with the particular product or company.

Ben & Jerry's Homemade Ice Cream, Inc., is an example of a company that has worked hard to sustain its areas of competence. Their super-premium, high-fat, expensive ice cream carries names like Cherry Garcia, Rainforest Crunch, New York Super Fudge Chunk, White Russian, and Coconut Almond Fudge Chip. They also publicize an adamant commitment to social causes. Many customers buy Ben & Jerry's ice cream partially because of the good taste and catchy names and partially because of the company's reputation for involvement in social causes.

Some companies, such as Columbia Sportswear (Profile 4.4), go to great lengths to protect their competencies.

### PROFILE 4.4: COLUMBIA SPORTSWEAR

Columbia Sportswear, of Portland, Oregon, in existence since 1938, expanded from hats into clothes for hunting and fishing. In 1986 it introduced the Bugaboo Parka, which, by virtue of removable and reversible lining and insulation, is three or four jackets in one. The product was a huge success, and Columbia sold its one-millionth Bugaboo Parka in 1992. The jacket is Columbia's best-selling item and makes up 13 percent of the company's $270 million in sales in 1994.

Naturally, along with success came the copycats. While the company's products are protected by registered trademarks, many copycat manufacturers routinely ignore the law, hoping that original manufacturers won't notice or care enough to search them out and prosecute. Protection of product designs and names are critical for Columbia Sportswear. Tim Boyle, Columbia's president, says he spends up to an hour a day addressing knockoff disputes. The company's employees monitor the marketplace closely for copycat parkas and notify Boyle immediately if they find any. In one case, an astute employee noted a copycat parka in a Sears catalog. Boyle immediately called Sears and learned that the goods were still enroute from a Taiwanese factory. He got Sears to cancel the order while the ship was still at sea. Boyle will, without hesitation, bring suit against either a manufacturer or a distributor of the copycat parkas. They are letting the industry know that Columbia is one company that will not tolerate competitors trying to overcome their distinctive competency.

(Source: Selz, p. B2)

---

Few competencies are sustainable forever. Even IBM, previously the epitome of success in the computer industry, has fallen on hard times in recent years. This occurs repeatedly among real estate companies in medium-size cities. For a few years, one company dominates the community's sale of real estate. A few years later, another firm leads the pack. Still later, another will take over as number one. A real estate firm is able to ward off competitors for a few years because of its size or because its key executives are well known in the city. The success of that firm, however, eventually fades when a competitor tries some other approach that customers find appealing. The tenuous nature of distinctive competencies should prompt small business owners to search for ways to sustain their competencies.

## Distinctive Competencies and Strategic Planning

The determination or recognition of a firm's distinctive competency is one of the critical, culminating events of the analysis phase of strategic planning. The distinctive competency of the business becomes the focus or driving force behind selecting relevant business opportunities, preparing mission and goal statements, and planning strategic actions.

It may be useful to refine the steps or processes that make up the analysis phase of the strategic planning model (see Figure 4.2). First, environmental analysis yields a series of environmental opportunities. These are then subjected to the scrutiny of internal analysis to determine if they are in fact relevant business opportunities. Additional analysis focusing on competitors and key internal strengths permits the firm to clearly recognize its distinctive competencies (or pinpoint those factors most fruitful for competency development). Then, the relevant business opportunities are evaluated in terms of the recognized distinctive competency. Those opportunities most consistent with the firm's competencies are the ones that are actively pursued and become the focus for subsequent planning efforts.

Figure 4.2

**DISTINCTIVE COMPETENCY IDENTIFICATION PROCESS**

Environmental Analysis → Environmental Opportunities

Internal Analysis → Strengths & Weaknesses

Environmental Opportunities + Strengths & Weaknesses → Relevant Business Opportunities

Relevant Business Opportunities → Competitive Analysis

Relevant Business Opportunities → Identification of Key Strengths

Competitive Analysis + Identification of Key Strengths → Distinctive Competencies

Distinctive Competencies → Strategy Focus

A caveat: a business may succeed without a specific distinctive competency. In particular, this may be true if consumer demand is strong in relation to industry supply: Simply presenting the product or service to a ready market assures at least short-term success. However, if business returns are attractive and there are no barriers to new entrants into the industry, there will be an eventual competitive shake out. Then, the businesses with firmly established competencies have the greatest likelihood of survival.

## Competitive Weaknesses

While careful environmental and internal analyses enable us to identify areas of distinctive competence, they also suggest areas of competitive weakness. A competitive weakness is an area of vulnerability, an area in which competitors have a meaningful edge. In a highly competitive situation, one firm's distinctive competency is often another firm's competitive weakness. Just as distinctive competencies are developed over time, competitive weaknesses typically evolve over time.

Throughout its business life, the things the company has done and failed to do can accrue into competitive weaknesses. Once recognized, however, competitive weaknesses can motivate the strategy process. Managers may respond by minimizing, mitigating, or overcoming areas of distinctive weakness.

Small business owners are a proud group. Often, they are enthusiastically enamored with their products and businesses. They may have great difficulty in recognizing competitive weaknesses. Generally, this stems both from an unrealistic analysis of the competitive environment and from an inadequate internal analysis. This is why it is so important to undertake a sound and objective analysis and why the owner must be open and ready to accept and respond to the outcomes of the analysis. Indeed, one or two key areas of competitive weakness can, if unrealized and unattended, destroy the base of strength derived from a series of distinctive competencies. Since few businesses are the best at everything, identifying competitive weaknesses is not a sign of failure. Instead, it signals the firm that there are factors to be dealt with in its development of goals and strategy for competitive action.

CHAPTER 4: RECOGNIZING DISTINCTIVE COMPETENCIES AND COMPETITIVE WEAKNESSES / 115

## Summary

Once the external analysis and the internal analysis are complete, the business owner should perform additional analysis to determine whether distinctive competencies or competitive weaknesses exist.

Distinctive competencies are areas of key strength in which a firm performs extremely well in comparison with its competitors. These strengths can be exploited to gain profitability or market share. Distinctive competencies can derive from high-quality products, excellent service, key locations, the ability to fill specific niches in the market, particular flexibility or adaptability, a strong consumer orientation, a significant reputation or image, exceptionally knowledgeable personnel, or a significant price advantage. A distinctive competency is seldom sustainable over the long run. However, business owners should do what they can to build and sustain distinctive competencies in order to maximize the return from them.

Competitive weaknesses make the business especially vulnerable to competitive threats. The areas in which a firm could possess a distinctive competency should be analyzed for the possibility of competitive weakness.

## Discussion Questions

1. How can distinctive competencies be identified?
2. Can distinctive competencies really be developed as part of a strategy or are they simply something a firm has or doesn't have?
3. How necessary is it for a firm to develop a particular distinctive competency?
4. Pick a company that you know something about. Does it have distinctive competencies? How does or should the firm exploit them?
5. What kinds of competencies might we expect in
    a. a shoe store?
    b. a grocery store?
    c. a pet shop?
    d. a heating and air-conditioning firm?
    e. a computer repair business?

## References

Michael Selz. "Columbia Sportswear Tackles Tidal Wave of Copycats." *Wall Street Journal*, May 24, 1993, p. B2.

# CASE STUDY

# Distinctive Competencies of Gaston Ridge Home Health Care, Inc.

AUTHORS' NOTE: Gaston Ridge Home Health Care, Inc., has a number of strengths. Close analysis, however, indicates that most of them do not differ significantly from those of their competitors. Pricing appears to be one area of distinctive competency. The caring nature of their personnel may be their most important distinctive competency.

## Distinctive Competencies

A careful look at Gaston Ridge's competitive and internal condition reveals some important strengths. One strength is the skilled nurses and the services they provide. However, this strength is not unique; as skilled nursing care is typical of Gaston's competitors.

While most competitors offer similar services, prices vary. Price is therefore a major differentiating factor, particularly given the cost sensitivity of consumers in the service area. We offer more moderate prices than do Ilini Home Health Care and Capital Center, our two most formidable competitors. This is a dimension of competence, but we must watch our competitors carefully to sustain our advantage.

Gaston Ridge benefits from its central location, which provides access to the broad service area. While important, the size of the service area requires extensive travel for all firms. Thus, this strength is not a significant advantage.

The most important distinctive competency is the culture and image of Gaston Ridge. Personal service and attention to building caring relationships with patients and their families differentiate Gaston Ridge from its competitors. Gaston Ridge's considerate approach is valued by consumers and is a key part of our approach to the target market.

## Competitive Weaknesses

Given the growing demand for physical therapy in the industry, the situation relative to physical therapists at Gaston Ridge is troublesome. While our current contractual arrangement is reasonable, Gaston Ridge lacks direct control, and there are questions about quality assurance. This deficiency is accentuated by the strong physical therapy services offered by competitors with hospital affiliations.

Meal provision is a service desired by significant numbers of patients and prospective patients. While no competitor is fully exploiting this opportunity, some do provide limited meal service. Gaston Ridge does not offer meal service and we may be missing an opportunity to serve larger numbers of clients.

The most significant competitive weakness facing Gaston Ridge is our lack of strong name recognition and identification. Consumer familiarity and physician and discharge planner referral bases are not strong. Further, there are few concerted programs in place to promote the agency, and we do no advertising. While this situation is not debilitating at present, it is a concern. And this deficiency looms larger because new competitors with hospital and nursing home affiliations may enter the industry. Their presence, with the name recognition and referral bases they bring, could be competitively troublesome for Gaston Ridge.

# PART III

# The Action Phase: Developing the Plan

THE PREVIOUS CHAPTERS have dealt with the analysis portions of the strategic planning process. We discussed in some detail how the firm's environment should be analyzed and how the firm itself must be thoroughly studied to determine strengths and weaknesses. We suggested that the macroenvironment should be analyzed first, focusing on key political, technical, social, and economic impacts, before moving on to the firm's industry and its immediate environment. We discussed how internal analysis reveals the firm's own strengths and weaknesses. Finally, we showed how the environmental and internal analyses together reveal distinctive competencies the firm possesses as well as vulnerabilities that competitors could exploit.

We turn now to the action phase of the process in which the actual strategic plan is developed. We begin, in Chapter 5, with a discussion of the all-important mission statement and the determination of the firm's strategic posture. Chapter 6 follows with a discussion of goal setting. This process takes the mission statement and strategic posture and breaks them into successively more specific, attainable goals. Chapter 7 then deals with various elements of a strategic plan, particularly the marketing strategy, the production strategy, the human resource strategy, and the financial strategy. Chapter 8 concludes with a discussion of actually writing the strategic plan. An appendix at the end of the text provides an example of an actual strategic plan.

# CHAPTER 5

# Defining the Firm's Mission and Strategic Posture

---

OBJECTIVES

In this chapter you will learn

1. the two parts of a mission statement.

2. how to define the nature of the business.

3. what is meant by a strategic posture.

4. the types of strategic postures common to small businesses.

5. how management's philosophy and strategic postures interrelate.

SOME BUSINESS OWNERS tend to write off or deemphasize this portion of the planning process, telling themselves that they already know where the firm is headed. However, the two steps discussed in this chapter are among the most important in the strategic planning process. A firm's basic mission and its accompanying strategic postures provide a focus. Without a mission statement, the company may flounder about, headed in no particular direction. Without a strategic posture, the firm may attempt a strategy that is not well grounded and does not translate well into specific actions.

## The Mission Statement

The mission statement is a concise statement of the general nature and direction of the company. By carefully delineating the underlying aim, scope, and direction of the business, the mission statement becomes an outline of what the company will do and what it will be. Although the mission statement is purposely broad, it must offer a clear word picture of the firm. Often, an elaborate-sounding, sweeping compilation of platitudes is offered as a mission statement. Such a statement fails to provide the precision and scope necessary to be useful as a meaningful planning tool. The owner should ask, "What separates us from other similar companies?" The answer becomes a unique mission statement that is the basis for a definitive corporate strategy.

## The Value of the Mission Statement

A written mission statement has two major values. The first is as a communication both inside and outside the firm. Naturally, the financial community will be interested in the direction the company is moving. But perhaps more important is the internal communication. Often, employees complain that they never know what is happening. They don't know what management's plans are nor how they, the employees, fit within those plans. This makes it difficult for them to be committed and motivated workers. The mission statement helps clarify the firm's vision and the employees' role in it.

The second major value is the commitment that the owner of the firm has to the mission once it is printed and publicized. If a concept or philosophy is believed strongly enough to put in writing, then everyone affected can expect the idea will be followed. It's like New Year's resolutions, but with higher stakes. If you make resolutions but tell no one, there is no particular incentive to keep them. But if you write them down, ponder them, type them up, post them on the refrigerator, tell your friends about them, maybe even wager that you will keep them, this public commitment means you can't break them without losing face (or maybe money). In the same way, the written mission statement commits the manager to the stated strategy and philosophy and may result in equal commitment by others in and around the business.

Such a commitment in no way suggests that a company's mission is cast in stone, never to be altered. Mission statements, as representations of the firm's place in a dynamic environment, may change over time. However, these changes evolve as the firm assesses movements in its competitive situation. The mission statement provides a central focus and unifying drive for the business within its planning horizon.

## The Parts of a Mission Statement

The mission statement contains two major elements. Each should be given careful consideration.

### THE NATURE OF THE BUSINESS

The first element of the mission statement defines and clearly specifies the basic nature of the firm's business. Four different areas must be considered:

1. The industry and product line of the company and the type of services provided

2. The firm's position in the distribution channel (is the company a wholesaler, a manufacturer, a retailer, or a mail-order business?)

3. The prime goals of the firm (quality, breadth of product line, price, or service?)

4. The target market (who does the firm presently serve? who does it intend to serve in the relevant future?)

By telling explicitly what the firm is, the mission statement also tells implicitly what the firm is not. These limiting statements serve as a control to keep the general direction intact, similar to fences on either side of a highway.

Consider the following example. A woman decides to start a bicycle shop that sells and services bicycles. After a few months, she is offered the opportunity to add a line of mopeds. Reasoning that mopeds are simply bicycles with a small motor, she adds the line. Later, the regional manager for Honda motorcycles stops by. The local Honda dealer is retiring, a once-in-a-lifetime opportunity to land a coveted Honda dealership. Now she has a bicycle/moped/motorcycle business. Somewhat later, the entrepreneur is presented the opportunity to take on a line of snowmobiles. Reasoning that snowmobiles really have much in common with motorcycles except that they run primarily on skis instead of wheels, she adds this line too. The story could continue indefinitely, as the woman adds garden tractors, lawnmowers, snowblowers, etc. The point is that the one-time bicycle shop has become a highly diversified dealership for a number of slightly related products. In the process, the owner has overextended herself, is no longer able to do any of it well, has incurred substantial debt—in short, has lost control of her operation.

A well-written and closely observed mission statement would allow the owner to specialize in bicycles until she decided it was time to expand. At that time she could carefully evaluate the market and her financial ability to take on an added line. Lines would be added at a controlled rate and with adequate financing.

Many businesses, large and small, fail because of rapid, uncontrolled growth. For example, large businesses often acquire unrelated firms or start up new businesses in unrelated areas with the stated goal of broadening their earnings base or gaining a countercyclical business. Many of these same subsidiaries are later divested as the parent firm's executives decide to "return to the things we do best." Obviously the corporation's management strayed from their basic mission and later realized their error.

## THE FIRM'S BASIC PHILOSOPHY

The second major element of the mission statement is an expression of the firm's management philosophy. While the mission statement, by itself, cannot create an organizational culture, it does define and espouse the kind of culture the owner wants. Over the last dozen years, much has been written about "corporate culture" and its impact, power, and influence on the behavior and activities of large organizations. The concept of culture is equally important for the small firm. The mission statement should capture the owner's basic philosophy of how business will be conducted. In simplest terms, the mission statement should explain the core values that are most central and most critical to the business. The result is a value orientation that becomes an important guide for subsequent management action.

For example, a small manufacturer included in its mission statement the phrase, "We build quality into every product we produce." The owner wanted to convey clearly to all customers and potential customers that the business was committed to the highest level of quality assurance. The owner emphasized the significance of this theme by including the phrase as the company motto on its business letterhead.

In making a philosophical or cultural declaration, the mission statement may say a great deal about the firm. Will the firm be a risk taker? Will it be employee oriented? Will the firm be run on the highest ethical standards? Will it be an aggressive competitor? Will it be a pioneer or a follower, me-too firm? The key is to include those items about which management feels strongly and omit those items about which it does not. For example, the mission statement may mention nothing about a promote-from-within policy and instead discuss the strategy of hiring young managers with new ideas.

Increasingly, small business owners are recognizing that while the formulation of the company mission is ultimately their responsibility, the vision process need not be an isolated activity. In fact, the formulation of a mission rarely comes from a flash of owner insight or inspiration. More typically, the owner engages in an active search and analysis process that involves the input of numerous sources, representing a range of stakeholders including suppliers, customers, and employees. Owners should recognize the significance and value of stakeholder input. In particular, employees, at all levels, often have important views and help guide and foster the mission's tone and direction.

Figure 5.1 is a mission statement for a small toy-manufacturing company. The statement clearly lays out the nature of the firm as well as the tone or philosophy of the company. At the same time it does not give away any proprietary secrets. Figure 5.2, p. 126, gives examples of some other company's mission statements.

---

Figure 5.1

### JOY'S TOY COMPANY MISSION STATEMENT

Joy's Toy Company produces a wide line of moderately priced educational toys for preschool and young school-age children. We service a four-state area surrounding Missouri and sell directly to schools or school district buying centers.

We care about children and view their education as the critical part of our task. Our toys are designed to enrich the child's educational experience.

All design work is done in-house to assure responsive, innovative products.

Our first product priority is quality. We would rather lose a sale by being overpriced than sell low-quality merchandise. We offer quick and accessible service and repair on all merchandise we sell.

In hiring sales representatives, we seek to attract former primary school teachers who are in tune with the needs and wants of children and who can identify with the concerns of parents. We exclusively promote from within.

---

In summary, the mission statement must do only two things, but it must do them well. First, it must set forth the direction of the business, thereby specifying what the business is and what it is not. Second, it must set forth the tone or culture of the business based on the owner's philosophy of how the business should be run.

---

Figure 5.2

### SAMPLE MISSION STATEMENTS

**Blazing Graphics**

Blazing Graphics will provide you with the most effective visual communication available. We will help you achieve all of your goals while providing you with the greatest value both seen and unseen.

Here at Blazing Graphics we take the time to do things right. We do this by controlling the entire graphic arts process. This enables us to better coordinate each job while providing a higher level of service.

Our mission is to ensure exceptional quality by opening up communication between crafts normally separated and at times adverse to one another.

Here at Blazing Graphics we have committed ourselves and our resources to being on the forefront of technology.

Creative technical know-how is the single most critical determinant of economic competitiveness.

It's our belief that together we can create an environment that will be both personally and professionally fulfilling for all the people who make up the Blazing Community.

*(Source: Nelton, p. 61)*

### Cascade Properties

Cascade Properties provides services for residential and commercial real estate sales. In addition, we have a property management firm that markets apartments, residential homes, office buildings, and commercial complexes. We are also involved in the environmental services area.

As the real estate industry continues to change, we will aggressively explore new market opportunities and continually educate our associates to provide outstanding service to our clients and customers.

*(Source: Company documents)*

### Lunar Productions, Inc.

Honor God in all we do.

Provide excellent and affordable corporate video, audio/visual, and broadcast production services to our valued clients.

Communicate with our clients and fellow employees as effectively as we communicate with our audiences.

Make a fair profit.

*(Source: Nelton, p. 63)*

### Ben & Jerry's

Ben & Jerry's is dedicated to the creation and demonstration of a new corporate concept of linked prosperity. Our mission consists of three interrelated parts.

PRODUCT MISSION: to make, distribute and sell the finest quality all natural ice cream and related products in a wide variety of innovative flavors made from Vermont dairy products.

ECONOMIC MISSION: to operate the company on a sound financial basis of profitable growth, increasing value for our shareholders, and creating career opportunities and financial rewards for our employees.

SOCIAL MISSION: to operate the company in a way that actively recognizes the central role that business plays in the structure of society by initiating innovative ways to improve the quality of life of a broad community: local, national, and international.

*(Source: Ben & Jerry's 1993 Annual Report)*

> **Bard Optical**
> Vision Statement
>
> Bard Optical provides the latest technological advances in vision care to meet the optometric needs of the retail consumer while providing the lowest possible price and highest quality service, while maintaining a reasonable profit.
>
> *(Source: Diana Hall, President, Bard Optical)*

## Developing the Firm's Strategic Posture

The mission statement, if well developed, conveys the general direction of the business and indicates its management philosophy. Before more specific goals can be defined or strategies developed to achieve those goals, the business owner needs to determine the firm's strategic posture.

A strategic posture is a general indication of how the business will behave in its attempt to achieve its overall mission and secure a competitive advantage. It is management's overall plan of action for running the business in response to external opportunities and threats, based on external awareness, assessment of internal strengths and weaknesses, and the set of distinctive competencies the business has developed.

Often, small businesses fail to give specific attention to a strategic posture and instead emphasize short-term goals and operational decisions. In this situation, the firm's strategic posture evolves as a reflection of past actions—it describes what the firm has done rather than prescribes what the business will do—and fails to reinforce the sense of direction generated by the mission statement.

### THE FOCUSED PRODUCT/MARKET POSTURE

The most prevalent strategic posture employed by the smaller business is to concentrate on a particular product or a single market. An aluminum garage door manufacturer, an automotive repair shop, or a family-style restaurant are examples of companies with a focused product or market.

The appeal of the focused product/market posture is its competitive advantage. This posture allows the small business to emphasize what it knows and does best. Small business success—at least initially—is greatly enhanced by limiting involvement to those areas where owners and managers have relevant business experience and understanding of the dynamics of the competitive market situation. This is especially true when the managerial staff is limited. Focusing on a single product or market allows the busy owner or manager to concentrate on the nuances of that particular situation. He or she can orient and target energies in a unique and focused direction and therefore stands a better chance of "staying on top of" relevant issues and competitive factors.

Similarly, a focused product/market posture allows the smaller business to develop a number of potential competitive advantages over larger firms. Small businesses are often characterized by flexibility and adaptability. These factors may enable the small firm to meet the special needs of their target market in a more timely and responsive way than larger businesses can. The smaller business can exploit opportunities that are normally overlooked or bypassed by larger firms. The case of Leegin Creative Leather Products (Profile 5.1) is an example.

---

### PROFILE 5.1: LEEGIN CREATIVE LEATHER PRODUCTS

Leegin Creative Leather Products makes leather belts. In a highly competitive industry with a stable product demand, Leegin's success has been staggering. That success has not come from unique twists or fancy gimmicks. "The company has neither uncovered nor created a burning new trend . . . it hasn't landed any make-or-break accounts . . . nor has the global economy boosted its growth." Relying on computer technology to pinpoint and direct customer orders and providing salespeople with portable computers so customers have up-to-the-minute sales information, Leegin is able to build excellent relationships with its customers. In turn, it makes sales—lots of sales! Leegin's production and support systems have been modified and refined to meet sales demands and customer expectations. The system is so fluid that Leegin's sales force can call on 180 customers a day and the company can produce and ship thousands of orders a week. In short, Leegin is able to offer customers better service and greater production variety than any of its competitors.

*(Source: Case, pp. 84-91)*

---

Of course, the focused product/market posture is not without risks. If the present product or market remains attractive, this posture can lead to significant growth. However, if either the product or the market loses its vitality, the business is on tenuous ground and may need to be repositioned. The essence of this posture can be found in Mark Twain's caveat, "Put all your eggs in one basket and watch the basket."

**THE NICHE POSTURE**

One of the most promising strategic postures for a small business is the niche posture. Here, careful environmental analysis identifies an important gap or niche in a market. If a business has the capacity and competency to enter these areas, it can capitalize on these unfulfilled opportunities. Recognizing and gearing business toward a promising niche may lead to substantial short-term profits, and the niche may remain viable for many years. Competitors may not recognize that the niche exists or be unwilling to move into it for economic or logistic reasons.

The niche posture can be a high-reward strategy, but there is always the risk that a more able competitor will suddenly close the gap. Profiles 5.2 and 5.3, are examples of creative niche postures.

---

### PROFILE 5.2: DESKTOP CHANNEL

It is quite common for small companies to seek niches in emerging industries. The computer industry is a prime target. Desktop Channel, for example, offers shoppers thousands of products through an on-line computer service. (Shoppers use their personal computers to contact Desktop and make purchases.) While other companies, including Prodigy and CompuServe, also offer on-line retailing, their product lines are limited. Desktop Channel is unique in its range of offerings. In fact, Desktop has been described as an on-line "superstore." With the on-line service industry booming, Desktop Channel seems positioned to capture part of this growing business.

*(Source: O'Brien)*

---

---

PROFILE 5.3: THE BLUE RIBBON CAR WASH

Sue and Jim Acres operate the Blue Ribbon Car Wash in an affluent part of the city. They do not market their car wash to the general public, and the general public would not typically frequent it. Charging more than $30 per wash ($50 for a wash and wax), Blue Ribbon caters only to those who drive expensive cars—Mercedes, BMWs, Audis, Cadillacs, and Lincolns. Cars are accepted by appointment only and must be left for at least four hours. The car is washed and polished by hand using only top-quality cleaners and waxes. The cars are cleaned and vacuumed inside, and fabric protector applied if desired. Wheels are scrubbed and wire wheels are carefully attended to—with a toothbrush if necessary. For an additional charge, the engine compartment can be cleaned, the trunk can be vacuumed, and the oil can be changed. Sue reports that business is brisk—ten cars a day—with some owners waiting as long as two weeks for an appointment.

---

## THE EXPANSIVE GROWTH POSTURE

A business that assumes an expansive growth posture builds on one or more of the previously discussed postures. Because of past success and a promising outlook, management realizes that there are opportunities to expand the company's scope of operations. An expansive growth posture will generally take one of two forms.

First, the business may expand its primary location. This may entail enlarging the present facility or relocating to a larger facility. There is no attempt to alter current products or markets. In fact, the overall strength of the market and product acceptance requires expansion to exploit the excess demand. In other words, the business will do the same things it has always done, but the additional capacity will enable it to reach larger numbers and thus realize greater returns.

In a second form of expansive growth, a business establishes additional facilities in promising new market areas. The multilocation approach is oriented toward new market areas, but not new or different target markets. The product remains unchanged, and the business still emphasizes the customer and product characteristics that have provided past success. New geographical markets for existing product lines are identified and tapped.

Crystal Rug Cleaners (Profile 5.4) adopted an expansive growth posture after it had successfully used the focused product/market posture. An expansive growth posture allows the business to increase capacity and garner returns from additional business. Of course, careful environmental and internal analyses are critical. Misreading competitive forces or target-market demands and characteristics could result in expensive capital expenditures and underutilized facilities.

Additional difficulties include questions of leadership and control. Often, small business owners have difficulty delegating authority, even when the level of business growth clearly extends beyond their control. Quality and production standards at the various facilities must also be addressed. In short, management structure, personnel, and operating policy must be reexamined as the expansive growth posture evolves.

---

### PROFILE 5.4: CRYSTAL RUG CLEANERS

Crystal Rug Cleaners was started in an exclusive section of Florida's Gulf coast in the mid-1960s by Michael Richards. Initially, Richards's environmental assessment revealed a promising opportunity. First, the market boasted extremely high income levels. Homes were quite large and expensive, and quality carpeting and rugs were common. Although there were a number of cleaning firms in the area, none had established themselves as quality businesses specializing in carpeting. The upper-income market was reluctant to entrust their cleaning needs to most of these operations, particularly since incorrect cleaning methods could damage or ruin their carpets. Richards trained extensively in cleaning methods and techniques, including those unique to high-grade and oriental carpets, and Crystal Rug Cleaners was licensed by the National Institute of Rug Cleaners, the first and only cleaner in the market area to earn such a distinction. In order to highlight his competence and expertise, Richards limited his firm's activities to carpet and rug cleaning. By distinguishing himself from his competitors and focusing on this single product/market posture, Richards made his business prosper and grow.

Within a period of three years, the demand for services outstripped the firm's internal capacity. Richards decided to expand the physical plant, and he eventually established satellite operations in nearby market areas. This expansion did not occur in piecemeal but was carefully planned. Richards made supportable projections of increased demand and budgeted his costs and returns. Expansive growth became the focus for modeling business decisions as the business developed.

## THE DEVELOPMENTAL GROWTH POSTURE

A business that uses a developmental growth posture decides to grow either by developing new target markets for its current products or by offering product variations to existing markets.

In market development, the business attempts to appeal to new and varied market segments whose characteristics or demographics differ from those of established primary markets. Product development stresses variations or improvements in the firm's primary products, which are introduced to current customers in the hope that the positive image customers have of existing products will carry over. Existing products are not changed: Growth comes because the same customers buy both the existing products and the new products.

One of the key advantages of a developmental posture is that the business maintains a high degree of consistency and stability. In product development, present customers (with assumed loyalty) are maintained and targeted while product variations are introduced. In market development, new market segments are tapped but products remain unchanged.

Crystal Rug Cleaners went on to assume a developmental posture. After the focused product/market strategy had proved effective and expansive growth had been undertaken, Richards took a developmental growth posture by targeting the middle-income market as well. Crystal's basic strengths of service, professionalism, and knowledge of proper cleaning procedures were maintained and stressed in advertising messages geared to this new market segment. Making such a strategic change requires care. The business must be sure that in addressing new markets, the needs of the established markets are not forgotten or confused. A developmental posture does add a fair amount of additional planning complexity, but remains a logical means of fostering continued growth.

## THE PRODUCT INNOVATION POSTURE

The distinction between product development and product innovation is a bit confusing, since the two certainly have common elements. Product development seeks product variations and improvements, but involves no overriding change in the fundamental product. Product innovation, on the other hand, seeks so novel an alteration of the existing product that a totally new or different product is created: Consumers shift their preferences away from the existing products to the newer ones.

Although product innovations are generally assumed to be outgrowths of larger firms with well-supported research and development staffs, many contemporary product advances have come from small, entrepreneurial operations. Advances in microcomputer hardware and software are common examples. Small businesses—working intensively with a particular product every day, hands-on—often generate meaningful product innovations.

An innovative strategic posture may be taken by service companies as well as by product manufacturers. For example, Copper's Cabinetry operated for four years as a fledgling operation that specialized in building and renovating closets in customers' homes. Today, operating as Copper's Consultants, they advise harried, time-conscious clients how to organize their lives to eliminate daily time wasters. This service includes everything from redesigning and rearranging wardrobe closets with customized modifications to adding mirrors to the shower stall so that shaving and tooth brushing can be done while showering. Consumers are willing to pay for the added control they gain over their time and routines. The company's business is steadily increasing among dual-income, upper-middle-class households.

One reason an innovation posture is so attractive is the possibility for high returns. Introducing new services or products can bring big profits—at least until competitors recognize and respond to the new changes. However, significant risks are also present: Being on the "cutting edge" demands a careful and accurate reading of environmental trends and necessitates a timely and cost-effective response.

## THE DIVERSIFICATION POSTURE

A diversification posture occurs when the business decides to grow by expanding operations into related but essentially different products or services. Although a core area of concentration may still command the bulk of the business energies, the business is broadened to include supporting or complementary products or services. For example, Leegin, the belt manufacturer profiled previously, recently diversified its operations to move beyond its focused product posture and now manufactures leather handbags as well. Similar raw materials, production processes, and distribution and retail sales outlets made handbags a logical diversification.

Determining where to expand is a function of two factors, competitive opportunity, and strategic fit. Competitive opportunity suggests that realistic gains may be achieved by moving into unexploited or untapped areas of consumer demand. Strategic fit means the firm should only grow into areas that are consistent with or complement existing operations.

The small firm must be sure that some logical relationship exists between primary, existing operations and the desired areas of diversification. This determination is often a function of the owner's capacity to understand and control the new diversified business. Extremely high risks occur when expansion extends beyond the entrepreneur's realm of experience or demonstrated competence. For this reason, unrelated diversification is typically not a reasonable option for the small firm.

Again, Crystal Rug Cleaners is a meaningful example. Crystal grew and prospered by selecting meaningful niches and appropriate strategic postures. When Richards realized that Crystal's level of professionalism and quality would prompt consumers to trust Crystal with other carpeting services, he added rug and carpet repair as a new service. The repair service was initially targeted toward the upper-income market needing delicate repairs of expensive oriental carpets. These were done, on a part-time, as-needed basis, by a retired master repair person. Soon the repair service was expanded to include other carpet groups and a range of repair needs. Within a year, a repair division, with a full-time expert concentrating solely on repairs, was added to the operation. A logical area of complementary growth was realized.

## The Choice of Strategic Posture

Given these six general, somewhat generic strategic postures available to smaller firms, small business owners must decide which posture or postures are most appropriate for their particular situation. Clear, obvious, straightforward answers are rare, and exceptions are common. However, certain considerations may help determine where each posture is likely to produce success. The four key variables are shown in Figure 5.3.

When choosing a strategic posture, first consider the present and future attractiveness of the firm's products and industry. Assessing attractiveness can be quite complex. At the most basic level, the owner must decide whether demand is stable or growing. Careful and thorough environmental analysis should provide enough information to decide if product and industry attractiveness is relatively strong or relatively weak. Of course, attractiveness must be assessed not only in the present, but projected over the firm's planning horizon.

A second variable is the firm's relative competitive strength. Through internal analysis, the firm must understand its strengths and potential in relation to its key competitors. This is especially important if one or more large firms dominate the industry.

The third variable is the personal desires, aspirations, and commitments of the owner. Essentially, different entrepreneurs have different views of their businesses and what they would like them to become. Some owners desire rapid growth and are willing to accept the accompanying risks in return for the potentially high returns. Others are content to remain small and modestly successful. No variable is more basic, and it frequently defines and limits the choices of strategic posture.

Figure 5.3

## VARIABLES AFFECTING STRATEGIC POSTURE CHOICE

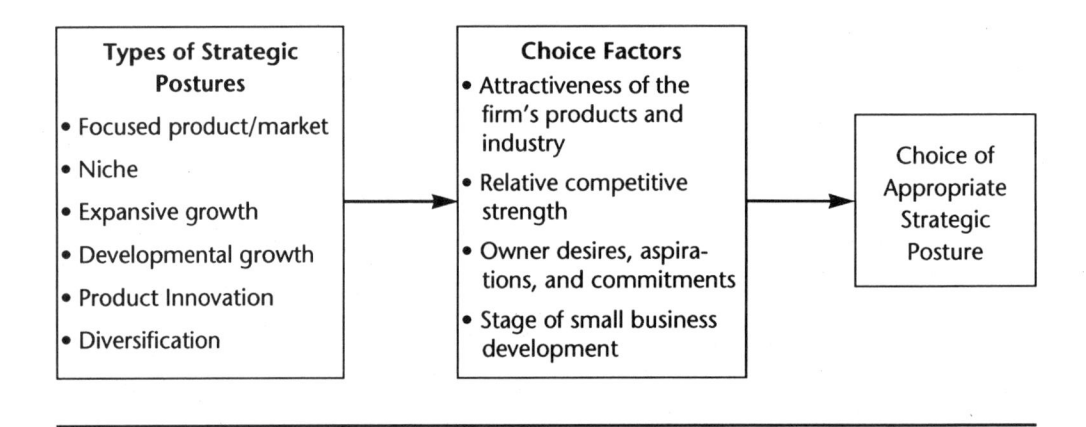

**Types of Strategic Postures**
- Focused product/market
- Niche
- Expansive growth
- Developmental growth
- Product Innovation
- Diversification

→

**Choice Factors**
- Attractiveness of the firm's products and industry
- Relative competitive strength
- Owner desires, aspirations, and commitments
- Stage of small business development

→

Choice of Appropriate Strategic Posture

The final variable is the stage of small business development. As the business moves from one stage to another—the start-up stage, stabilization stage, and growth stage—its emphasis shifts. Different strategic postures seem appropriate for different stages and conditions within stages. Arnold Cooper has developed a typology of small business growth stages that offer some meaningful insights (Cooper).

## START-UP STAGE

The first stage in Cooper's typology is the start-up stage, beginning with the decision to start a new business and encompassing the initial period when the business attempts to become established and "get on its feet." During the start-up stage, the underlying concern is typically survival. Often, the firm's products or services are adequate and properly conceived, but the owner doesn't know how to create public awareness of and desire for these products or services. The owner struggles with where and how to position the business within the chosen industry.

Typically, a business in this stage limits its scope to one or two products, using a focused product/market posture. Given the limited financial and human resources available to businesses during this phase, a single product/market posture is generally the most realistic. A small, fledgling operation with limited resources, struggling to create market awareness in order to survive, is best served by focusing its energies in a concentrated direction.

The variables of relative competitive strength and product/industry attractiveness must be considered at this initial stage, even though they may be difficult to ascertain. Since there is little in the way of existing, ongoing business operations to observe, internal analysis is limited. Instead, the owner's experience, background, philosophy, knowledge, and skills form the basis of these assessments.

The business should be started in an area that the owner knows and understands. However, this in no way ensures that either product/industry characteristics or relative competitive position will be attractive. Therefore, the business must be open to signals that the current area of concentration appears risky or is rapidly becoming unattractive. Generally, the business can change directions at this initial stage more easily and more quickly than during subsequent stages. But the owner must be willing to read the signals, appraise them accurately, and respond objectively. The entrepreneur must fight the urge to become enamored of a pet product and consequently refuse to perceive and react to important critical feedback.

If either product/industry attractiveness or relative competitive strength are low, the firm should consider a niche posture to search for and develop new areas of concentration. As Cooper notes, it is quite common for businesses to change products or services during the start-up stage. New niches and areas of concentration should be limited to areas that are in demand and where true entrepreneurial skill and knowledge exist. If such a venture cannot be identified, one should realistically consider leaving the business arena.

## STABILIZATION STAGE

Once the business becomes established and survival seems probable, the owner must decide whether to pursue further business growth aggressively. Although we often assume that growth is a natural and underlying assumption held by all businesspersons, that view is inaccurate. Often, the owner is content with the present level of business activity and decides to stabilize at the current level of activity even though growth opportunities are possible.

There is nothing bizarre or wrong with such a decision. It often reflects a personal lifestyle choice. If growth is not desired, the established product/market posture that has provided past successes is again the most appropriate. This does not mean that the firm's owners are lulled into a passive complacency. To concentrate on the existing posture and still be responsive to changing customer needs and competitive demands and threats requires an open and aware management. Environmental analysis, internal analysis, and creatively planned strategies are as important as ever. The focused product/market posture can be retained as long as the firm's relative competitive position and product and industry attractiveness remain positive.

## GROWTH STAGE

Although Cooper distinguishes between early growth and later growth, his model has been modified and simplified here to suggest a single, more encompassing growth stage. A growth-stage business has weathered the storms of early business life and has gained a level of consumer acceptance and establishment. However, rather than maintain current business levels (as is the case in stabilization), the owners desire continued growth.

As the business develops, it encounters, for the first time, some of the problems and demands of growth. For example, owners must add employees, delegate some operating decisions, formalize standards and controls, and delineate job responsibilities as a workable organizational structure evolves.

As noted previously, the choice of the proper strategic posture is strongly influenced by the firm's relative competitive position and its product/industry attractiveness. Two caveats must be stressed. First, attempts at securing growth are risky if the business is experiencing a relatively weak competitive position in its original product/market areas. Second, if product/industry attractiveness is becoming or is projected to become less favorable, one should be cautious about further growth.

These caveats are not meant to suggest that a business is precluded from growth opportunities if either relative competitive position or product/industry attractiveness is unfavorable. Still, the additional risk involved must be noted. Unfavorable readings signal a need for change. But should this change be oriented toward further growth or rectifying the areas of difficulty? Coping with the additional pressures and demands of growth without a strong primary base of operations is difficult. The business may need to firm up its current situation—perhaps by exploring new competitive niches or searching out new, more promising product/market areas—before moving on to the challenges of growth. Growth efforts are best and most safely pursued when relative competitive position and product/industry attractiveness are positive.

Given relative competitive strength and product/industry attractiveness, a number of growth-oriented strategic postures are possible. Depending on the nature of the industry and the specifics of the business, any of the six strategic postures—focused product/market, niche, expansive growth, developmental growth, product innovation, or diversification—may foster effective growth. Rather than attempt to prescribe specific postures, it is best simply to encourage planners to choose postures that complement the existing business and its present strategic posture. If at any time during growth the business realizes that its relative internal or competitive strength is being diminished, growth will need to be stabilized until the internal condition is rectified.

## Assessing Progress

In developing a strategic plan and selecting appropriate strategic postures, the owner of a small business must clearly recognize the firm's present stage of development. Then the owner is ready to assess future growth potential and growth-related aspirations. Realistically, one should not expect a detailed or specific response: A broad indication of the extent of growth commitment is more likely.

Remember that growth potential is a function of environmental factors, internal strengths and weaknesses, and owner attitudes. After carefully examining these considerations, the owner may wish to proceed with or reevaluate growth projections.

## Summary

In this chapter we have presented two important facets of the action phase of the strategic planning process for small businesses. At the outset, a mission statement must be carefully prepared that sets forth the general direction the business will take, states the management philosophy to be followed, and implicitly indicates where the business is not headed.

Once the mission statement has been drawn up, the next step is to determine the strategic posture the firm will assume. These may be the focused product/market posture, the niche posture, the expansive growth posture, the developmental posture, the innovation posture, or the diversification posture. The particular posture assumed will depend heavily on the strengths and weaknesses of the firm, the nature of the firm's environment, and the personal desires of the owner/manager. There is, however, some relationship between the stage of development that the business is in and the most appropriate posture to take.

## Discussion Questions

1. Why is the mission statement so important for small firms?

2. Is it necessary to have written mission statement? Why or why not?

3. Is it easy to identify a company's management philosophy? Can significant information about a firm's philosophy be determined in a 30-minute interview with a key manager?

4. How do strategic postures relate to the stages of business development?

5. Which strategic posture might be most appropriate for
   a. a new computer chip manufacturer?
   b. a real estate firm dealing with commercial property?
   c. an older grocery store located in a growing community?
   d. a business that is seeing sales decline steadily?

## References

Sharon Nelton. "Put Your Purpose in Writing," *Nation's Business*, Volume 82, February, 1994, pp. 61-64.

John Case. "A Business Transformed," *Inc.*, vol. 15, no. 6 (June 1993), pp. 84–91.

Timothy L. O'Brien. "Company Has Head Start in Electronic Computer Sales." *Wall Street Journal*, March 10, 1994, p. B2.

Arnold C. Cooper. "Strategic Management: New Ventures and Small Business." In *Strategic Management*, edited by Dan E. Schendel and Charles W. Hofer, pp. 316–27. Boston: Little, Brown, 1979.

CASE STUDY

# Mission and Strategic Posture of Gaston Ridge Home Health Care, Inc.

AUTHORS' NOTE: The mission of Gaston Ridge can be stated quite succinctly. It states that Gaston Ridge is a full-service agency providing high-quality services in a specific geographical area. The strategic posture that follows illustrates the focused product/market posture. The services offered are similar to those provided by the major competitors in the service area. The focused strategy is reasonable given the growth in demand for existing services that is being experienced and is projected in the foreseeable future. A niche posture is also being considered. This posture would be increasingly viable if additional hospital and nursing home affiliates enter the service area.

## Mission

Gaston Ridge Home Health Care, Inc., provides a full range of quality home health care services to patients in smaller and rural areas of an eight-county licensed service area of Southern Illinois.

## Strategic Posture

Gaston Ridge's strategy is to focus on the needs of homebound patients in rural areas. Services are provided in 15 categories that duplicate many of those provided within a hospital setting. We do not compete in larger cities. Although 15 services are provided, we focus primarily on services prescribed by physicians, such as injections, medications, applications of bandages, etc. To a lesser extent, we are involved with education and training of patients and in occupational and physical therapy. Other services will be added as client demands and expectations arise. We are studying the demand for and our ability to provide meals.

CHAPTER 6

# Setting Goals

---

OBJECTIVES

After studying this chapter carefully, you should know

1. the relationship of goals to the mission statement, strategic posture, and actual strategies.

2. how major goals can be determined.

3. the difference between horizon goals and near-term goals.

4. how to prioritize goals.

---

THIS CHAPTER IS designed to help you determine specific goals for the business. We discuss the value of clear goals, the process of determining goals, and how to refine the goals into more and more specific targets, along with actions necessary to achieve them. In addition, we focus on the value of the goals to different people within the company. Incidentally, some writers emphasize the differences between *goals* and *objectives*. For our purposes, the differences are negligible and we use the term *goal* exclusively.

## Benefits of Specific Goals

Suppose you and a friend are leisurely driving around the city some Sunday afternoon, and you discover that you have no idea where you are. Are you lost? The answer—no. Now suppose one of you suddenly says, "It's four o'clock! We were supposed to be at a meeting fifteen minutes ago!" *Now* you are lost.

The leisurely Sunday afternoon drive was fine as long as the only "goal" is to have a good time. But once you needed to get somewhere, there is a problem. You looked around for landmarks or asked directions in order to find the way. Only if you have a specific goal to strive for do you take the actions necessary to achieve it.

Once a goal is set, performance can be measured in terms of that goal. Thus, a goal is simultaneously a planning tool and a control. It is a planning tool because it must precede the actual development of a plan. It is a control because it is a preset standard against which performance can be measured. If the goals have not been achieved, corrective steps may be taken to improve performance.

Goals also motivate employees. Achievable goals can become a rallying point for the entire company. Recently, the owner of a small manufacturing firm attributed her firm's ability to weather some tough economic and competitive times to the fact that the employees knew where the company was headed. They knew what the owners expected and had a good sense of what was likely to happen. She noted that sharing goals built a sense of identity. She was convinced that the open sharing of goals fostered a "we're in this together" spirit that helped the firm rebound from some bleak days.

If goals are to have meaning and the process of goal setting is to work, certain basic rules, guidelines, or considerations must be noted. In general these rules apply to all types of goals.

First, goal statements should be phrased in terms of outcomes or results rather than actions. We must focus on desired accomplishments, not the series of activities undertaken to achieve these accomplishments. There is a world of difference between saying, "This week we'll work on the budget," and "By the end of this week, the budget will be completed."

Second, goal statements should be clear, specific, and to the extent possible, quantifiable or measurable. The clearer and more precise the goal, the greater the likelihood that it will be pursued and attained.

Third, effective goal statements should be challenging, yet realistic. Challenging goals are essential for growth-oriented businesses and growth-oriented people. Goals that are too simple or too easily reached cheat the business of its full potential. They can cause employees to feel underutilized in their jobs and contribute to declines in morale and job satisfaction. On the other hand, goals that are too lofty may quickly be perceived as unreasonable or unrealistic, and employees won't even try to achieve them.

Finally, goals must be communicated throughout the organization. Regardless of how impressive a goal statement may be in meeting the foregoing criteria, its potential to influence behavior is lost if it isn't communicated to the employees. Many managers interpret communication even more broadly and include their employees in the goal-setting process. This not only enhances the goals, it also becomes a key to motivation. The empowerment movement of recent years focuses on mutual understanding, involvement, and agreement between owners and employees with regard to goal setting. The characteristics of good goals are summarized in Figure 6.1.

---

Figure 6.1

**CHARACTERISTICS OF GOOD GOALS**

1. Goals should be phrased in terms of outcomes rather than actions.

2. Goals should be measurable.

3. Goals should be challenging, yet realistic.

4. Goals should be communicated.

---

## How Are Goals Created?

Although setting viable goals is largely a judgmental process, it should not be done by the seat of your pants. In part, it is based on historical data. To a greater extent, however, it is based on the analysis discussed in Part II of this book.

The focus of goals may change from time to time. Suppose, for example, that sales have increased as planned over the past several years, but costs have risen dramatically. The goal for the next period may focus on cost containment. Sales increases may still be encouraged, but the primary emphasis will be on reducing expenses per sales dollar.

A specific numerical goal will often be a compromise among key management personnel. The marketing manager may suggest a target increase in sales of, say, 10 percent. The controller may be more pessimistic and feel that 6 percent is the most that could be expected. The production manager may be pretty sure that 7 or 8 percent is the maximum increase obtainable without a substantial capital outlay. The owner, working with these managers, encourages each person to offer his or her sales forecast for the coming year along with related information, and together they set final goals for the year.

## Conflict Among Goals

No business will have a single overriding goal. All groups, all businesses, all individuals, have multiple goals. Many of the goals are congruous, but some will be in conflict. For example, goals to be successful business owners sometimes conflict with goals to be successful parents.

Conflicts among goals within a business can affect the strategy of the firm.

### MUTUALLY EXCLUSIVE GOALS

Managers of a business may have mutually exclusive goals. One manager may have a goal in conflict with another manager, or a manager may have two goals that conflict with each other. In either case the exclusivity means that one cannot be achieved without serious damage to the other. These goal conflicts must be resolved.

### GOAL PRIORITIES

Everyone establishes priorities for themselves. People can never attain all that they want to attain nor do all that they want to do. Somehow they learn to prioritize their lives and determine which of life's objectives are most important.

The same holds true for businesses. Businesses will have multiple opportunities and multiple goals, and it is difficult, if not impossible, to achieve all of them. It is necessary, then, to prioritize the company's goals. Owners may decide that the major emphasis *this* year will be on hiring new employees because the major emphasis last year was on expanding into a new area. Sales may have increased dramatically, but personnel needs must now be addressed.

Although growth and expansion received first priority last year, they now must take second place to human resource considerations.

Prioritizing goals is particularly important in product development. If our firm has a number of products that could be marketed, we may decide that products A and B will receive attention next year, with products C, D, and E being funded the following year. Similarly, we may budget to replace some of our old equipment this year and schedule the remainder for replacement two years from now.

## Levels and Time Frames

Goal setting is often seen as a complex process, and owners of small firms bristle at the thought of wading through the necessary procedures. This is unfortunate, because goal setting need not be overly cumbersome.

All goals are not the same—there are different levels and types. While such distinctions may appear to complicate the goal-setting process, they are the basis for a logical system that allows the power of strategic goal setting to emerge.

### LEVELS OF GOALS

As noted in Figure 6.2, p. 150, two levels of goals—company and unit—are typical for small businesses. Company goals relate to the performance or accomplishments of the overall business. Unit goals relate to the performance or accomplishments of one or more departments or units within the business. Figure 6.3, p. 150, shows how company and unit goals differ, yet relate to each other. A company goal establishes certain demands and requirements that need to be reflected in the unit goals.

For example, if a manufacturing business is to secure a 5 percent growth in revenues (company goal), marketing must develop a more effective advertising and promotion scheme, operations must increase its capacity, the sales force must secure new contracts, and human resources must hire and train new workers (all unit-level goals). Unit goals, then, help individual workers realize how their specialty fits into the overall business plan.

Unit goals must mesh with one another and with the overall business goals. One of the important problems plaguing contemporary business is the

Figure 6.2

**LEVELS OF SMALL BUSINESS GOALS**

COMPANY GOALS
(Relate to performance or accomplishments of the overall business)

UNIT GOALS
(Relate to performance or accomplishments of each functional area within the business)

ADVERTISING   OPERATIONS   SALES   HUMAN RESOURCES

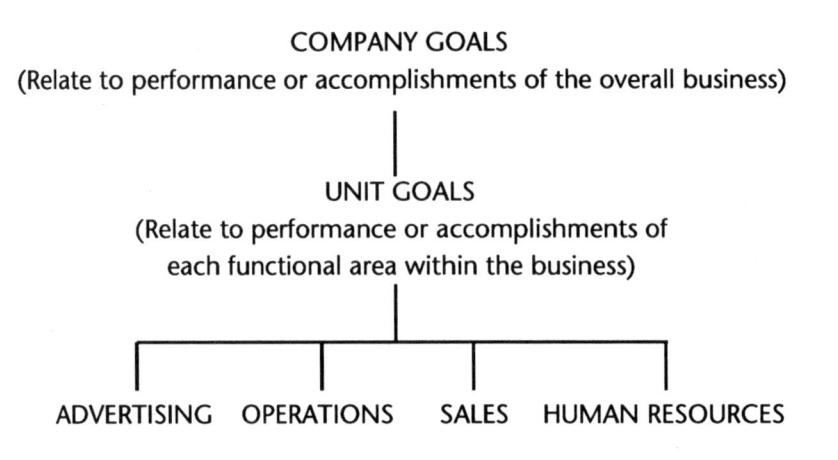

Figure 6.3

**EXAMPLES OF COMPANY AND UNIT-LEVEL GOALS**

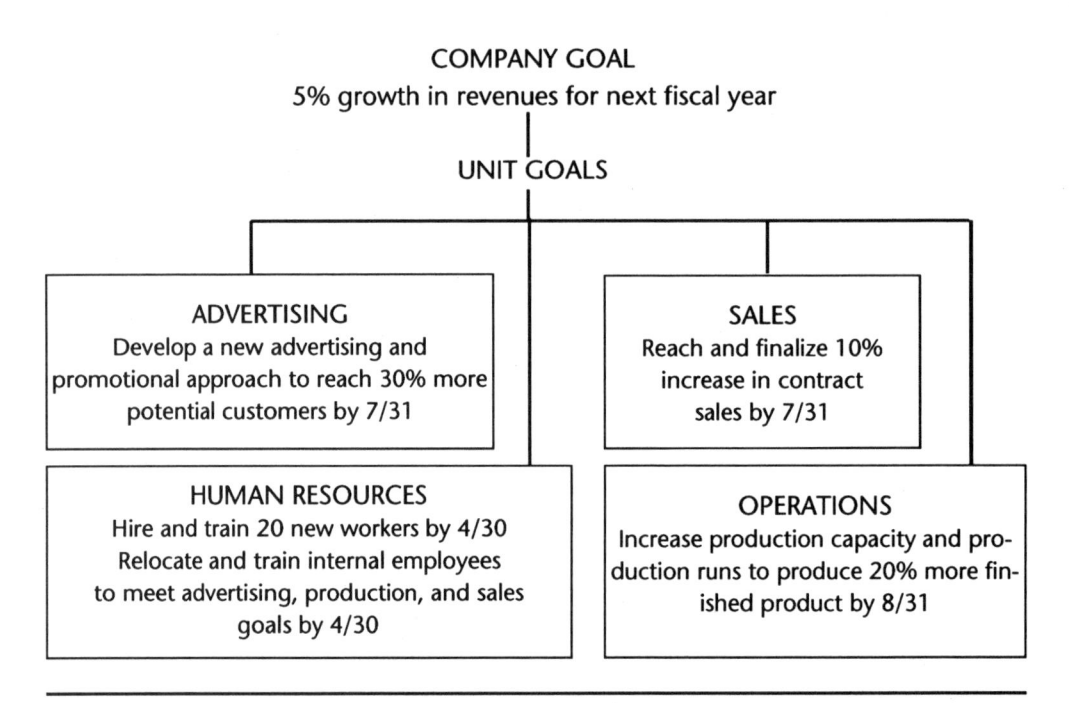

COMPANY GOAL
5% growth in revenues for next fiscal year

UNIT GOALS

**ADVERTISING**
Develop a new advertising and promotional approach to reach 30% more potential customers by 7/31

**SALES**
Reach and finalize 10% increase in contract sales by 7/31

**HUMAN RESOURCES**
Hire and train 20 new workers by 4/30
Relocate and train internal employees to meet advertising, production, and sales goals by 4/30

**OPERATIONS**
Increase production capacity and production runs to produce 20% more finished product by 8/31

lack of integration of unit goals. For example, the marketing department may develop new promotional programs without much regard for how this affects other functional areas or the overall efficiency of the business. They may do an excellent job of securing new contracts or additional orders but, in the process, outsell the business's capacity to produce on time. Each unit must see itself as a part of the whole business. All must recognize that each part complements the other.

Company goals must precede unit goals. Company goals are established and then communicated to units. Unit managers then develop goals and review them with the owner to ensure that they fit properly with other unit goals and make an appropriate, balanced contribution to the business goals.

**GOAL TIME FRAMES**

Small firms typically establish goals within three different time frames, as shown in Figure 6.4. These three time frames—horizon goals, near-term goals, and target goals—are interrelated and interdependent.

Horizon goals focus on accomplishments expected over the course of the firm's planning horizon. The longer-time nature of these goals means they involve relatively high levels of uncertainty. Horizon goals therefore tend to be broader and less specific than other types of goals.

---

Figure 6.4

**GOAL TIME FRAMES**

HORIZON GOALS
(Cover the firm's planning horizon)
↓
NEAR-TERM GOALS
(Cover the firm's next operating cycle)
↓
TARGET GOALS
(Cover the short run; i.e., weeks or days)

---

Near-term goals are established to delineate results or accomplishments expected within the firm's next operating cycle. Although that period is industry and company specific, normally near-term goals deal with the next six months to a year.

From a planning perspective, horizon goals should be established before other goals. Often there is a strong temptation to think of the shorter-run, near-term goals as a starting point. If horizon goals are set first, however, the business must necessarily be analyzed with an eye on the distant future. All subsequent plans aim toward the longer-term goal rather than being unduly constrained with meeting near-term profitability or sales targets. At the very least, horizon goals should be developed for sales dollars, market share, dollar profits, cash flow, and return on investment.

Near-term goals are those portions of the horizon goals that can logically be obtained in a short period of time. For example, if the planning horizon for a manufacturing firm is five years and the horizon goal is to increase sales by 50 percent, then the near-term goal could logically be to increase sales by 10 percent over the next year. Similarly, if a restaurant manager has a three-year planning horizon and desires to have a new restaurant in place at the end of the three years, a near-term goal may be to accrue $10,000 in interest-bearing accessible funds by the middle of the current fiscal year while keeping the current ratio above 2.0. Near-term goals are the in-progress portion of horizon goals.

Once horizon and near-term goals have been determined, the final goal-setting task is to segment the near-term goals into target goals. Target goals refer to very short-term goals that are quite specific as to time and measurability. Target goals may generate actions that must be completed in a few weeks or even a few days.

Suppose a real estate business in Indianapolis has as one of its horizon goals to increase its market share for residential sales by 10 percent within five years. This goal may then be segmented into the near-term goal of increasing market share by 1 percent in year one, 2 percent in each of years two, three, and four, and 3 percent in year five. Target goals are then developed to refine the near-term goals into smaller, more workable units: increasing home sales by 10 percent in the first quarter, increasing listings by 20 percent, increasing sales per broker by 5 percent, or any other goals that will ultimately lead to the first-year 1 percent increase in market share. Finally, specific actions are developed to achieve those target goals.

The key to target goals is to make them very specific, measurable, and attainable. Once all the target goals are defined, they must then be checked to ensure that they mesh with the larger or longer near-term goals. Some target goals will change monthly, some will change weekly, and very specific targets might change daily. Although target goals should be included in the strategic plan, they should be physically easy to remove (included in an appendix, for example), since the targets may change frequently. But it is still necessary to write down the target goals and related activities in order to communicate them, get commitment, and help direct employees.

## Goal Segmentation Process

The process of strategic goal setting is the same for company-level and unit-level goals. In fact, there should be horizon and near-term goals for both company and unit levels (see Figure 6.5). Target goals are generally developed for the units of the company.

Figure 6.5

**LEVELS AND TIME FRAMES OF GOALS**

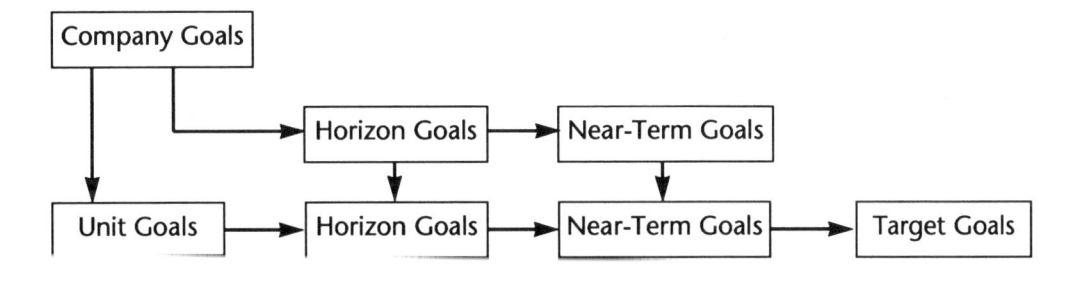

```
Company Goals ──┬──► Horizon Goals ──► Near-Term Goals
                │         ▲  │                │
                ▼         │  ▼                ▼
Unit Goals ────► Horizon Goals ──► Near-Term Goals ──► Target Goals
```

Unfortunately, many small business owners develop goal statements that are so broad and ambiguous that they are merely platitudes. These dream-list approaches do little to provide a clear focus and direction for business activity or to offer meaningful indicators of business progress or necessary corrective actions. Moving incrementally from horizon to target goals forces owners to work through this potential goal stalemate and to produce a series of relevant and significant target goals.

## Target Action Plans[1]

Once a set of horizon, near-term, and target goals has been developed and communicated, many owners think that planning has been accomplished, that further refinement is unnecessary. These people will rarely see their goals reach fruition and will be understandably frustrated at having wasted so much time on the process. A target action plan forces you to move beyond this scenario. This target action plan, outlined in Figure 6.6, itemizes a series of tasks to be prescribed and accomplished in meeting each target goal. Figure 6.7, p. 156 shows the target action plan for Rabek Manufacturing, Inc., which has decided to use an advertising specialty campaign to promote their sales of printing supplies.

The first step in the target action plan is to restate the target goal in clear, precise, objective, results-oriented terms. In the Rabek example, the target goal is to develop an advertising specialty campaign within the next month. Note that this is part of a larger near-term goal to increase market share by three percent over the next year. Note also that even though the decision to use the advertising specialty approach had already been made, staff commitment to this approach has not been secured. With the target goal firmly in mind, a series of important action steps come into play, including determining any barriers that must be overcome, determining specific tasks that must be done, setting deadlines for completion, and identifying elements of feedback to use to assess results.

### BARRIERS

Barriers are the obstacles or bottlenecks that must be overcome or circumvented before target goals can be reached. It is critical that owners take the time to consider, in detail, the barriers that stand in the way of reaching target goals. Barriers typically relate to human resources, other resources, and time. There are three types: (1) insurmountable barriers, (2) barriers that can be overcome but only with a concerted redirection of effort toward the barrier, and (3) barriers that can be hurdled while enroute to the target goals.

The first type is a barrier or a series of barriers so overwhelming and significant that it is clear the target goal will never be attained. Suppose, for

---

[1] Many of the ideas for this target action plan are drawn from the goal-planning work of Robert S. Bailey of the Center for Creative Leadership, Greensboro, North Carolina.

CHAPTER 6: SETTING GOALS / 155

Figure 6.6

**TARGET ACTION PLAN**

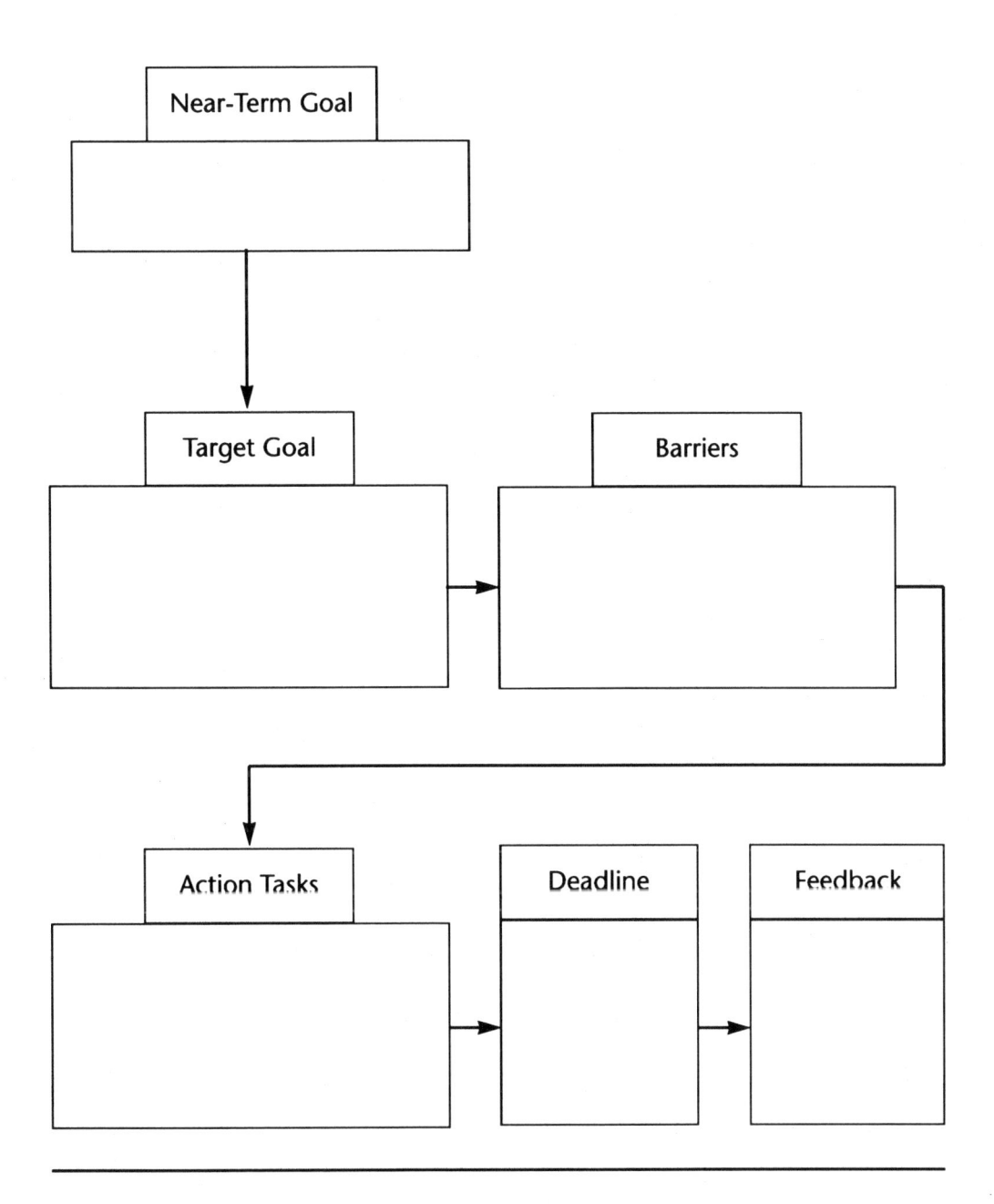

Near-Term Goal

Target Goal

Barriers

Action Tasks

Deadline

Feedback

Figure 6.7

**TARGET ACTION PLAN FOR RABEK MANUFACTURING, INC.**

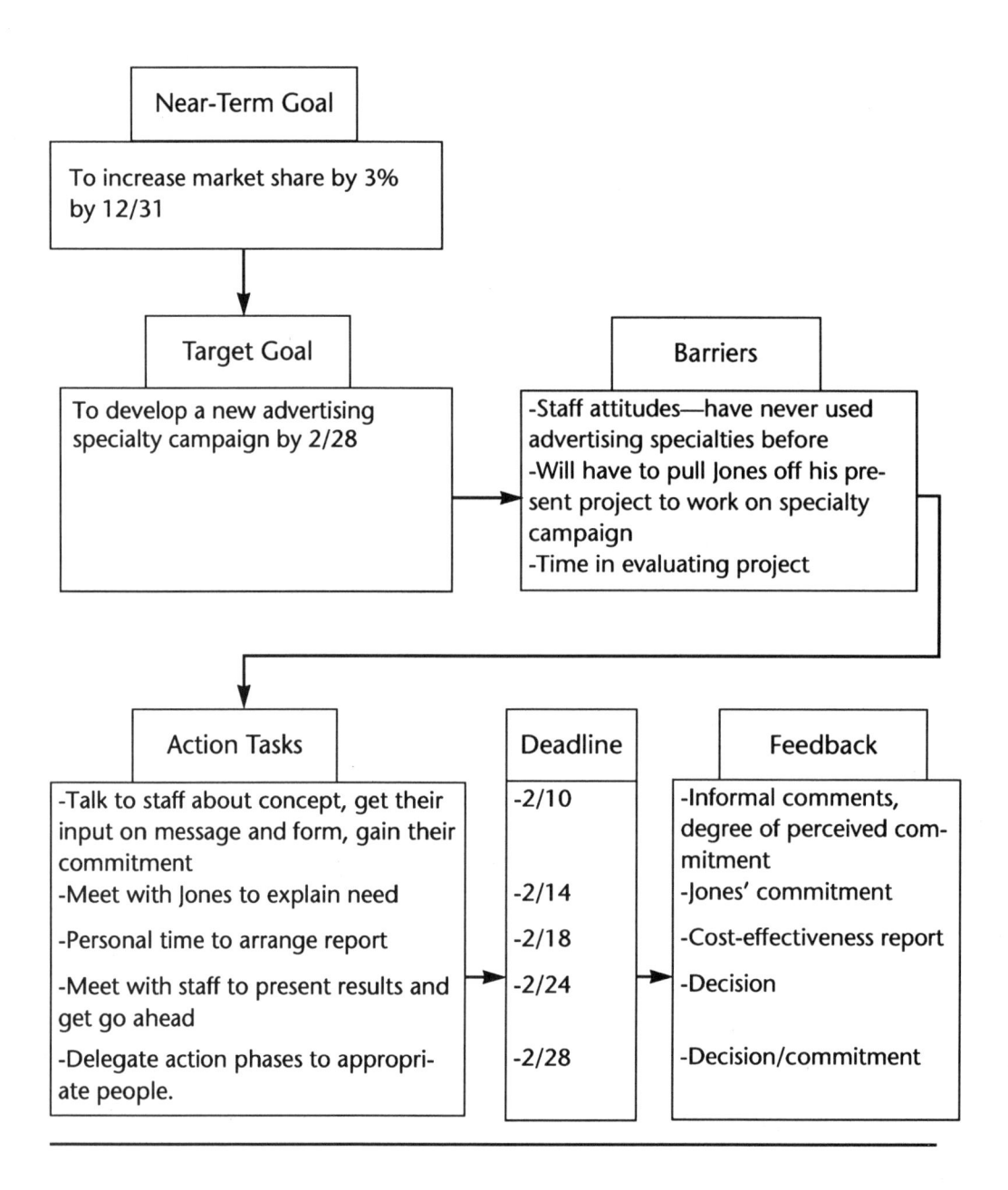

**Near-Term Goal**
To increase market share by 3% by 12/31

**Target Goal**
To develop a new advertising specialty campaign by 2/28

**Barriers**
- Staff attitudes—have never used advertising specialties before
- Will have to pull Jones off his present project to work on specialty campaign
- Time in evaluating project

**Action Tasks**
- Talk to staff about concept, get their input on message and form, gain their commitment
- Meet with Jones to explain need
- Personal time to arrange report
- Meet with staff to present results and get go ahead
- Delegate action phases to appropriate people.

**Deadline**
- 2/10
- 2/14
- 2/18
- 2/24
- 2/28

**Feedback**
- Informal comments, degree of perceived commitment
- Jones' commitment
- Cost-effectiveness report
- Decision
- Decision/commitment

example, a company has a target goal of completing a marketing research project by the end of the month. If the two primary researchers on this project suddenly resign, the goal becomes unreachable. It is important to recognize an insurmountable goal early in the action process, before you waste important resources and become frustrated. When you hit an insurmountable barrier, you need to abandon your target goal and consider alternatives.

The second type of barrier must be resolved before target goals can be addressed. This kind of barrier forces the owner to abandon the target goal temporarily and focus on overcoming the barrier. For example, if a machine is not performing to specifications, the target goal must be set aside and energies directed toward repairing the machine or acquiring a new one. Only then can the original target goal be readdressed.

The third type of barrier is not as pervasive or overwhelming but still requires some element of sacrifice, in terms of either resources or time. Owners must be aware of these sacrifices and be open and responsive to addressing these difficulties and explaining likely benefits if they are overcome. In the Rabek example, the owners must convince the marketing department that time spent on advertising specialties is worthwhile and meaningful. They must also let the staff know what is expected of them, allaying their fears and apprehensions and encouraging a positive, supportive attitude.

## ACTION TASKS

Action tasks are the specific tasks that must be completed if target goals are to be achieved. They are the final refinement in the process of segmenting goals into smaller, incremental units. These tasks are the most basic and narrowly defined.

Each necessary action task must be noted. (Some action tasks may focus on dealing with barriers.) Once action tasks have been prescribed, they must be arranged or prioritized into a logical sequence. The specificity of the actions depends on the owner's confidence in the employees. If employees are knowledgeable, dedicated, and innovative, action tasks are best stated in broad parameters, leaving it to the employees to determine specific activities. Conversely, if employees are new or unskilled, they may need more specificity and direction.

**DEADLINES**

It is important to establish deadlines, or completion dates, for each task in the sequence. These deadlines must be real, not arbitrary, so that employees treat them seriously. Imposing an artificially early deadline only frustrates employees, who no doubt have a number of simultaneous responsibilities. Deadlines should also be meaningful. Deadlines for the most critical tasks—those that if delayed will cause severe problems—should be set first. Deadlines for other tasks can then be assigned and prioritized accordingly.

**FEEDBACK**

Some method of securing feedback should be determined in order to evaluate whether a task has been completed or is progressing as required. Feedback needs to give the owner a solid feel for the success of the task. Feedback regarding individual tasks may be easily identifiable, as when an employee obtains a contract, or may be more qualitative, such as favorable comments from customers or an apparent increase in the ratio between sales calls and sales dollars. Monitoring feedback forces the owner to concentrate on action tasks and evaluate efforts to meet each part of the action task sequence. In the Rabek Manufacturing Inc. example, action tasks are listed in their prioritized sequence, along with deadlines and a means of evaluative feedback for each.

## The Integrative Goal Model

Thus far, we have identified three elements of strategic planning. First, a broad situational analysis is performed, allowing the business to recognize its threats, opportunities, strengths, weaknesses, and relevant competencies. Taking the analysis into full consideration, a series of goals is then developed in the form of written, measurable goal statements. This series of goals clearly and specifically designates desired results. Finally, a target action plan is enacted to detail the process of bringing the goal statements to fruition. Figure 6.8 outlines this integrative goal model.

Figure 6.8

**INTEGRATIVE GOAL MODEL**

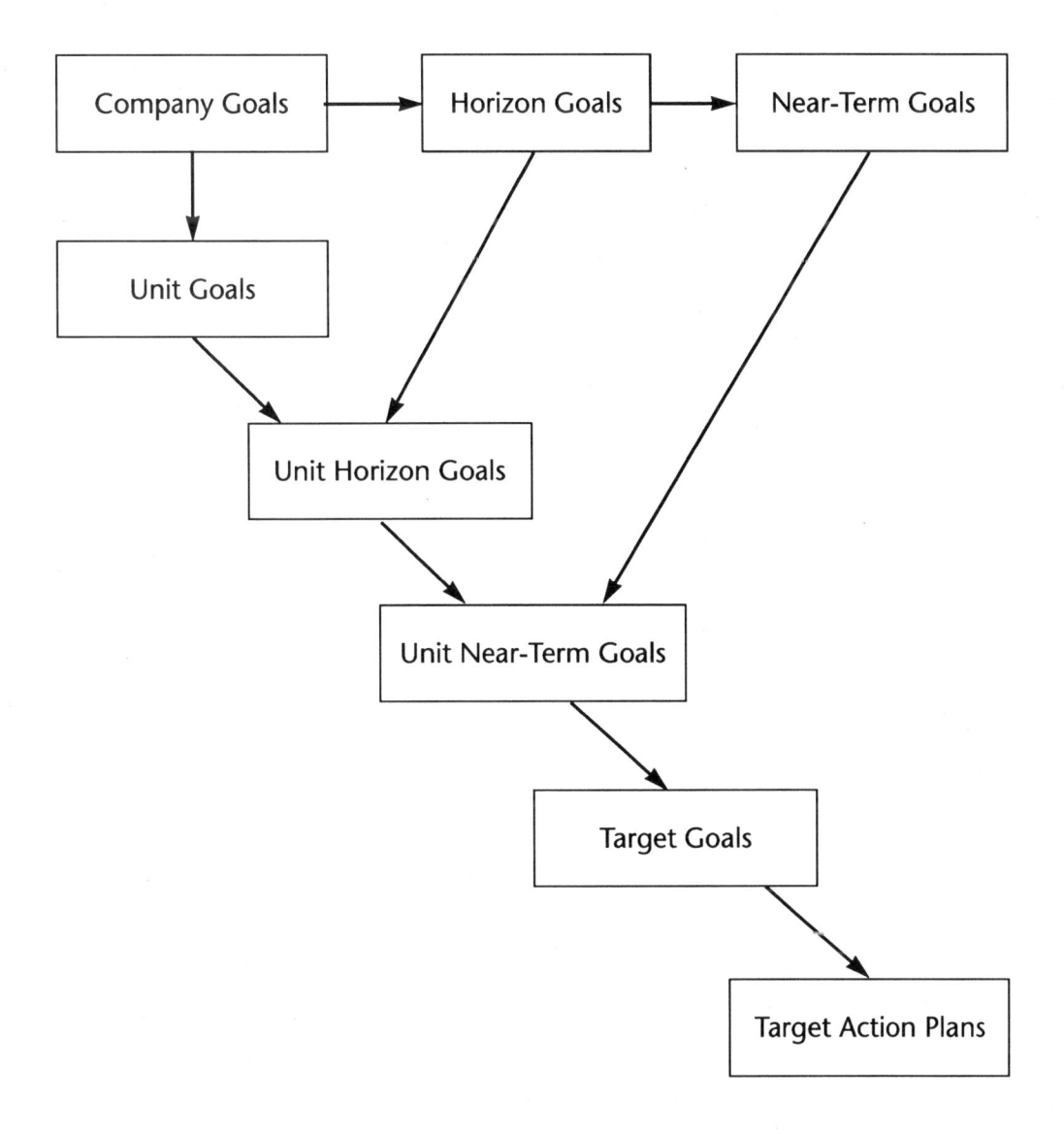

```
Company Goals ──► Horizon Goals ──► Near-Term Goals
      │                │                    │
      ▼                │                    │
  Unit Goals           │                    │
      │                ▼                    │
      └──────► Unit Horizon Goals           │
                      │                     │
                      ▼                     │
               Unit Near-Term Goals ◄───────┘
                      │
                      ▼
                 Target Goals
                      │
                      ▼
              Target Action Plans
```

## Summary

This chapter stressed the nature and importance of a written mission statement and its accompanying goals and objectives. We emphasized the importance of determining an appropriate planning horizon and discussed the process of formulating both near-term and horizon goals and turning them into action tasks.

## Discussion Questions

1. How do a company's goals differ from its mission?

2. Historically, what is the relationship between goals and actual performance? Is the relationship different for a fast-growing firm and a slow-growing firm?

3. What process should be used to determine specific goals for a business? Is this process any different for a larger firm? For a not-for-profit organization?

4. What is the similarity between action tasks as they relate to specific goals, and strategies as they relate to broader goals?

5. How can specific functional areas have horizon-level goals?

# CASE STUDY

# Company Goals for Gaston Ridge Home Health Care, Inc.

AUTHORS' NOTE: Two company horizon goals are currently emphasized. These goals are clearly interdependent, because the development of one affects the other. Near-term and target goals are also presented. (Note that there is a brief justification for each of these goals. That way, when you refer back to them at a later date you can also see why the goals were selected.) Unit goals relating to marketing and human resources are also noted.

## Horizon Goals

1. Increase the patient base by 100 percent over the next three years.

*Rationale:*
The demographic profile of the service area reveals that a considerable percentage of the area's population is over 65, providing a large potential client base. Further, economic, legal, and political forces indicate strong growth in the home health care field. We should have a large and growing target market from which to draw clients. Further, the current client base of 52 is not large, although it is quite respectable for a relatively new entrant in the market. Growth to 104 clients is a realistic yet challenging goal over the next three years.

2. Increase awareness of Gaston Ridge and the services we offer over the next three years so that 90 percent of physicians and 75 percent of the customers in the target market are familiar with us.

*Rationale:*
The proposed goal of client growth can only occur if awareness of Gaston Ridge and its services is enhanced. Promotional and advertising efforts have

been quite limited. The goal is important and achievable. Figures for both physicians and customers are about double the rates noted in recent physician and customer surveys.

## NEAR-TERM GOALS

1. Develop and implement a new promotional campaign to introduce Gaston Ridge personnel and services to all physicians in the service area within the next twelve months. This goal is segmented into target goals of reaching eight designated physicians every six weeks.)

*Rationale:*
The two most tangible ways to increase awareness and enhance the client base are to focus efforts toward both physicians and end users. We know that physician familiarity and willingness to refer is affected by their perception of the breadth and quality of services available.

2. Add two physical therapy assistants to the staff within the next year.

*Rationale:*
A recent survey of area physicians indicated that most physicians making referrals to home health care agencies list physical therapy as an important service. We will maintain our contractual arrangement for the very expensive and highly demanded physical therapists, but by employing two physical therapy assistants, we will build a stronger working relationship in this service area. It is the physical therapy assistant who actually administers the treatment prescribed by the physical therapist. Assistants are more affordable and appear to be in ample supply within the market area.

## TARGET GOALS

1. Hire a physical therapist as soon as we are sure that the physical therapy client load will reach 35 visits a month.

*Rationale:*
As business grows and in order to assure higher levels of control, we will benefit from hiring our own physical therapist. Currently, however, only 15 monthly visits are done.

2. Provide a meal delivery service within the next six months.

*Rationale:*
The environmental analysis clearly highlighted the need within the market for this service. This service adds benefit to current clients and the care they receive. In addition, the meal service can be an effective form of advertising. Many elderly persons may use the meal service even though they do not need home health care at the present time.

## Unit Goals

1. Design a new physician-focused promotional campaign by July 31.
2. Secure promotional materials and arrangements by August 31.
3. Begin initial promotional contacts by September 15.
4. Determine new job responsibilities for physical therapy assistants and home health aides by August 15.
5. Recruit and hire a full time additional home health aide and the first physical therapy assistant by September 30.

*Rationale:*
These target goals support the near-term goals stated above.

# CHAPTER 7

# Developing Unit Strategies

OBJECTIVES

After studying this chapter, you should understand

1. the relationship between goal setting and unit strategies.

2. the major parts of each of the unit strategies.

3. the importance of each part of the unit strategies.

4. the need for consistency among the parts of the plan.

ONCE THE FIRM'S goals have been set, unit strategies can be developed. A unit strategy is a plan of action indicating how managers within a given unit area go about achieving near-term goals.

Figure 7.1 incorporates the role of unit strategies into the goal-planning model. Recall that company goals must first be prescribed for the relevant planning horizon and the near term. Then, managers in each unit area can develop relevant horizon and near-term goals for their areas. With these unit-level goals firmly in mind, the planner then considers unit *strategies* that are appropriate for that area and are consistent with both the unit-level goals and the overall company goals. In the marketing department, for example, managers will look at the overall business goals, determine marketing's role in achieving those goals, and then set unit goals for the marketing area. They will then develop a set of marketing strategies to

Figure 7.1

**RELATIONSHIP BETWEEN GOALS AND STRATEGIES**

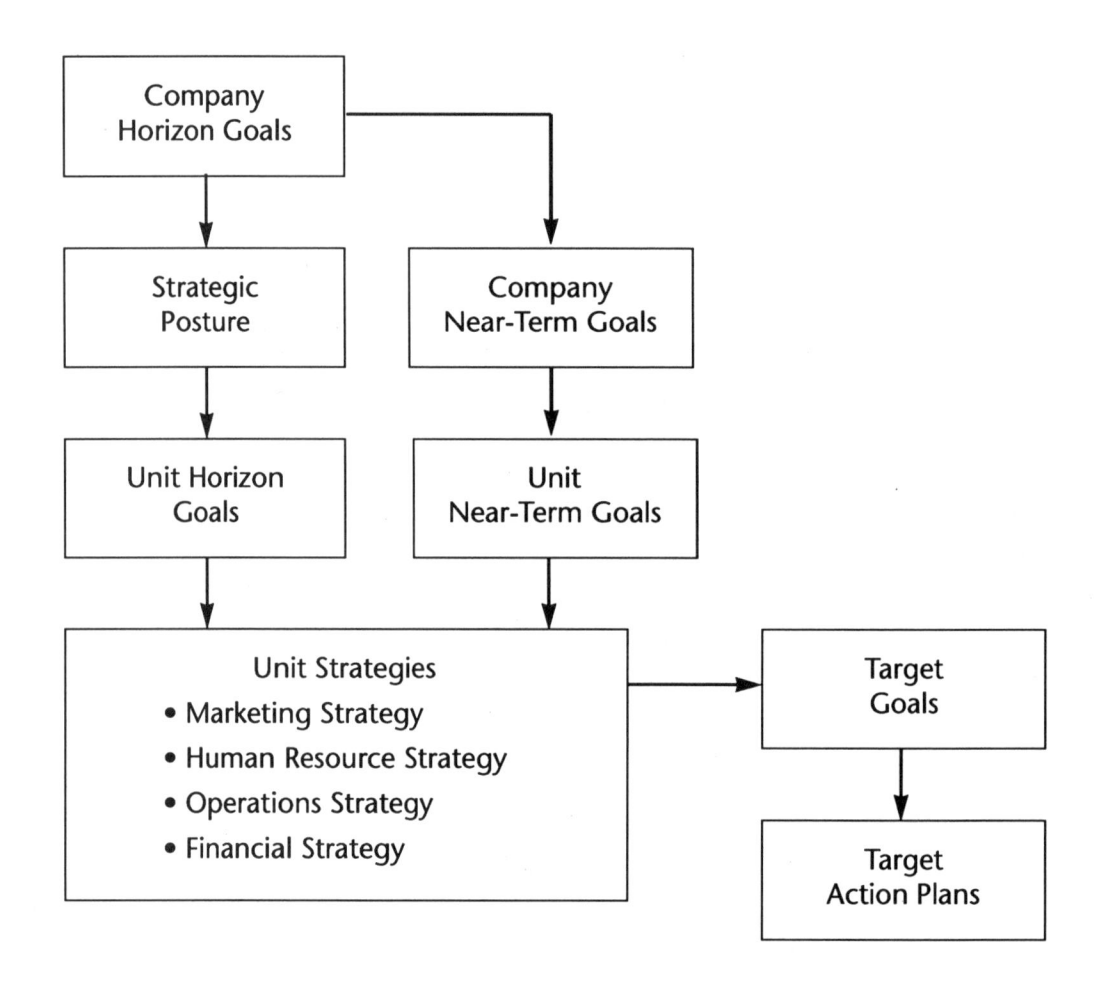

```
┌──────────────┐
│   Company    │─────────────┐
│ Horizon Goals│             │
└──────┬───────┘             │
       │                     ▼
       ▼              ┌──────────────┐
┌──────────────┐      │   Company    │
│  Strategic   │      │Near-Term Goals│
│   Posture    │      └──────┬───────┘
└──────┬───────┘             │
       ▼                     ▼
┌──────────────┐      ┌──────────────┐
│ Unit Horizon │      │     Unit     │
│    Goals     │      │Near-Term Goals│
└──────┬───────┘      └──────┬───────┘
       │                     │
       ▼                     ▼
┌─────────────────────────────────┐     ┌──────────┐
│        Unit Strategies          │     │  Target  │
│   • Marketing Strategy          │────▶│  Goals   │
│   • Human Resource Strategy     │     └─────┬────┘
│   • Operations Strategy         │           │
│   • Financial Strategy          │           ▼
└─────────────────────────────────┘     ┌──────────┐
                                        │  Target  │
                                        │Action Plans│
                                        └──────────┘
```

achieve those goals, ensuring that the marketing strategy meshes with the firm's overall strategy.

Once unit strategies are in place, managers in each area can refine their relevant goals. Each group within an area creates its particular target goals and target action plans.

It should be clear that although unit strategies are addressed in this chapter, they cannot be viewed independently of or in isolation from the goal development discussed in Chapter 6.

This chapter discusses issues that must be addressed as a prerequisite to writing the actual business plan. They fall into four general categories: marketing, operations, human resources, and the all-important financial elements. This chapter focuses on the strategic nature of the issues. Chapter 8 discusses the actual writing of the plan.

# The Marketing Strategy

The marketing strategy must be detailed enough to help the owner establish, for example, how many salespersons to hire, the type and amount of advertising to use, the pricing strategy, the product mix, and the selling strategy. The strategic plan may not answer specific questions, but it should set forth general guidelines and *relatively* specific details. It should be sufficiently detailed so that it easily distinguishes the business from its competitors and that employees can identify and understand their relative roles in accomplishing the firm's objectives.

### THE TARGET MARKET SEGMENT

Perhaps the most important marketing issue is the market segment the business will target. One of the biggest failures of many new businesses (and some not so new) is that they attempt to be everything to everyone. Marketing dollars are spread too thin and are therefore often wasted. If a company is trying to reach all the customers it possibly can, few will be properly served.

Defining a market segment does not mean that customers outside that segment will be unwelcome. It only means that they will not receive strategic attention. That is, they will not receive primary emphasis. If customers outside the defined segment purchase the firm's goods or services, that's fine. (If enough customers outside the target market purchase from the company, the target market may need to be redefined.) But the point is this: There will never be enough marketing dollars. Thus, by targeting more specific segments, we can do a better job of marketing and can serve our customers better.

Take the following example. Although many people buy waterbeds, most customers are either teenagers or adults under thirty. Targeting this market will limit radio advertising to rock stations and TV advertising to certain shows. Newspaper ads can be placed on those pages most read by the 15-to-30-year-old bracket. Marketing dollars can also be concentrated into time/media combinations that hit the target audience most directly. Waterbed styles most ordered by the target market are stocked, and other styles can be special ordered, thus limiting inventory while still giving most of the customers immediate service.

## THE PRODUCT IMAGE

The difference between Wal-Mart and Neiman-Marcus is readily apparent. Similarly, Häagen Dazs connotes a different image to the consumer than Dairy Queen does. These are extreme examples, but a product's image is an integral part of the corporate marketing strategy whether the firm does $50,000 in sales or $5 million in sales.

Let's return to the waterbed example. A father and son started selling waterbeds direct from the manufacturer. They had no showroom, instead operating the business out of their home. They listed no address, only a phone number. Handwritten, photocopied advertisements for waterbeds were tacked to grocery store bulletin boards. They had also "done some advertising in the newspaper," which consisted of a three-line ad in the classified section. Although they apparently were selling good-quality waterbeds, their marketing strategy gave them a low-quality, low-price image.

This is not to say that either a high- or a low-quality image is better, only that the product or service *will have an image* whether one is desired or not. A specific image should therefore be purposely determined, cultivated, and maintained. A specific image is as necessary for a manufacturer of industrial components as it is for retailers. No business, whatever its size, can escape the image issue.

## THE PRICING STRATEGY

A firm's pricing strategy is important for two reasons. The first relates to image. Part of the overall image of the firm and its product line or service is the perceived price of the product or service. There is obviously a relationship between price and quality. But the actual relationship is not as important as the perceived relationship. Most people perceive higher-priced goods to be better whether they are or not. Aspirin is a good example. FDA regulations require all aspirin to have the same active ingredients. Any brand differences are in either the coatings or the bonding agents. Yet millions, encouraged by advertising, are convinced that the national brands are worth the substantial difference in price.

In many cases, the higher-priced product is the better-quality product. Pennsylvania House stands out as a premier-quality brand of furniture. Cadillac, Mercedes, and Volvo carry distinctive automobile images and distinctive prices. Ben and Jerry's ice cream and Hummel figurines are other examples where price and quality are both high and well accepted.

Businesses may sometimes successfully confuse the price-image relationship (Profile 7.1 is one example). In general, however, price and image go hand in hand.

---

### PROFILE 7.1: CAN MANUFACTURER'S OUTLETS BEAT THE PRICE/IMAGE RELATIONSHIP?

One retailing method is the manufacturer's outlet store. A current trend is the outlet mall containing as many as fifty different outlet stores. These stores sell national brand name products at somewhat lower than retail prices. Whether the stores sell first-quality products or seconds, this year's styles or last's, overruns or normal production runs, is a matter of opinion. And in some cases the savings are questionable. Yet these off-price stores seem to flourish. Why? Don't they violate the price/image relationship? Isn't the customer suspicious when buying a coat for half the normal price?

The success of these stores is rooted in the general public's continual search for a bargain. That and extensive highway advertising attracts many customers. Interestingly, the same type of advertising for a normal store would have little effect, nor would an outlet store that did not convince the public of the alleged savings.

---

The second issue surrounding the pricing strategy has to do with margins. One business may sell at low prices in hopes that high volume will offset low margins. Others, such as high-quality furniture stores, will depend on high margins to offset obviously lower volume. The pricing strategy depends on the elasticity of the product. That is, if prices are raised by 10 percent, will sales decrease by less than or more than 10 percent? What will be the effect if competitors raise their prices 10 percent?

Neither high nor low pricing strategies are advocated, but some strategy should be used. A combination strategy may be used. A high-end pricing strategy may be used with most of the product line, while loss leaders are used to attract customers to the store. Consistency is important. It is difficult to change an image, and it is perhaps even more difficult to change the perceived price/quality relationship.

## THE PRODUCT MIX STRATEGY

The mission statement and the other marketing issues largely determine the product mix. The business owner must still decide (1) whether to carry a full line or be a specialty store, (2) whether or not to offer service after the sale, and (3) the depth and breadth of the product line.

These decisions are largely dictated by the owner's personal desires, the amount of financing available, the market niche, the nature of the industry, and the capabilities of the personnel. For example, a retail craft store may only sell craft supplies, may offer craft classes as well, or may sell finished craft projects in addition to both of these services. It may carry a broad product line or specialize in only a few types of projects. It may carry several manufacturers' brands of the same product or carry only one brand per product.

Similarly, a manufacturer must determine whether to produce a broad line of products or a single product. Several models or variations of a given product may be produced (colors, sizes, extras) or only a single version.

## THE SELLING STRATEGY

The selling strategy ties in very closely with the image of the company. The selling strategy affects whether a high-quality or a low-quality image is projected. You need only count the number of salespeople to differentiate between the self-service store and the full-service store.

Store layout is also a part of the selling strategy. A store whose aisles are cluttered with merchandise that is buried or out of reach projects a different image than one with wide aisles and easily accessible merchandise.

The selling strategy depends on the target market. Sophisticated and prosperous customers may prefer personal attention when buying clothes, depend on in-home decorators when purchasing home furnishings, and want an expert to recommend art objects for their living room. Those not interested in these expensive frills may want to browse, try on clothes without being hassled by a sales clerk, or pick out their own home furnishings from the selection on the sales floor.

The selling strategy is at least as important to a manufacturing firm as it is to the retail stores discussed above. This is especially critical when launching a new firm. Should the manufacturer attempt to market the product directly, using a company sales force? Should representatives be used? Should the firm only manufacture the product, relying totally on a marketing company for distribution? Or should the owner of a manufacturing firm license the product to someone else to manufacture? There are a variety of ways the product can reach the final customer.

Two of the most important factors affecting the selling strategy for small firms are the up-front investment and the day-to-day costs. A new firm that manufactures a single product may be forced to go with a manufacturer's representative because of the high unit cost associated with an in-house sales force. The initial cost of hiring sales people is prohibitive if a wide geographical area is being targeted. In new retail situations, day-to-day costs may be the overriding factor. Stories abound of retail stores that, in the interests of quality and personal service, staff their stores with too many clerks and find later that their wage and salary costs are excessive. Profile 7.2 is an example.

### PROFILE 7.2: ANTIQUES UNLIMITED

Bill and Sandy Houlihan opened their dream business, an antiques mall called Antiques Unlimited. They sensed antiques dealers wanted a year-round showroom where they could exhibit their wares without needing to hire sales help. Bill and Sandy rented dealers space in a large building they owned and provided all sales floor personnel, who floated from area to area monitoring and assisting customers. Bill and Sandy agreed to provide one sales clerk for every three shops or every 750 square feet.

This agreement was quite beneficial for the dealers but a killer for the Houlihans. Although there were times when all staff members were busy, there were far more times when the only people in the mall were the clerks. There was a limit to how much dusting, arranging, and bookkeeping they could do.

Attempting to renegotiate the agreement with dealers, the Houlihans encountered a lot of resistance from the dealers of small but expensive antiques, who were concerned about shoplifting. Furniture dealers, on the other hand, were not overly concerned. The problem was partially resolved when the Houlihans agreed that the store would be fully staffed on weekends and other days or times when traffic was expected to be heavy. At other times, there would be one clerk for every five shops or 1,200 square feet.

Later, the Houlihans rearranged the shops so that the large-products stores were in one area and the small-products shops were in another area. This arrangement permitted the Antiques Unlimited staff to monitor the mall more closely, paying particular attention to those areas that needed it.

---

There are a myriad of other short-run tactical or operational issues, such as commissioned versus salaried sales people, appropriate attitudes among the sales force, and part-time versus full-time workers. All are part of the overall marketing strategy. While it is beyond the scope of this book to consider each specific issue, owners must address all of them and more as part of their planning process.

## The Operations Strategy

The operations strategy includes those decisions related to the actual manufacture of goods or provision of services and to the facilities issues associated with them. Operations issues affect all kinds of firms. For example, inventory is a strategic issue in both manufacturing and retail businesses. Purchasing and scheduling are important in all businesses. Layout concerns are important in retail stores as well as manufacturing firms.

We are concerned here with strategic issues relating to operations. Perhaps no other area involves more day-to-day decisions than operations in a manufacturing firm, but our interest here is on the development of an operations strategy.

## FACILITIES

Strategic decisions about facilities are necessarily related with marketing and financial strategies. For example, major investments in facilities may be required to meet increasing demand. But investing thousands of dollars in plant and equipment may take resources away from marketing that will be needed to sell the very products produced in the expanded facilities.

Forecasting sales is critical to facilities decisions. Since facilities use extraordinary amounts of capital, the business owner must carefully project how large the firm's operations are expected to be or are expected to grow in the foreseeable future. One of the first decisions to be made must be the acquisition of the appropriate amount and type of space for the firm's operations.

Two errors are common when making space decisions, either of which can adversely impact a firm's ability to compete in the long run. The first is overcapacity. The owner assumes the firm will grow quickly and leases or buys more capacity than the firm can use or afford. Later, the firm is in trouble because of the financial drain caused by the overcapacity. The second error is to acquire insufficient space, which leads to undercapacity. Operations are so cramped that they become severely inefficient. There is no room for expansion, so the firm must relocate. Retail stores often lose customers when they relocate. For a manufacturing operation, the expense of relocating equipment and retrofitting a new facility may be excessive, creating financial difficulties.

Another space-related issue is the type of space needed. Unfortunately, in many cases, the small business starts out by using the most easily available space rather than the most appropriate space. An entrepreneur starts a home-based business and stays there even though better space is sorely needed; a budding retailer decides to open a shop near home when space is available across town in a well-traveled shopping center; a manufacturer accepts space in an old warehouse and then finds that the costs of remodeling and rewiring is excessive.

The key is to somehow find a location that has enough space, yet not too much. There are no hard-and-fast rules. A rough guide is to acquire space that is 15 to 20 percent too large or that may be fully utilized within a year to 18 months. This will ensure that space is available, and it will offset the near-term undercapacity problem. Although this strategy does present an immediate overcapacity problem, it is not as serious a problem as being under capacity a short while after moving into the facility. The extra space is a necessary hedge at a relatively small cost. An alternative is to acquire somewhat more capacity than initially needed and sublet the excess. This not only ensures the needed capacity later but also brings in a small amount of income in the interim. Caution should be taken, however, not to overdo. Plans should be made realistically, adhering to the 18-month or 20 percent limits.

Facility strategies may take a variety of forms dictated by the unique needs of the business and its situation. The facility option highlighted in Profile 7.3 is becoming increasingly popular.

---

### PROFILE 7.3: BUSINESS TECHNOLOGY CENTER

The Maple City Business Technology Center is one of a growing number of facility arrangements available to new and small businesses. The technology center concept is an interesting one for new business owners that don't need a lot of administrative services. A technology center is a large building (sometimes an abandoned warehouse or factory) that has been remodeled to house a number of diverse small businesses and provide them with administrative support. The business owners rent exactly as much space as they need, but can usually add space as necessary. Administrative services such as receptionists, computer support, and secretarial and bookkeeping help are provided, along with moral support.

The last item, moral support, is often the most important factor. The owners share ideas, techniques, and problems with other owners as well as the center manager. Sometimes the businesses purchase goods and services from other businesses in the center.

Some centers are run with private dollars on a for-profit basis. Others are run on a not-for-profit basis with state or federal dollars in the interest of creating jobs or boosting the economy. The concept's central thesis is that businesses can operate efficiently by sharing administrative services and assistance.

---

## MAKE-OR-BUY STRATEGIES

The make-or-buy decision is among the most important strategic operations decisions. It involves a great deal of money and is irreversible—at least in the short run. For a manufacturing firm, the choices are:

1. Manufacture all products in-house.

2. Manufacture one or more prime products in-house and purchase other products finished, perhaps in packaging bearing the company name.

3. Assemble some or all products from finished components and package them.

4. Produce nothing. Contract all production. Do only packaging, or perhaps not even that. Be responsible only for marketing the finished product.

Several factors influence the decision, and the firm's financial condition is certainly one. A business that is not able to invest large sums of money in manufacturing facilities may be forced to contract most of its production. Insufficient space may also force a firm to contract some of its production. On the other hand, a desire for quality may lead a firm to keep all of its production in-house. Lower production costs may also be a reason to produce components in-house, if the firm can make them for less than they could be purchased outside. In some cases, higher quality or lower costs may not be as important as the availability of goods. If components must be purchased from suppliers that are unreliable in meeting delivery dates, the company may be forced into producing its own components.

## VENDOR SELECTION

An issue being increasingly considered by both large and small businesses is vendor selection. Many large companies have switched from using several vendors who each provide perhaps 20 percent of the firm's component needs to using a single vendor who satisfies the firm's entire demand for the product. In the former system, the firm uses the multiple vendors as a hedge against one or more of them becoming unreliable. In the latter case, called just-in-time inventory, the firm contracts with a single vendor who agrees to provide the inventory precisely when needed and at a competitive price. The contracting firm works hand-in-hand with the vendor to ensure that problems do not arise.

Small businesses cannot use just-in-time inventory to the same extent as large firms because they don't have the clout to ensure that a supplier meets all demands. However, the basic concepts of this method are still available. Reducing the number of suppliers increases vulnerability to supplier reliability, but it can also result in increased quality if only the best supplier is used. It can sometimes also result in price breaks. Also, the ease of working with a single supplier may offset other risks.

### FINISHED INVENTORY STRATEGY

The preceding section dealt with supplier strategies regarding raw materials. Owners must also adopt a strategy for finished goods inventory. Here, the cost of maintaining substantial inventory must be weighed against two other factors. The first is the problem of stock outs. If inventory is kept too close to demand, any sudden changes can result in stock outs that cause a company to lose both sales and customer goodwill. In addition, maintaining minimal inventory causes production runs and personnel needs to fluctuate. This is particularly true for manufacturers who produce seasonal goods. Producing inventory in the off-season allows the owner to have a more level production schedule and to avoid adding and laying off workers. Complicating finished goods inventory even more is the cost of the inventory and its storage and the effect of that cost on the company's financial condition.

## The Human Resources Strategy

Many of the human resources–related issues fall more within operational policies than under the larger strategic plan. Our focus here is on those major organizational issues that affect the overall business and its owners.

### MANAGER SELECTION STRATEGIES

Perhaps no strategic issue is more important than the selection of competent managers. The managers are responsible for both the strategic direction of the firm and its day-to-day operations. There are no-hard-and-fast rules for how to choose managers. Some suggestions are in order, however:

1. Hire based on ability, not on friendships. Most people like to work with others when the relationship is comfortable and friendly. However, the skills and talents brought to the position are far more important. It may be fun to work with friends, but they may not have the background and ability to contribute in the manner needed. In addition, it is very difficult to fire friends if they do not perform adequately.

2. Hire to offset existing weaknesses. Frequently, the tendency is for company managers to hire others who think just like they do. The greater need, however, may be to hire those whose strengths offset current managerial weaknesses.

3. Develop the position and then fit a person to it. Don't hire a person and a then find a job to match the individual.

4. Think strategy! Many people can handle day-to-day administrative duties. Finding someone with entrepreneurial capabilities who can think toward the future is considerably more difficult.

5. Once a manager is chosen, the key words are train and delegate. Give the new person sufficient guidance to develop important skills and understanding of the business, and then delegate authority and responsibility. This allows the owner to concentrate on the overall company strategy rather than spend too much time with routine decision making.

Profile 7.4 illustrates the problem one small business owner experienced in dealing with a newly hired skilled worker. On the other hand, Ted Turner, the entrepreneurial genius who now owns the Atlanta Braves baseball team, the Atlanta Hawks basketball team, super station WTBS, and other ventures is noted as being an impetuous, shoot-from-the-hip entrepreneur. But he is also recognized as an excellent delegater. He chooses good managers and then turns them loose to run their operations.

---

### PROFILE 7.4: THE YARN AND HOOP SHOP

Jerry Jacobs started The Yarn and Hoop craft store. The store was well stocked with a wide variety of craft supplies. In addition to selling craft supplies, Jacobs gave classes in a number of different crafts, such as tole painting, decoupage, silk flower arranging, and macrame.

Following suggestions 1 and 2 on how to hire a good manager, Jacobs hired a person who was an expert in all forms of decorative painting. She had taught classes on her own, had exhibited some paintings, and was well respected in the community. He followed suggestion 3 and designed the job before hiring his painting assistant. Unfortunately, he suffered from a disease that strikes many entrepreneurs. He could not delegate. He could not accept that his assistant knew more than he did about painting-related crafts. And he could not accept that customers would ask specifically for her instead of talking to him. He could not follow suggestion 5, and fired his assistant in less than a month. As a result, customers were disappointed, some goodwill was lost with both customers and employees, and sales experienced a pronounced decline.

### WAGE AND SALARY STRATEGIES

Wage and salary strategies are different from wage and salary policies. The policies deal with the technical aspects of implementing the wage and salary strategies. The strategic emphasis of wage and salary issues deals with those items that may significantly affect the overall operation of the business. One important strategic issue is whether the firm will have a high-salary strategy or a low-salary strategy. Coupled with this is the combination of salaries and benefit packages. These are strategic issues, since they can affect the firm's ability to attract and retain key qualified workers.

The benefit issue is particularly important from a strategic viewpoint since benefits do not directly add to the productivity of the firm. The basic value the business gains from providing additional employee benefits may come from having a more dedicated, more loyal work force. One example is the employee stock option plan. Here, the owner is willing to share increasing amounts of ownership in exchange for presumed increases in employee commitment and dedication to the business.

## The Financial Strategy

Most analysts of small business failures suggest that they occur for two main reasons. One is a general lack of managerial planning. The second is the failure to finance the business adequately. Of course, inadequate financing may be a result of poor planning! Many small businesses are undercapitalized and do not have adequate resources to weather economic downturns or to take advantage of opportunities. Most financial strategies available to the small business fall into two general categories, equity strategies and debt strategies. There are also some funding strategies, which do not fit cleanly into either.

Most businesses will use a combination of financial sources as their overall financial strategy. These combinations may include federal and state government funds, venture capital, partnerships, and debt.

The amount and source of funding is an integral part of the firm's strategy, since it will affect the growth potential and the control of the business. For example, an owner who uses a high-debt strategy will maintain full control of the operation but will have a high debt service expense. Conversely, a company that has a high-equity strategy will have relatively less debt to service but must share some amount of profit and control with investors.

**DEBT STRATEGIES**

It has been said that it is easier to obtain a $100,000 loan than it is to get a $10,000 loan. Some may even say that obtaining a $1 million loan is easier still. Although this debate is unresolvable, the point is significant. Different strategies may be used depending on the size of the loan needed and the use of the funds.

The small start-up business may have relatively few alternatives. This is especially true if the start-up is a retail or a service business. The options may be personal loans by the owner, loans from friends or relatives, or a commercial bank loan. In the latter case, a percentage of equity capital will be a prerequisite. For example, a firm needing $50,000 may be able to get only $35,000 from a bank; the remaining $15,000 will need to be owner's equity. Banks tend to be wary of small start-ups, since many fail.

Related to bank financing is the Small Business Administration's guaranteed loan program. In this program, a bank agrees to the financing but 80 percent of the loan amount is guaranteed by the SBA. Thus, a bank is risking only 20 percent of its funds even though it is loaning the entire amount. This encourages a bank to work with small businesses to which they might not otherwise offer a straight commercial loan.

## EQUITY STRATEGIES

A variety of financing strategies fall within the area of equity financing. As before, the type of strategy chosen may be a function of what is available. However, it may also be a function of the owner's overall strategic plan.

Partnerships are an obvious source of equity funding, but it is a strategy that the primary owner must consider carefully. This method of financing has merit in that a working partner not only provides capital but also provides additional management skills. On the other hand, taking in a partner changes the nature of the business. The primary owner is no longer the sole decision maker. Further, taking in a partner requires that the profits also be shared. In some cases, a limited partner or silent partner can be found. In this case, decision making normally rests with the primary partner, but any profits or losses still must be split with the other partners.

A second strategy for raising equity capital is to sell stock either to individuals or to the general public through an initial public offering, or IPO. Small companies will typically sell stock either to wealthy acquaintances or to individual investors, or "angels," who invest in a number of high-potential businesses. Selling stock in this manner will normally require that a financial business plan be prepared. Much of that information, however, can be taken from the written strategic plan. Businesses that have already had some success may consider going public through an IPO. This is a complex process requiring assistance from investment bankers and underwriters. However, if successful, it can bring in a substantial amount of funds.

Venture capitalists are an attractive avenue for financing in some situations. There are many varieties, each with their own preferred investments. Some venture capitalists will invest only in high-tech companies. Some venture capital firms are associated with industrial firms and only invest in those companies that complement the parent firm's operations. Some venture capital firms insist on majority ownership, although most take a minority but significant ownership position. All venture capitalists require an extensive business plan. Further, they typically underwrite only about one percent of companies whose plans they review.

Government funds may come in either debt or equity form. In some cases, either the Small Business Administration or a state agency loans money directly to the business owner. In others, funds are loaned to "Certified Development Companies," which, in turn, lend the money to businesses. In some cases, a state agency may take an equity or quasi-equity position in the company. In some infrequent cases, an agency may make grants to the firm. These situations vary from state to state. Some states are very interested in economic development and are quite willing to be involved in "creative financing," particularly if the firm is located in an economically depressed area. Acquiring government funds is not necessarily easy, but it may be an attractive strategy, particularly if private funding is unavailable.

## OTHER FUNDING SOURCES

Some funding sources do not fall neatly into either the debt or equity category. They must still be considered as part of the financial strategy.

Leasing equipment rather than purchasing equipment is attractive in some cases, especially when equipment has a relatively short life or may become obsolete within a few years. Although leasing may ultimately be more expensive than owning, it does not tie up corporate funds and eliminates the need to incur debt.

Suppliers often provide short-term inventory financing. Technically, this is debt financing, since there is an obligation to pay. However, the payment may be made a few weeks later or, more rarely, at the end of the season.

Customers can also be a source of financing. This often involves complex equipment that is specially ordered. The manufacturer requires partial payment on order, with the remainder due on delivery. The manufacturer has thus shifted the part of the financial burden away from the firm to the customer, thus reducing debt.

## THE NEED FOR A PLAN

While there are several sources and possible strategies for financing, remember the underlying importance of developing a financial strategy. Financing should never be ad hoc. The owner should always be aware of the various sources and uses of funds. A financing discussion often revolves around building a business plan that can be taken to lenders or equity sources. The point we emphasize here is the role of financing in the firm's strategic plan.

The overall strategic plan must include the financial strategy. This allows the effective merging of the financial strategy, the marketing strategy, the human resources strategy, and the operations strategy.

## Summary

This chapter has discussed the refinement of overall strategies by breaking them into unit strategies. Discussion has focused on four primary areas—the marketing strategy, the operations strategy, the human resources strategy, and the financial strategy. The discussion has emphasized the relationship between the unit strategies and the fit of the unit strategies with the overall company strategy.

## Discussion Questions

1. How will the marketing strategy of a discount firm differ from that of a "top of the line" firm?

2. How does its pricing policy relate to a firm's image?

3. Is it possible to have a manufacturing strategy that is relatively independent of the other parts of a firm's strategy?

4. How does the human resources strategy relate to the marketing strategy? The financial strategy?

5. Determine the overall strategy of a small manufacturing firm in your area.

# CASE STUDY

# Unit Strategies for Gaston Ridge Home Health Care, Inc.

AUTHORS' NOTE: In the Gaston Ridge Home Health Care case, specific strategies are needed that relate to and build on the goals previously noted. These are presented and explained below. In some cases, supporting policy actions are also noted, as these emphasize how given strategies will be carried out. Many of the strategies take time, planning, and money to effect. However, the strategies will help establish Gaston Ridge as a solid and respected business, which will, in turn, affect profitability.

## Marketing Strategies

We must engage in advertising, public relations, and personal contact activities to enhance the image and awareness of the agency. The following strategies will be used:

1. Monthly blood pressure and cholesterol screenings will be conducted in Perryville and the surrounding communities of Ellsworth, Corrington, Wood Ridge, and Brookside. These activities will be arranged through senior citizen centers and local churches. The screenings will be free of charge. Notices of the screenings will be public service advertisements in the local weekly newspapers and radio stations in the area.

2. Informational and goodwill advertising will be carried in the weekly newspapers on a monthly basis.

3. Frequent efforts will be made to inform and influence physicians and their nurses. Gaston Ridge will offer 45-minute breakfast or luncheon meetings with physicians and their nurses at the physician's office. These will be scheduled on Tuesdays and Thursdays, our slow days. These meetings will

begin with a 15-minute formal presentation about our services followed by a question-and-answer period. At the conclusion, coffee mugs with the Gaston Ridge logo will be given to the physician and his or her staff. Personalized thank you notes will be sent the following week. New brochures and follow-up thank you notes for referrals will be sent every six months.

4. We will form a strategic alliance with a local provider of food services such as the Perryville High School or a local restaurant. Initially, the service will provide a weekday hot lunch, with enough left over for the evening meal. This service will be limited to the Perryville area until demand warrants expansion to other areas. Prices for the meals will be our cost of the purchased meal plus fifty percent.

## Human Resources Strategy

1. Because of the expected demand for physical therapy, which is offset by the high cost of a licensed therapist, we will hire a physical therapy assistant from the community college physical therapy assistant program. The assistant will work with a contracted physical therapist until demand grows enough that we can hire our own physical therapist. Once the case load grows, we will hire a part-time physical therapist until demand warrants one full-time.

2. The pay and benefits for all personnel will be competitive with the industry as adjusted to a smaller community. We will monitor our competitors' rates and adjust ours as necessary.

## Financial Strategy

We currently have a loan from Perryville County. We plan to retire the debt within nine months unless other major expenditures are necessary. As a contingency plan, we will forecast our needs at the end of six months and extend the loan if necessary, since the rates are favorable.

# CHAPTER 8

# Writing the Plan

---

OBJECTIVES

Readers of this chapter should achieve a single objective: to gain a better understanding of how to write a strategic plan.

THIS CHAPTER REVIEWS the items to be included in the strategic plan and discusses the actual format and writing of the plan. As you recall, the strategic planning model was divided into two phases. Phase 1 dealt with the analysis. Phase 2 concentrated on the actions necessary to develop the strategy. The final step of this action phase is the actual writing of the plan.

While we have followed Gaston Ridge Home Health Care, Inc., through most of the chapters in the book, it is important to see the written, integrated strategic plan, which follows this chapter in Appendix A. It is an example of a plan that can be used to guide the company's business decisions.

Before getting into the actual details, we must reemphasize the reasons for writing the plan in the first place. Frequently small business owners make the dangerous assumption that a plan can be stored in their minds and still give them needed direction and guidance. Although the strategic plan is primarily an instrument for guiding the owner, it is also to be read by employees and others such as potential investors and key suppliers. Though some of the items may seem trite or self-evident to the owner, they may be necessary for the other potential readers.

Reasonably specific detail should be included—as much detail as confidentiality will allow. This, too, may seem unnecessary. Remember, however, that a second key use of the plan is to review progress. The more specific the plan is, the better can progress be evaluated. Less obvious is the motivational effect of putting the plan on paper—the owner and employees are likely to be more committed to such a plan. Consider Reder Electronics, in Profile 8.1.

---

### PROFILE 8.1: REDER ELECTRONICS

Reder Electronics sets forth a strategic plan for the business at the beginning of each fiscal year. The plan specifies relevant aspects of the environment, presents an assessment of internal strengths and weaknesses, and lays out rather clearly the firm's goals. A strategy for the year is then presented that will be used to achieve the company's goals.

This plan is not filed away, never to be seen again. Rather, it is a working document, referenced and reexamined regularly. Scott Reder feels that such checks are critical and encourages quarterly reviews.

During these progress checks, Reder compares both the internal analysis and the external assessment in the plan to the current situation. If necessary, the plans may be changed. (Remember, they are not etched in stone.) The important thing, according to Reder, is that this process allows the business to "note where we have been and how far we have to go to attain either the goals we set for ourselves or the new goals that have developed since that writing."

Sometimes the quarterly analysis is favorable and encouraging. Sometimes it is not. But the reexamination procedure allows Reder to know where the company is compared to where he wants it to be and then to focus on corrective action.

---

Figure 8.1, p. 188, shows the format for a strategic plan. The discussion throughout the rest of this chapter will follow that format.

## The Nature of the Business

This section of the plan is a broad overview of the business designed to give potential readers a feel for the business and its operating environment.

The initial description of the business will be broad, noting whether the business is wholesale, manufacturing, retail, or service. This should give the reader an idea of where the business fits within the overall industry.

Next, provide a fairly detailed discussion of the industry in which the firm competes. It should include the industry's sensitivity to the economy, the intensity of competition, the nature of competition (price versus quality versus product differentiation), and the size of the total market.

Specific information on competitors should follow. Estimate each competitor's market share and other significant competitive factors. Include any additional, relevant information on key competitors. Taken together, the industry and competitors' data should provide a reasonably clear idea of the size of the market and the degree of turbulence to expect in the industry.

Next, discuss the general location. This may include overall community characteristics as well as comments on the specific location of the business. The key here is to include information that will be valuable for comparison later. Itemize the unemployment rate in the local community, the general outlook for the community, the relative locations of competitors, and the strengths and weaknesses of the precise location within the community.

Finally, explain the company's distinctive competencies. The degree of detail included in the actual written plan depends on the intended audience. If the primary readers are inside the organization, a rather specific rendering of distinctive competencies should be included to give employees management's perception of the firm's key strengths. This may also be useful if lenders or other investors will be reading the plan. On the other hand, if suppliers, customers, or others outside the firm may have access to the plan, then a more conservative, less detailed presentation of the distinctive competencies should be given in order not to tip off competitors about proprietary information.

## The Mission Statement

Chapter 5 discussed in some detail the need for a definitive statement of the company's mission, as well as the components of the mission statement. The

Figure 8.1
## STRATEGIC PLAN FORMAT

I. **The Nature of the Business**
   A. Description of the business
   B. Industry characteristics
   C. Competition
   D. Location Description
   E. Distinctive Competencies

II. **Mission Statement**
   A. Product line or services provided
   B. Philosophy of the business

III. **Posture and Goals**
   A. Strategic Posture
   B. Company Goals
      1. Horizon Goals
      2. Near-Term Goals

IV. **Unit-Level Goals and Strategies**
   A. Marketing
      1. Target market
      2. Product-line strategy
      3. Pricing strategy
      4. Distribution strategy
      5. Promotion strategy
      6. Service strategy
   B. Operations
      1. Location in distribution channel
      2. Make-or-buy decisions
      3. Lease/purchase of equipment
      4. Sourcing strategy
      5. Production methods
   C. Human Resources
      1. Employment strategy
      2. Promote from within versus hiring outside managers
      3. Wage/salary/benefit strategy
   D. Financial
      1. Debt/equity Strategy
      2. Capital sourcing strategy
      3. Growth/stability strategy
      4. Financial projections

V. **Target Goals and Target Action Plan**

actual written mission statement need be no more than one or two paragraphs, although some may be a bit longer. The mission statement must lay out the general direction of the company and describe the firm's product line or groups of product lines. It should also briefly discuss the owner's business philosophy. It should be specific enough to allow the reader to assess how the business operates and how its culture, tone, or climate appears to the public.

## Posture and Goals

This section lays out in more detail the direction in which the firm is headed. It also focuses on more specific goals, both for the business as a whole and for the units within the business.

### THE STRATEGIC POSTURE

The strategic posture that the business will pursue should be well explained, including the justification for the posture. Remember that the strategic posture is an overall, general plan or approach for running the firm in response to its external and internal condition. Chapter 5 discusses six specific strategic postures. The description of the posture must be detailed enough to make the precise nature of the posture clear.

### COMPANY GOALS

While the mission statement lets readers know where the business is headed and the strategic posture prescribes a general business approach for getting there, company goals enable the reader to see the specific achievements or results the owner expects the business to reach. Company goals covering both the horizon and near term should be included. The two time frames should be presented so that readers can clearly see the relationship between the near-term goals and the broader horizon goals.

As noted in Chapter 6, since horizon goals are oriented toward the overall planning horizon, these goals will be stated in broader terms. Near-term goals concentrate on the next business operating period and require greater precision, detail, and specificity.

Horizon and near-term goals are fundamental, critical elements in the written plan. Goal statements are one of the primary factors outside readers focus on in assessing the business, its scope of activities, and the plausibility of its intended direction. Additionally, near-term goals become the key benchmarks for monitoring and evaluating business operations. Their effects on internal direction and control, as well as on external perceptions of the business, are quite significant.

## Unit Goals and Strategies

Once company goals have been written into the plan, enumerate the unit-level goals and strategies for both horizon and near-term time frames. Unit goals are written in the same manner as company goals, except that they focus on issues relevant to a functional area. Of course, unit goals must mesh with and complement each other and relate and support the fulfillment of the broader company goals.

Once unit-level goals are written, add statements of unit strategies relevant to the achievement of these goals. Four areas of unit strategies have been stressed. These relate to marketing, operations, human resources, and financial issues. Although these are not necessarily an all-inclusive listing of concerns, they do represent the key unit areas of importance for most small businesses.

### MARKETING

At least six items should be identified as part of the marketing strategy. Address each separately in order to have a clear understanding of the firm's total marketing strategy. In general, these strategy decisions will be led or primarily determined by the unit goals.

The target market should identify, specifically, the primary customers of the business. As discussed in Chapter 2, note the demographic makeup of the target market, including age ranges, socioeconomic status, customer location if relevant, and any other distinguishing characteristics. It may be helpful to include target market A and target market B, where the A group includes those in the primary target market and the B group includes those in an important but secondary category. Profile 8.2 shows the target market discussion for Haberkorn Ace Hardware.

## PROFILE 8.2: HABERKORN ACE HARDWARE

The geographical area targeted by Haberkorn Ace Hardware is the area roughly bounded by Prospect Road on the east, Sheridan Road on the west, Northmoor Road on the north, and Forrest Hill Avenue on the south. This forms an approximately two-mile square centered on the store's location. Customers living outside this area will live closer to a competitor than they do to Haberkorn Ace Hardware. The customers inside the square can be counted on because of the convenience of the store. Those who live outside the area and still shop at Haberkorn will do so because of the perceived quality of Haberkorn Ace Hardware. Since quality is an important but not overriding variable in hardware store selection, those people are considered part of our secondary market. Customers who live in the northern and western edges of the target market are vulnerable because of the new discount home improvement stores that have arisen in the last five years. Customers who live more than three miles from the store are not considered part of our target market.

The demographic/psychographic characteristics of members of the target market are: a do-it-yourselfer; married; living in single-family housing; between 30 and 70 years old. Approximately three-fourths of the customers will be male. About 60 percent will pay by check, 30 percent will use a major credit card, and some preferred customers such as contractors will use store credit. Small purchases are almost always in cash. The income range within the target market varies, but generally the area has a family income of between $35,000 and $75,000 per year.

---

The product line strategy consists of a description of the general lines carried by the firm, including whether the products are considered top of the line, moderately priced, or economy priced. It should indicate the breadth and depth of the line and if special orders are accepted or encouraged. It should indicate whether the firm intends to increase its line over time, maintain the line, or phase out portions of the line.

The pricing strategy should follow the product strategy. Very simply, it should state whether the pricing strategy is to price higher than, competitive with, or lower than competitors. It may include more specific information, such as "Our pricing strategy is to consistently price 15 percent below the competition and to honor competitors' prices in those cases in which their prices are lower than ours."

The distribution strategy should have been determined as a result of earlier analysis. The task here is to write it down clearly, so that readers inside and outside the business can understand and evaluate it easily. Include the types of distribution used, the method of accessing those channels, the reasons those particular channels are used, and the impact the distribution system should have on sales.

Again, the reason for writing this on paper is not only to have it available for others to see, but also for the business owner to review at a later date. As a business grows, the most effective and efficient method of distribution may change. At one stage, the manufacturers' representative may be the most efficient method of distribution. But as the business grows, an in-house sales person plus an on-the-road commissioned sales force may be more effective and more efficient. In some situations, the opposite case can be made. Here, the company sales force introduces the product, and manufacturer's representatives take over once the product becomes established and well known in the industry.

The promotion strategy is certainly one of the key aspects of the overall marketing strategy. Chapter 7 suggested the importance of determining an overall promotion strategy, budgeting for it correctly, and staying with that strategy. It is very important that the selected strategy be defined as specifically as possible in order to serve as a control later on.

The promotional plan includes the total budgeted amount to be spent on advertising and other promotional activities; a month-by-month breakdown of the annual promotional budget; and a description of the media to be used, the frequency of advertising, whether (and which) advertising agencies will be used, the nature of the advertising, and the image to be conveyed.

It is important to write down the promotional strategy, because it encourages consistency. Each of the above factors should be laid out in as much detail as possible and then regularly reviewed. A haphazard promotion strategy can confuse customers and allow promotion resources to be used inefficiently. At the very least, the written strategy should eliminate spur-of-the-moment acquiescence to some aggressive ad salesperson who walks in the door.

The service strategy should be straightforward. It should be the basis for day-to-day service policies. Although specific policy issues such as price per hour or number of service representatives is not really a part of the strategy per se, issues such as degree of service performed, warranties, subcontracting, and whether to advertise service should be included.

**OPERATIONS STRATEGY**

Strategies relating to operations tend to be more stable than those relating to marketing simply because they deal with fixed assets rather than annual expenses. Far more care is involved in determining the initial strategy, and equal care is taken when changing the strategy. The operations strategy is much less frequently changed than are some of the others discussed throughout this book. However, it is still wise to write the operations strategy on paper for employees and other key people to read. Also, the strategies serve as the basis for developing cohesive policies to guide the day-to-day actions within the core part of the business.

For product-related firms, the location in the distribution channel and the make-or-buy decisions are key parts of the operations strategy and should be clearly delineated in the strategic planning document. Included here are whether the firm plans to be a full manufacturer, an assembler, a distributor, or some combination of the above. These decisions will typically also answer the make-or-buy questions, but more specifications should be included if the firm makes part of its components and purchases the rest outside.

In the Joy's Toys Company example in Profile 8.3, the operations strategy combines some longer-range strategies with some shorter-term ones. This is perfectly acceptable, since the entire strategy should be reviewed at least semiannually anyway. The strategy statement serves as a later check against whether the marketing department did cooperate successfully, whether the market research did show increased sales projections, and whether the building plan was, in fact, completed.

---

PROFILE 8.3: JOY'S TOYS COMPANY

*Production Strategy*

Joy's Toys Company's production strategy is to do all assembly work on their stuffed animals and produce all the clothes for all the models. Parts for the animals will be purchased from reputable suppliers only, thereby reducing the need for 100 percent inspection of purchased materials. Cloth for the skin will be purchased ready to cut. Stuffing will be purchased in the largest quantities that inventory space will allow, in order to take advantage of volume discounts. Hard pieces (eyes, noses, and buttons) will be standardized as much as possible throughout all models in order to reduce both ordering and inventory costs.

Attempts will be made to retain workers as long as possible, in order to reduce assembly defects. Cutting machines are scheduled to be replaced on a rotating basis beginning the last quarter of this year, with one machine replaced each of the next six quarters.

If market research indicates that sales of the newest models will continue to expand, new facilities for storage of finished inventory will be necessary by early 1997. Therefore, preliminary plans for the building should be developed by the end of the second quarter of 1996.

Cost reductions will be necessary throughout the next several quarters, especially on the older models. Discussions will be held with marketing personnel to encourage distributors to make larger orders in order to increase the size of production runs.

---

Make-or-buy decisions should be included in the operations strategy. Joy's Toys consciously decided to purchase most material from reputable suppliers rather than to manufacture the cloth, eyes, buttons, etc. This does not mean that the company should proceed in this manner forever. In later strategy reviews, a decision might be made to manufacture the eyes and buttons in-house. This would be a significant change in strategy, however, and that decision would be made only after careful study.

Leasing equipment rather than purchasing it is a decision in which individuals both inside and outside the business may have an interest. Those inside the organization may be interested because of the ramifications related to service, equipment replacement schedules, warranties, etc. Those outside the business may be interested because of the financial ramifications. Financiers may want to know the impact of leasing on both the cash flow of the company and the balance sheet and income statements. In other words, purchasing the equipment outright may require significant debt, but the equipment appears as an asset on the balance sheet. If the equipment is leased, the initial expenditure and debt are not as significant, but lease payments become a substantial expense.

Vendor strategies should be included. The primary issue is whether to have a single source or multiple sources for a given part. Having a single source suggests larger quantities, thereby allowing the possibility for quantity discounts. On the other hand, having multiple sources for each part is a lower-risk strategy, assuming all suppliers can meet quality standards.

A remaining aspect of the operations strategy is to list and discuss any production methods issues that are germane to the firm's strategy. Included here, for example, would be strategies for reducing defects, plans for adding a second shift, or any of a variety of cost/volume objectives. Strategies for training or development of production personnel may be included either here or under human resources strategies.

## HUMAN RESOURCES STRATEGY

There are a myriad of human resources policies within the personnel function—testing policies, interviewing policies, evaluation policies, and termination policies. But there are some human resources strategies that must be considered and included in the written strategic plan.

First is the employment strategy. Of particular importance are sources of managers and line workers and the method of hiring them. For example, it may be part of the strategy to hire only college graduates from accredited business schools. Some large firms hire liberal arts graduates, whom they then train in-house. Other firms hire only experienced workers, thus alleviating the need for all but orientation training once they are hired.

The second aspect of the human resources strategy is the promotion strategy. This may appear more a policy than a strategy, but it really does fit the definition of strategy, since it can determine the future effectiveness of the company's personnel. Indicate whether the firm typically promotes from within or hires managers from outside. A case can be made either way. The point is that the strategy should be communicated to interested people—most important, the employees.

A third strategic issue to be delineated is the compensation strategy. This, of course, must be kept relatively broad so as not to cause internal problems. But items such as a bonus plan, insurance benefits, company cars, and stock options should be included. If the company has a history of paying higher-than-competitive wages, this should be noted and periodically reviewed. Any other items in the wage and salary area that might make the company better than its competitors should also be included.

## FINANCIAL STRATEGY

Much of the financial strategy is included in more depth in a financial plan than it is in the strategic plan. However, it is important to include major factors of the financial strategy in the strategic plan both as a guide for future direction and as a control.

A major portion of the financial strategy deals with debt versus equity. In new businesses, the strategy may be the default strategy—whatever strategy is successful will be used. The most successful strategy may be the only strategy available.

Once a business has stabilized, it typically has more options. Some owners prefer to rely totally on internally generated funds, taking on little or no additional equity or debt financing. This may limit growth, of course, but it is a viable strategy. Others may rely primarily on debt financing. Still others may rely on additional equity financing or on a combination of debt and equity financing. As we've said many times throughout this chapter, the concern is not what is included in the strategy, but that the strategy be presented in written form so that it can be read and reviewed.

Strategies for capital sources should be listed, since these will change over time. Numerous sources are available including bank financing, venture capitalists, state and federal loans, and supplier financing. If the firm is to use a combination of these sources, a rough estimation of the relative proportion of each should be stated.

An additional item that should be included in the discussion of sources of capital is the rate of growth the firm will want to achieve. Will the firm use all available sources of financing to the maximum in order to achieve the highest possible growth, or will growth be a function of the amount of financing that can be obtained with minimum risk? The growth question must be answered early on in the strategic planning process, because it affects nearly all other areas of the business. Since the wisdom of a high-growth strategy will change over time, it should be included in the written plan for later review. Growth projections will also be covered in the mission and the postures sections.

Financial projections are one of the most important parts of the strategic plan and the most important part of a financial plan. Lenders or venture capitalists want to see monthly projections of income statements for one or two years, along with quarterly or annual projections for up to five years. In small businesses, particularly new ones, a cash flow projection is perhaps even more important than the income statement projection, simply because the owner of a small business is often strapped for cash and constantly needs to be aware of the relative cash inflows and outflows. It is not uncommon for a small business to be in serious trouble, even though it is making a profit, because the outflows of cash necessarily precede the inflows. This is especially true if the business deals in credit or does work for the government, which is often slow in paying for goods or services.

Similarly, the balance sheet should be completed for the year-end of each of the next several years.

## Target Goals and Target Action Plans

Although it is important to write down target goals and target action plans, they are so specific that they are typically presented in a separate document. Readers outside the company will find the detail of these areas unnecessary for their purposes. For the owner and employees, however, they offer daily guidance.

Details regarding target goals and target action plans were presented in Chapter 6 and are not repeated here. Remember, target goals and action plans are very short run. They therefore need to be flexible and adaptable.

## Sharing the Plan

Once the task of writing the strategic plan is complete, what should you do with it? It is of course important to communicate the plan to key people in the firm (although many of them were no doubt involved in developing the plan)—the debate arises around how widely to distribute the plan. If the work force is small and viewed as quite stable and loyal, it is a good idea to share part or all of the plan with everyone. The risk, however, is that an employee will take the information from the plan and either join a competitor or start a competing business. In some cases, excerpts from the plan—especially the goals section—may be given to employees and the more sensitive items shown only to top management.

The complete plan or portions of it may need to be shown to investors, suppliers, or key customers. It is probably a good idea not to show any sensitive information to any outside groups unless it is specifically required.

## Summary

Throughout this chapter, we have restated the importance of writing very specific items into the final strategic planning document. We have risked seeming redundant because it is crucial to end up with a document that is so detailed and clearly written that all interested parties can understand where the firm is headed and how they plan to get there. In addition, the written document serves as a control measure and an evaluative device at the end of the quarter, fiscal year, or other key time period.

## A Final Caveat

Our attempt throughout this book has been to provide as much information as possible to aid in the creation of a strategic plan for a small business. Small business owners are naturally reluctant to take the time necessary time to analyze the environment, assess the strengths and weaknesses of the firm, and develop a strategic plan based on the distinctive competencies the firm possesses. However, the effort should be highly rewarded, not only because of the strategies actually developed, but because the owner has taken the time to analyze the firm and its environment objectively. This objective analysis alone is worth the time and effort!

Additional benefits of having a written plan are that it encourages the commitment of the owner to a specific plan and it offers a mechanism for reviewing progress later. The plan becomes both a measure of success and a method of achieving success. The development and writing of a strategic plan won't guarantee success, but it is a giant stride in that direction.

## Discussion Questions

1. What items should appear in the section entitled Nature of the Business?
2. How often should the entire strategic plan be rewritten?

3. Are each of the items under the Unit Goals and Strategies section necessary for all firms? Which should always be included and which are optional?

4. What can be done to ensure that the plan is reviewed periodically?

5. How should the plan be shared?

# APPENDIX A

# Sample Strategic Plan

AUTHORS' NOTE: The following strategic plan is a compilation of the previous case notes for Gaston Ridge Home Health Care, Inc. Remember, not every section of the plan will be relevant for every business. Service businesses have different styles of plans than manufacturing businesses. Owners or consultants writing strategic plans should adapt the plan format to their particular needs.

## GASTON RIDGE HOME HEALTH CARE, INC. STRATEGIC PLAN

### I. THE NATURE OF THE BUSINESS

A. Description of the business
Gaston Ridge Home Health Care, Inc., owned and operated by four experienced registered nurses, began operations in 1993. The agency provides home health care services to patients in small communities and rural sections of an eight-county area of Southern Illinois. Most of the current clients are homebound by advanced age or disability.

B. Industry characteristics
Home care is the fastest-growing segment of health care. Because of the anticipated interaction of political issues, social and demographic changes, and technological advances, the home health care industry should incur significant growth over the next decade. Further, the home health care industry will remain in the growth stage of the product life cycle for some time. Much of this sustained growth is due to the fact

that the costs of traditional health care will continue to increase, prompting alternative considerations such as home care.

C. Competition

Gaston Ridge has 16 competitors that operate in at least one of the counties within its service area. However, some of these agencies have only a minor presence. Six major competitor agencies are key players in the area and pose the strongest competitive threat to Gaston Ridge. They are Illini Home Health Care (an affiliate of Illini Medical Center), Capital Center Hospital, Mid-Central Home Health Association, Pioneer Homecare, Cashing Home Health Care, and Senior Dimension Home Care. Both Illini and Capital possess strong services in physical and occupational therapy relative to the competition. However, these services are costly, so their prices are above average. Mid-Central provides meals but quality is perceived as low. No doubt because of their hospital affiliations, Illini and Capital possess strong physician and discharge planner referral bases relative to other competitors. No competitor possesses strong consumer familiarity.

D. Location Description

Gaston Ridge operates in an eight-county service area of Southern Illinois. It is located in Perryville, a small community centrally located in the eight-county region. Gaston Ridge is housed in a medical building. The site is used primarily for administrative purposes, although some consultation with families of patients and prospective patients is conducted at this location. The site is acceptable and its central location is critical, because employees need to travel to patients' homes.

E. Distinctive Competencies

The most important distinctive competency is the culture and image of Gaston Ridge. The personal service and attention to building caring relationships with patients and their families differentiates Gaston Ridge from its competitors. Gaston Ridge's considerate approach is valued by consumers and is a key part of Gaston Ridge's approach to its target market. In comparison to Illini Home Health Care and Capital Center, the two most formidable competitors, Gaston Ridge offers more moderate prices.

## II. MISSION STATEMENT

Gaston Ridge Home Health Care, Inc., provides a full range of quality home health care services to patients in smaller and rural areas of an eight-county licensed service area of Southern Illinois.

   A. Product line or services provided

      Although 15 services are provided, we focus primarily on services prescribed by physicians, such as injections, medications, applications of bandages, etc. To a lesser extent, we educate and train patients and offer occupational and physical therapy. Other services will be added as client demands and expectations arise.

   B. Philosophy of the business

      Gaston Ridge operates in a team-oriented manner, with open communication and group consensus guiding major decisions. All employees are encouraged to contribute ideas and suggestions. Gaston Ridge staff spend considerable time and energy building strong relationships with patients and patient families. We are extraordinarily sensitive to the unique needs of patients and their loved ones. Employees are encouraged to build rapport, confidence, and trust as they attend to their patients.

## III. POSTURE AND GOALS

   A. Strategic Posture

      Gaston Ridge's strategy is to focus on the needs of homebound patients in rural areas. Services are provided in 15 categories that duplicate many of those provided within a hospital setting. We do not compete in larger cities.

   B. Company Goals

   1. Horizon Goals

      a. Increase the patient base by 100 percent over the next three years.

      b. Increase awareness of Gaston Ridge and the services we offer over the next three years so that 90 percent of physicians and 75 percent of the customers in the target market are familiar with us.

2. Near-Term Goals

   a. Develop and implement a new promotional campaign to introduce Gaston Ridge personnel and services to all physicians in the service area within the next twelve months. This goal is segmented into target goals of reaching eight designated physicians every six weeks.

   b. Add two physical therapy assistants to the staff within the next year.

   c. Hire a physical therapist as soon as we are sure that the physical therapy client load will reach 35 visits a month.

   d. Provide a meal delivery service in Perryville within the next six months.

## IV. UNIT-LEVEL STRATEGIES

A. Marketing

   1. Target market
   Gaston Ridge serves an eight-county, 490-square-mile area of Southern Illinois. Over 60 percent of Gaston Ridge's market resides in rural areas, with most of the remainder living in small communities. The target market is primarily aged or disabled people who are homebound.

   2. Product line strategy
   Gaston Ridge Home Health Care, Inc. offers services in 15 areas: new diabetic teaching, venipuncture, intromuscular injections, intravenous therapy, medication teaching, hypertension management, diet instruction, home catheter insertion and maintenance, feeding tubes, postoperative care, wound care, hot/cold applications, physical therapy, occupational therapy, and speech therapy. Physical therapy, occupational therapy, and speech therapy services are contracted through outside sources.

   3. Pricing strategy
   Gaston Ridge's pricing structure is average relative to competitors in the service area.

   4. Promotion strategy
   Minimal advertising is currently done to increase awareness and obtain new patients because of the rural nature of the target market

and the lack of a single medium that covers the entire area cost effectively. The following actions comprise the promotion mix:

a. Monthly blood pressure and cholesterol screenings will be conducted in Perryville and the surrounding communities of Ellsworth, Corrington, Wood Ridge, and Brookside. These activities will be arranged through senior citizen centers and local churches. The screenings will be free of charge. Notices of the screenings will be public service advertisements in the local weekly newspapers and radio stations in the area.

b. Informational and goodwill advertising will be placed in the weekly newspapers on a monthly basis.

c. Frequent efforts will be made to inform and influence physicians and their nurses. Gaston Ridge will offer 45-minute breakfast or luncheon meetings with physicians and their nurses at the physician's office. These will be scheduled on Tuesdays and Thursdays, our slow days. These meetings will begin with a 15-minute formal presentation about our services followed by a question-and-answer period. At the conclusion, coffee mugs with the Gaston Ridge logo will be given to the physician and his or her staff. Personalized thank you notes will be sent the following week. New brochures and follow-up thank you notes for referrals will be sent every six months.

B. Operations and Human Resources

1. Rene Price, RN, is the administrator and president of Gaston Ridge. She is responsible for payroll, insurance, benefits, and scheduling. Jane Heske, RN, is the director of nursing services. Her responsibilities include Medicare filing, operating the computer, and billing. Michelle Lewis, RN, and Tami Skinner, RN, are case managers in charge of all patients. These four principals each draw a salary from the business.

2. Gaston Ridge employs one full-time health care aid and three part-time time health care aids. These women are paid an hourly wage competitive for the industry and area. Physical therapy, occupational therapy, and speech therapy are handled, as needed, on a contractual basis through outside sources. These therapists are also paid an hourly wage.

3. Currently, Gaston Ridge has standard technology and equipment consistent with most of its competitors. However, it does not possess, nor does it have ready access to, some of the newer equipment and machines such as mobile EKG and X-ray machines.

4. Clients are billed on an accounts receivable basis. The average accounts receivable collection period is three months after the date of billing.

C. Financial

Gaston Ridge has received strong community support in the Perryville area and has been able to obtain funds as needed. The county has provided a low-income loan of $17,000 at 5 percent interest. Further, Legion Bank, located in Perryville, has offered a $20,000 line of credit at 10 percent.

## V. TARGET GOALS AND TARGET ACTION PLAN

1. Design a new physician-focused promotional campaign by July 31.

2. Secure promotional materials and arrangements by August 31.

3. Begin initial promotional contacts by September 15.

4. Determine new job responsibilities for physical therapy assistants and home health aides by August 15.

5. Recruit and hire a full time additional home health aide and the first physical therapy assistant by September 30.

# APPENDIX B

# Managing the Consulting Process

CONSULTING WITH A small business can be an exciting and challenging experience, allowing consultants to put their knowledge of strategic planning to use in concrete situations. No longer merely an academic undertaking, strategic planning becomes a mechanism for helping real people deal with real small business issues. The twists and complexities encountered in this process are always somewhat novel. The frustrations are numerous. But the rewards derived from helping small business owners grasp and deal with their competitive situations are significant and far-reaching.

Recently, a Small Business Institute (SBI) student consulting team was approached by clients who requested a complete internal and competitive analysis, along with precise recommendations of what should be done to reverse a downward spiral in revenues. The students realized that the business owners, a middle-aged husband and wife, were nice people literally at their wit's end. One student noted, quite appropriately, "These clients are depending on us. They intend to do whatever we tell them. It's kind of scary to think we are going to play a key role in the fortunes of these people and their livelihood."

Certainly, all consulting interventions do not hold the same dramatic prospects these students faced. Yet, working with owners of new and ongoing small businesses poses unique demands and can be rather intimidating. At the same time, business owners must realize that consultants are only advisers. They do not dictate what the owner must do, and owners are under no legal pressure to accept what the consultants recommend. Each party to the consulting process should have realistic expectations both of the process and its possible results.

This appendix will briefly discuss the nature of consulting. We will then present a recommended four-phase consulting process.

## The Nature of Consulting

The consulting process obviously includes two parties. The first is the client. The client is typically seeking assistance for one of two reasons. The first is that the company is experiencing some type of problem. The business owner may or may not be aware of what the problem is but knows that something is wrong. The owner contacts a consultant to come in to the business, study it objectively, identify the problem, determine its causes, and recommend solutions.

The second reason for using a consultant is more opportunistic. In this case, the business may be doing well, but the owner is interested in pursuing a new opportunity. A consultant is brought in to analyze the feasibility of the new opportunity.

For example, a dentist has an excellent practice involving two offices, another dentist, and a number of hygienists. One of the offices is in a major department store in the city, while the other is in a nearby small town. Even though the practice is going well, the dentist is interested in expanding—especially into the growing senior citizen market. He calls in a consultant to identify ways to attract that market segment. During their early meetings, the dentist reveals his interest in the possibility of emphasizing dental implants for senior citizens and wonders how he might convince customers to take advantage of this service. Accepting this challenge, the consultant decides to use focus groups to gather the views of the prospective target market. The consultant assembles groups of eight to ten people. Their ages range from 55 to 70. The consultant facilitates group discussion and gains important ideas that help him formulate recommendations for the dentist.

### TYPES OF CONSULTANTS

Consulting is one of the fastest-growing industries today, and there are a number of different types of consultants. The first type is the large consulting firm such as Andersen Consulting, Hewitt Associates, or Coopers and Lybrand. These large firms often have specialties in addition to doing general consulting. Andersen, for example, specializes in information systems, while Hewitt specializes in employee benefits.

The second category is the small consulting firm, which may consist of only one or two individuals and a support staff. These firms, too, may be either specialists or generalists. Some firms, for example, specialize in business valuation. Others may primarily offer accounting services. Still others may be small market research firms.

A third type is the part-time consultant who has another job and does consulting on the side. Many business professors do consulting in their areas of specialty and are even encouraged to do so by their universities. Some part-time consultants work for large companies and do consulting after hours. For example, a person may work in the information systems area of a hospital and moonlight as an information systems consultant.

The fourth kind of consultant is the not-for-profit organization. These organizations, such as those underwritten by the Small Business Administration (SBA), provide free or low-cost consulting by staff, volunteers, or students. The Service Corps of Retired Executives (SCORE) is a group of retired volunteers who previously worked in business. Their minor expenses are covered by the Small Business Administration. Another SBA-funded group is the Small Business Development Center, which typically receives both state and federal funding in order to provide staff consultants to area businesses. A third SBA-funded consulting source are the Small Business Institute (SBI) program in approximately 500 colleges and universities. Begun in 1972, the programs use teams of senior or graduate business students to do in-depth analyses for small companies. The SBI team members gain extensive hands-on consulting experience while providing supervised consulting to hundreds of small companies each year. In addition to the SBA-sponsored consulting, many universities have a Center for Business Research that provides fee-based consulting. Other not-for-profit and trade associations also provide consulting either free or for a modest fee.

## The Phases of the Consulting Process

The four phases of consulting are the rapport-building phase, the problem-identification phase, the data-gathering phase, and the recommendations phase.

## Building Rapport

No matter how talented consultants may be, those talents are only recognized and appreciated by the client when a base level of rapport and trust is established. Some clients are by nature open and accepting people. Others are more guarded and uncertain. However, all clients must feel confidence in their consultants if they are to work with them to produce valued changes in the business. When a business owner engages a consultant, the owner is entrusting certain business revelations and outcomes. For most small business owners, who have a tendency to value independence and self sufficiency, this act of trust is not taken lightly or entered without serious deliberation. The consultant must act to build rapport, ensure confidence, and establish a working foundation of trust.

## CONFIDENTIALITY

Small business clients need assurance of confidentiality. The consultant must explain to the client that all information received about the business will be treated with strict and absolute confidence. If there are exceptions to this statement, those exceptions need to be delineated and explained at the time of engagement. For example, SBI teams will routinely have to share information with the faculty member directing their project. Further, the final summary report is submitted by the college or university to the SBA Regional Office. Consultants must present their claims of confidentiality in a serious and convincing manner if they are to win the acceptance of their clients. More important, it is the professional and moral responsibility of the consultant to abide by the terms of the confidence they have guaranteed.

## COMPETENCE

The underpinning of confidence and trust rests on competence. If clients feel that consultants are skilled and knowledgeable, they are more likely to reveal and share information and ideas. Consultants must provide information to the client that establishes that competence. Student teams sometimes have difficulty here, but may find that providing résumés showing classes completed and jobs held may add to their credibility.

## DEADLINES AND COMMITMENTS

Confidence and trust are built incrementally through seemingly small actions. A key initial factor here is the way deadlines and commitments are honored. If you tell the client you will have a summary of the initial meeting prepared by Tuesday, it must be delivered by Tuesday. If you agree that the entire team will meet with the client at 6:00 P.M. Friday, you'd all better be there. These small commitments are really the only way a client can judge whether you will treat more sensitive and important revelations with the appropriate scrutiny and diligence.

It is also important not to make commitments you cannot keep. Owners should recognize that consultants are busy and the owner's business is one of many responsibilities facing the consultants. Both the client and the consultants must be clear and up front about expectations and schedules.

While we refer to a confidence-building phase, confidence building is ongoing. Every contact and every interaction between client and consultant shape the perception of confidence.

## Defining the Problem

Early in the consulting relationship, business owners should be encouraged to define their problems or needs as carefully as possible. This step is quite important for two reasons. First, it forces owners to think through the factors and issues they are confronting. This may produce valuable input and information the consultant can use. Second, it often helps clients move beyond symptoms, pushing beneath the surface to reveal underlying causes of organizational problems. Of course, this presumes that the clients are aware of their needs, and that often is not the case. In fact, this issue of awareness becomes a key factor in moving toward problem definition.

### PROBLEM AWARENESS

Frequently small business clients are aware of their needs but simply do not have the expertise or time to address the area of concern on their own. For example, a client may be aware that current advertising efforts are woeful yet be so embroiled in day-to-day operations that there is simply no time to analyze and develop a well-orchestrated advertising plan. Or, perhaps even more typical, the client has wonderful technical expertise in the design and manufacture of the product line but virtually no understanding of or interest in the dynamics of the marketing function.

In these situations, the client understands the strategic necessity of getting help in developing an area of the business. Accordingly, the client has decided to entrust this area to the expertise of the consultant.

It is not unusual, however, as the consultant engages in the details of strategic analysis, to uncover concerns and needs that the client did not know about. Here, the consultant's first task is to educate the client. Generally, this means that a client must not only be told that an unrecognized need exists, but the client must be convinced that the need is real.

The best way to convince clients is to show them clear, documented evidence. Small business owners respond to the bottom line, and if they can be shown the bottom-line implications of dealing with a problem, the likelihood that they will go along with a solution is greatly enhanced. For example, showing a client that the firm's financial ratios vary dramatically from industry averages may encourage the owner to pay attention to what is causing the variance.

Care must be exercised at this stage. Some clients feel threatened because the consultant has uncovered new concerns. Often, their pride and egos are bruised. It is important for the consultants, therefore, to be firm but supportive. The consultants must convey a positive image that encourages the client to accept the issues and become part of the plan to remedy the concerns.

## STATEMENT OF WORK

At a point early in the consulting intervention, a clear statement of work should be developed by the consultants and presented to the client. While responsibility for drafting the statement of work rests with the consultant, the development of the statement cannot be a unilateral effort. The client must contribute to the development of the statement, and points of disagreement must be discussed and negotiated. Consultants must understand the client's business situation and relevant issues to such an extent that the statement responds meaningfully to the needs of the business.

In all likelihood, some problems will not be addressed. Rather, consultants may select particular areas in which immediate action is necessary. Or they may select areas that mesh best with their own background and experience. Or they may select areas in which it is clear that the owners do not have the time or expertise.

The statement of work becomes an agreement between the parties that outlines the nature and scope of the consulting that will be performed. This statement establishes and formalizes each party's expectations of the other. The statement should clearly indicate the type of work to be done. However, it will not and cannot, at this early juncture, prescribe many of the specifics and details that will no doubt occur during the consulting process. The statement should be rather broad, while still defining the topic of coverage. For example, if a client is seriously questioning the effectiveness of current advertising approaches, the statement may focus, broadly, around that issue. The consultants may indicate that "an evaluation of the current advertising strategy will be performed and appropriate changes will be recommended." While such a statement provides the consultants with considerable flexibility in terms of approaches and execution, the client clearly knows what outcomes to expect.

## Gathering and Analyzing Data

A common cliché in woodworking is, "measure twice, cut once." This is also good advice for consultants. Consultants who do a thorough job of gathering data and analyzing that data (measuring twice) will have a more successful relationship because their solutions (the cut) will be better.

### PREPARATION

There is no alternative to hard work and diligence. Consultants must be thoroughly prepared when they meet with clients. Realize that for most small business owners, their most precious and most limited resource is time. Nothing frustrates owners more and is more destructive to the client-consultant relationship than the client's perception that their time is being wasted.

Consultants must review documents and know as much as possible about clients before the initial meeting. Consultants should understand what they already know and what they must learn. They must coordinate their questions so that the client's time is used most efficiently. Consultants often study the industry in some depth as well. (Faculty members often require this of student teams.) Then when the initial meeting occurs, the consultant is knowledgeable about the industry and the firm's placement in it.

## LISTENING

When meeting with clients, it is critical to let them talk. Often, consultants—especially student teams—think they have to impress the client with their knowledge and background. While some of that is necessary to build client confidence, many consultants are reluctant to step back and let the clients express their views and impressions. Consultants must listen to what the client says and they must take notes so they have a record of points to ponder and evaluate after they leave. Asking questions about areas of confusion or areas where more focus needs to be exerted helps clarify both the problem and possible solutions. For example, if the client says she is having difficulty securing funds, probe for her impressions of why there are problems.

## CONTACT

One of the most common complaints clients have of consultants is that the consultants do not let them know what is being done and what progress is being made. It is critical for consultants to keep their clients well informed. Often, consultants are working hard analyzing data and searching for information and see no reason to contact the client. The client, unaware of all that is going on, sees the lack of contact as a lack of interest. Have regular informational updates with the client. The schedule and frequency of these is really a function of both the consultant's and the client's needs. The contact does not always have to be in person, but it must occur. Since credibility and trust are built over time, these contacts are the building blocks of the consultant/client relationship.

## SEARCH FOR PRACTICAL ANSWERS

This is one of the greatest challenges a consultant faces. Frequently, consultants search for ideal and optimal ways to address client concerns and needs, assuming that the business resources are unlimited. Unfortunately, small businesses rarely operate in an ideal or optimal world. This realization in no way suggests that the consulting analysis should proceed without careful scrutiny and rigor. However, a consultant must always be aware of the realities the client faces. These realities, such as depleted finances, tight cash flows, and short-run commitments to existing technology, may limit the possible solutions.

The ideal solution may do little to advance the small business in its strategic efforts. Shenson and Nicholas note that successful consultants suboptimize—they consciously realize that while an optimal solution may exist, it may be too costly to be reasonable and practical. Consultants must propose the best solutions possible given the constraints of time, money, and resources.

## Making the Recommendations

A successful consulting engagement culminates in recommendations being shared and understood. This does not presume that the owner and the consultant will always agree. Nor does it assume that clients will act on and implement all recommendations. Rather, the client must understand the complexity of the consultant's recommendations and the reasoning behind them. A client who refuses to hear the final presentation or a consultant who simply mails the final report to the client is guilty of a breach of faith in the process.

### FINAL WRITTEN REPORT

After conducting all analyses and determining the business recommendations, consultants must formalize their conclusions and rationale in a written document to be presented to the client. Prescribing the exact form and content of this document is difficult—it's largely a function of the nature and scope of the project. In the case of Small Business Institute projects, the final SBI report format may be prescribed by either the supervising faculty member or the Small Business Administration. Yet, certain themes should be considered and included in the written report. These are outlined in Figure C.1, p. 216.

The report must be written to the client and written for the client. Thus, the tone of the report should take the client's background and level of comprehension into consideration. If the client is likely to be unfamiliar with specific jargon and terminology, avoid those phrases even though they may be accurate and technically correct. In some cases, reasoning and rationale for certain conclusions may require a detailed explanation. In all cases, present the logical development of the consultant's case clearly and succinctly.

The written report should begin with an executive summary. This summary should be only one or two pages long. It provides the client with a snapshot of the conclusions reached and recommendations offered. Detail and rationale are not possible here. The executive summary captures the client's interest and provides the impetus for digging into the heart of the study.

---

Figure C.1

**OUTLINE OF THE FINAL WRITTEN REPORT**

1. Executive Summary

2. Purpose of the Consulting Project

3. Methods and Procedures

4. Findings and Recommendations

5. Implementation

6. Appendices

7. Bibliography

---

After the executive summary, the purpose of the consulting project should be detailed. This is a refinement of the statement of work that was developed early in the consulting relationship, and notes the areas covered in the report and the basic expectations that the report seeks to meet. This section may also note any constraints that limited the consultant in executing the statement of work.

Next, the report should indicate the methods and procedures used to gather data and structure the conclusions and recommendations. This section may be detailed, but should not ramble. The intent is to demonstrate to the client the thorough and complete nature of the processes used to reach final decisions. Beyond that fundamental perspective, most clients do not care about the details and nuances of the procedures, and these should not take up extensive portions of the report. If particular methodologies need to be detailed, such as the procedures used to do original market or consumer research, these should be mentioned in the methods section and explained in more detail in appendixes. This allows those who are interested to examine the methods without frustrating the typical reader or draining the focus from the action items of the report.

The main portion of the report presents the findings and recommendations. Both conclusions and rationales must be carefully and fully developed.

As noted earlier, small business owners tend to be bottom-line people. Therefore, arguments that demonstrate financial or competitive advantages are particularly effective.

A final implementation section should discuss how recommendations can be implemented. Again, the practical nature of small business owners suggests that they appreciate ideas and thoughts on how recommendations can be effectively put into action.

Appendixes that provide more specific explanations of methods, offer supporting evidence and documentation, and present graphs and exhibits should come at the end of the report. These are often interesting additions that augment and support the narrative portions of the report. A bibliography should be included if appropriate.

Throughout the writing process, every effort should be made to be direct and succinct. The goal is not award-winning literature: The purpose is to explain findings and help guide the client to necessary action.

## ORAL PRESENTATION

The consultant should meet with the client and summarize the written report orally. The consultant should be open to questions from the client. This presentation is a chance to communicate the importance of the recommendations and the impact they can carry for the business. Don't just read the written report—that's a waste of time. Present highlights. It's helpful if the client has had a chance to review the written report.

The oral presentation is also an opportunity for the consultants and the client to discuss ideas not included in the report. Ideas that the client recently developed should be discussed. Possible problems with implementation should be noted. Potential developments in the industry might be discussed.

Finally, always leave the door open for additional meetings and additional consulting. Repeat business is easier to get than new business. A client who has been happy with a consultant often uses one again. Since the consulting process began with building rapport, it should end in a way that allows the rapport to continue.

# Reference

Howard Shenson and Ted Nicholas. *The Complete Guide to Consulting Success.* Chicago: Dearborn Financial Publishing, 1993, p. 74.

# GLOSSARY

ACCOUNTS RECEIVABLE: Sales or revenues extended to customers on credit that has not yet been collected.

ACID TEST RATIO: A liquidity ratio that measures a firm's ability to pay its short-term bills; measured by subtracting inventory from current assets and dividing the result by current liabilities.

ACTIVITY RATIOS: Ratios that indicate the movement of items through the business. These include the inventory turnover ratio and the accounts receivable turnover.

ASSETS: Things a company owns. These include current assets such as cash, fixed assets such as equipment, and intangible assets such as patents.

AVERAGE COLLECTION RATIO: The average amount of days required to collect accounts receivable; calculated as the accounts receivable turnover divided into 365 days.

BALANCE SHEET: The financial statement that describes the condition of the business. Consists of assets, liabilities, and equity.

CULTURE: The tone or climate of a firm. The organizational or corporate culture in a new or small firm is strongly affected by the firm's owner. It, in turn, affects how the firm will address the market in which it competes.

BUSINESS PLANS: Either of two major types of plans for a business. The strategic plan focuses on the strategies for the business. The financial plan focuses on the acquisition and use of funds and is used primarily for acquiring external financing.

CASH FLOW: The movement of cash into and out of the business. For small and new businesses, this is often more important than net income.

COMPANY GOALS: Overall goals for a firm. These may be either horizon goals or near-term goals.

COMPETITIVE WEAKNESS: A weakness in a firm that makes it especially vulnerable to moves of competitors. The opposite of a distinctive competency.

COMPETITIVE OPPORTUNITY: A situation in the firm's environment that can be exploited if appropriate firm capabilities exist.

COST CONTAINMENT: Actions taken to reduce or limit costs of operations. This can be very important in a highly competitive situation.

CURRENT RATIO: The measure of a firm's ability to pay its bills; calculated as current assets divided by current liabilities.

DEBT TO ASSETS RATIO: A liquidity ratio indicating the degree to which assets are funded by debt; measured as total debt divided by total assets.

DEBT TO EQUITY RATIO: A liquidity ratio indicating the percentage of total funding of the business provided by debt; measured by dividing total debt by total equity.

DEMOGRAPHIC CHANGES: Changes in the make-up of society, particularly regarding the number in particular age brackets, education levels, or income groups.

DISTINCTIVE COMPETENCY: A particular strength a company has that not only is exceptionally strong but is significantly better than that of competitors.

DIVERSIFICATION POSTURE: A firm's strategic posture based on an intention to expand into completely different product markets.

ENVIRONMENTAL ANALYSIS: The analysis of a firm's external environment, including economic, social, technological, political, industry, and competitive factors.

ETOP (Environmental Threats and Oopportunities Profile): A process for identifying both opportunities and threats by comparing competitors and other environmental situations on a "strong threat" to "strong opportunity" continuum.

EQUITY: The amount of ownership one has in a business. Also, the residual when total liabilities are subtracted from total assets.

EQUITY FUNDING: External funding provided in the form of ownership as opposed to debt. It may include shares of stock sold to the public or a percentage of ownership held by partners.

FACILITIES: Fixed assets usually consisting of plant and equipment, regardless of whether they are owned or leased.

FINANCIAL RATIOS: One of the primary means of assessing the financial performance of a firm. The ratios compare two or more items from the firm's balance sheet, cash flow statement, or income statement.

FIRM ANALYSIS: See Internal analysis.

GOAL: A stated objective for the firm; usually expressed in terms of dollars of sales, return on investment, market share, or other financial measure. May be either long term (horizon) or near term, and may be for the company or one of its units. To be differentiated from strategies, which are actions taken in order to achieve a goal.

GROSS PROFIT MARGIN: Gross profit (revenues less cost of goods sold) divided by sales.

HIGH (LOW) MARGINS: A pricing strategy in which the unit price is high (or low) in comparison with the unit cost.

HIGH (LOW) VOLUME: Typically the result of a low-(or high-)margin pricing strategy. The volume times the margin gives gross profit.

IMMEDIATE (TASK) ENVIRONMENT: The part of a firm's environment that directly affects it and that the firm's strategy may affect. This includes the firm's customers, competitors, suppliers, and the community in which it operates.

INCOME STATEMENT: The financial statement that presents details of a firm's revenues, expenses, and profit or loss. May be calculated on a monthly, quarterly, or annual basis.

INITIAL PUBLIC OFFERING: The first offering of a firm's stock to the general public. The process is very expensive, but it may bring in substantial capital for the firm and its owners.

INTERNAL ANALYSIS: The steps taken to analyze a firm's strengths and weaknesses. The analysis should include all aspects of a firm, including its human resources, financial resources, marketing procedures, products, and operations. It is useful to do this in comparison to competitors if possible.

INVENTORY TURNOVER: An indicator of the speed with which inventory is moving through the firm; measured by dividing cost of goods sold by average inventory.

IPO: Initial public offering

JUST-IN-TIME INVENTORY: An inventory strategy in which components arrive at the company immediately before they are needed rather than being stockpiled.

LEVERAGE RATIOS: Ratios that measure the degree to which a firm is financed through debt rather than equity. These include the debt to asset ratio and the debt to equity ratio.

LIABILITIES: The total owed by the firm's owners. The firm's debt; includes current liabilities and long-term liabilities.

LIQUIDITY RATIOS: Ratios that measure a firm's ability to pay its bills. These include the current ratio and quick (acid test) ratio.

LOSS LEADERS: Products that are purposely priced below cost in order to attract customers into the store.

MACROENVIRONMENT: The portion of a firm's environment beyond its capability to affect. This includes economic, political, technological, and social factors within the environment. To be differentiated from immediate or task environment.

MANAGEMENT PHILOSOPHY: The basic philosophy management uses in operating the business. A key part of the firm's mission statement.

MARKET DEVELOPMENT: A strategic posture in which the firm attempts to expand the market to which it sells its products or services.

MARKET NICHE: The specific portion of an industry in which a firm competes. Also, a portion of the industry market ignored by competitors.

MARKET SHARE: The percentage of the total industry sales held by a single firm.

MISSION STATEMENT: A firm's overall guiding statement of purpose. A broad statement including the basic description of a firm, its nature, and its philosophy.

OPERATIONAL RESOURCES: Those resources that are directly related to producing a firm's products or services.

PLANNING HORIZON: The length of time into the future that a firm should consider. The horizon varies by type of firm and industry.

PRICE ELASTICITY: The sensitivity of a product's volume to changes in price. Must be considered in making pricing-strategy decisions.

PROACTIVE MANAGEMENT: Management that carefully considers the firm's current and future environment and makes plans to take advantage of developing changes rather than reacting to those changes only once they occur.

PRODUCT LIFE CYCLE: The variation in the sales of a product as it moves from introduction to growth to stability to decline.

PRODUCT LINE: The entire offering of a firm's products with broadly similar characteristics. Many small manufacturing businesses offer only a single product line but may have a number of similar products in the line.

PROFITABILITY RATIOS: Ratios that measure a firm's degree of profitability in comparison with sales, assets, or investment. These include return on sales, return on investment, and return on assets.

PRODUCT DEVELOPMENT POSTURE: The strategic posture in which a firm develops new variations or improvements of existing products.

PRODUCT INNOVATION POSTURE: The strategic posture in which a firm develops significantly new and different products or services.

PRODUCT MIX: The total offering of a firm's products. It may consist of a number of product lines.

QUICK RATIO: See acid test ratio.

REACTIVE MANAGEMENT: Management that does not plan ahead and, instead, reacts only to immediate changes in its environment.

REPOSITION: A change in how a firm's product is compared with competing products. The positioning of a product affects how it will be marketed.

RETURN ON . . .: A profitability ratio in which a firm's net income is divided by one of three variables—assets, income, or investment.

SELLING STRATEGY: The particular strategy used to sell a product to a customer. The strategy used will vary depending on the type of product and the industry.

STOCK OUT: A term describing what happens when a firm is able to sell more of its product(s) than it can produce or buy. The result is often a disappointed customer.

STRATEGIC FIT: The degree to which a firm's strategy meshes with its basic mission and management philosophy. This is particularly important when considering acquiring another firm or introducing a new product.

STRATEGIC POSTURE: The broad strategy adopted by a firm. There are several different strategic postures that new and small firms may take.

STRATEGIC REACTION TIME: The length of time between an environmental change and a firm's change in strategies to take advantage of it.

SUSTAINABLE COMPETENCY: A distinctive competency that can be continued over time. This usually requires either patents, unique designs, or specific skills that cannot be duplicated by competitors.

TARGET ACTION PLANS: Very specific short-run actions to achieve unit or company goals.

TARGET MARKET: The group of customers most likely to buy the firm's products. This is the group on which the firm should focus most of its marketing resources.

TOTAL ASSET TURNOVER: An activity ratio that measures the extent to which assets are used in the production of goods; measured by dividing sales by total assets.

TRADE AREA: The geographical area in which most of the firm's customers reside. This may be a few blocks for a grocery store, an entire city for a specialty store, or an entire country or the world for a major manufacturer.

UNIT GOALS: The goals of the individual units within the firm. These may consist of marketing goals, human resources goals, operations goals, or financial goals, and they may be horizon, near term, or target goals.

UNIT STRATEGIES: The strategies developed by units within the firm to achieve unit goals and contribute to the overall company strategies and goals.

VENTURE CAPITALISTS: Financing organizations that specialize in high-risk, high-return ventures. Venture capitalists will typically insist on significant ownership of the firm in exchange for providing equity capital.

# RESOURCES

**Upstart Publishing Company, Inc.** These publications on proven management techniques for small businesses are available from Upstart Publishing Company, Inc., 12 Portland St., Dover, NH 03820. For a free current catalog, call (800) 235-8866 outside New Hampshire, or (603) 749-5071 in state.

*The Business Planning Guide*, 6th edition, 1992, David H. Bangs, Jr. and Upstart Publishing Company, Inc. A manual that helps you write a business plan and financing proposal tailored to your business, your goals, and your resources. Includes worksheets and checklists. (Softcover, 208 pp., $19.95)

*The Market Planning Guide*, 4th edition, 1995, David H. Bangs, Jr. and Upstart Publishing Company, Inc. A manual to help small-business owners put together a goal-oriented, resource-based marketing plan with action steps, benchmarks and time lines. Includes worksheets and checklists to make implementation and review easier. (Softcover, 180 pp., $19.95)

*The Cash Flow Control Guide*, 1990, David H. Bangs, Jr. and Upstart Publishing Company, Inc. A manual to help small-business owners solve their number-one financial problem. Includes worksheets and checklists. (Softcover, 88 pp., $14.95)

*The Personnel Planning Guide*, 1988, David H. Bangs, Jr. and Upstart Publishing Company, Inc. A 176-page manual outlining practical, proven personnel-management techniques, including hiring, managing, evaluating, and compensating personnel. Includes worksheets and checklists. (Softcover, 176 pp., $19.95)

*The Start Up Guide: A One-Year Plan for Entrepreneurs*, 2nd edition, 1994, David H. Bangs, Jr. and Upstart Publishing Company, Inc. This book utilizes the same step-by-step, no-jargon method as The Business Planning Guide to help even those with no business training through the process of beginning a successful business. (Softcover, 176 pp., $19.95)

***Managing By the Numbers: Financial Essentials for the Growing Business***, 1992, David H. Bangs, Jr. and Upstart Publishing Company, Inc. Straightforward techniques for getting the maximum return with a minimum of detail in your business's financial management. (Softcover, 160 pp., $19.95)

***Building Wealth***, 1992, David H. Bangs, Jr. and the editors of Common Sense. A collection of tested techniques designed to help you plan your personal finances and how to plan your business finances to benefit you, your family and employees. (Softcover, 168 pp., $19.95)

***Buy the Right Business—At the Right Price***, 1990, Brian Knight and the Associates of Country Business, Inc. Many people who would like to be in business for themselves think strictly of starting a business. In some cases, buying a going concern may be preferable—and just as affordable. (Softcover, 152 pp., $18.95)

***Borrowing for Your Business***, 1991, George M. Dawson. This is a book for borrowers and about lenders. Includes detailed guidelines on how to select a bank and a banker, how to answer the lender's seven most important questions, how your banker looks at a loan, and how to get a loan renewed. (Hardcover, 160 pp., $19.95)

***Can This Partnership Be Saved?***, 1992, D. Peter Wylie and Dr. Mardy Grothe. The authors offer solutions and hope for problems between key people in business. (Softcover, 272 pp., $19.95)

***Cases in Small Business Management***, 1994, John Edward de Young. A compilation of intriguing and useful case studies in typical small business problems. (Softcover, 258 pp., $24.95)

***The Complete Guide to Selling Your Business***, 1992, Paul Sperry and Beatrice Mitchell. A step-by-step guide through the entire process, from how to determine when the time is right to sell to negotiating the final terms. (Hardcover, 160 pp., $21.95)

***Creating Customers***, 1992, David H. Bangs, Jr. and the editors of Common Sense. A book for business owners and managers who want a step-by-step approach to selling and promoting. Techniques include inexpensive market research, pricing your goods and services, and writing a usable marketing plan. (Softcover, 176 pp., $19.95)

*The Entrepreneur's Guide to Going Public*, 1994, James B. Arkebauer with Ron Schultz. A comprehensive and useful book on a subject that is the ultimate dream of most entrepreneurs—making an initial public offering (IPO). (Softcover, 368 pp., $19.95)

*Export Profits*, 1992, Jack S. Wolf. This book shows how to find the right foreign markets for your product, cut through the red tape, minimize currency risks, and find the experts who can help. (Softcover, 304 pp., $19.95)

*Financial Troubleshooting*, 1992, David H. Bangs, Jr. and the editors of Common Sense. This book helps the owner/manager use basic diagnostic methods to monitor the health of the business and solve problems before damage occurs. (Softcover, 192 pp., $19.95)

*Financial Essentials for Small Business Success*, 1994, Joseph Tabet and Jeffrey Slater. Designed to show readers where to get the information they need and how planning and recordkeeping will enhance the health of any small business. (Softcover, 272 pp., $19.95)

*Keeping the Books*, 1993, Linda Pinson and Jerry Jinnett. Basic business recordkeeping both explained and illustrated. Designed to give you a clear understanding of small business accounting by taking you step-by-step through general records, development of financial statements, tax reporting, scheduling, and financial statement analysis. (Softcover, 208 pp., $19.95)

*The Language of Small Business*, 1994, Carl O. Trautmann. A clear, concise dictionary of small business terms for students and small business owners. (Softcover, 416 pp., $19.95)

*Launching New Ventures: An Entrepreneurial Approach*, 1995, Kathleen R. Allen. Emphasizes growth-oriented entrepreneurial ventures and focuses on venture creation in the global economy. Each chapter contains learning objectives, a "New Venture Checklist" for launching new businesses, and real-world case studies. An instructor's manual is available. (Softcover, 350 pp., $32.95)

***The Small Business Computer Book***, 1993, Robert Moskowitz. This book does not recommend particular systems, but rather provides readers with a way to think about these choices and make the right decisions for their businesses. (Softcover, 190 pp., $19.95)

***Steps to Small Business Start-Up***, 1993, Linda Pinson and Jerry Jinnett. A step-by-step guide for starting and succeeding with a small or home-based business. Takes you through the mechanics of business start-up and gives an overview of information on such topics as copyrights, trademarks, legal structures, recordkeeping, and marketing. (Softcover, 256 pp., $19.95)

***Target Marketing for the Small Business***, 1993, Linda Pinson and Jerry Jinnett. A comprehensive guide to marketing your business. This book not only shows you how to reach your customers, it also gives you a wealth of information on how to research that market through the use of library resources, questionnaires, demographics, etc. (Softcover, 176 pp., $19.95)

***On Your Own: A Woman's Guide to Starting Your Own Business***, 2nd edition, 1993, Laurie Zuckerman. On Your Own is for women who want hands-on, practical information about starting and running their own business. It deals honestly with issues like finding time for your business when you're also the primary care provider, societal biases against women, and credit discrimination. (Softcover, 320 pp., $19.95)

***Problem Employees***, 1991, Dr. Peter Wylie and Dr. Mardy Grothe. Provides managers and supervisors with a simple, practical and straightforward approach to help all employees, especially problem employees, significantly improve their work performance. (Softcover, 272 pp., $22.95)

***Problems and Solutions in Small Business Management***, 1994, the editors of Forum, the journal of the Association of Small Business Development Centers. A collection of case studies selected from the pages of Forum magazine. (Softcover, 200 pp., $21.95)

***The Restaurant Planning Guide***, 1992, Peter Rainsford and David H. Bangs, Jr. This book takes the practical techniques of The Business Planning Guide and combines it with the expertise of Peter Rainsford, a restaurateur and a professor at the Cornell School of Hotel Administration. Topics include: establishing menu prices, staffing and scheduling, controlling costs and niche marketing. (Softcover, 176 pp., $19.95)

***Successful Retailing***, 2nd edition, 1993, Paula Wardell. Provides hands-on help for those who want to start or expand their retail business. Sections include: strategic planning, marketing and market research, and inventory control. (Softcover, 176 pp., $19.95)

# INDEX

## A

Accounts receivable turnover ratios, 77-79, 206, 219
Acid test ratios, 76, 219
Action phase, 17-18, 119
Action plan. *See* Target action plan
Action tasks, 155-157
Activity ratios, 76-79, 219
Adaptability, 109
Advertising, 5, 87-88; and promotion, 126, 188, 192, 195, 204-205
Advisory board, 11
*Almanac of Business and Industrial Financial Ratios*, 67
Ambiance, community, 44
Analysis: competitive profile, 4-5, 41-43, 58, 202, 207; environmental, 15-17, 23-58, 220; financial, 66-82; internal, 59-101, 207, 221. *See also* Internal analysis; internal firm, 15-17; internal profile, 65, 101; vertical, 71, 72
Andersen Consulting, 208
*Annual Statement Studies*, 67
Antiques Unlimited, 171-172
Area, trade, 225
Aspirations, personal, 136
Asset turnover ratios, 77
Assets, firm's, 219
Associations. *See* Trade associations
Athletic footwear industry, 34-35
Atmosphere Processing, Inc., 11

## B

Balance sheet, 197, 219; percentages, comparative, 69, 71, 72
Bank financing, 179. *See also* Capital; Debt strategies; Financing
Bankruptcy: factors causing, 63; filing for, 4
Bard Optical, 128
Barriers, 154-157
Ben & Jerry's Ice Cream, 111, 127
Blazing Graphics, 126
Blue Ribbon Car Wash, 131
Board of directors, 11
Business: description of, 201; nature of, 187, 188, 201-202; plan, 219. *See also* Financial plan; Strategic plan; small. *See* Small business
Business opportunities, relevant, 103-104
Business publications, general interest, 50
Business Technology Center, Maple City, 174
*Business Week*, 29, 50

## C

Capital: ability to raise, 82; cost of, 39; sources of, 38-39, 188, 196; venture, 39
Cascade Properties, 127
Cash flow: analyzing, 72-74, 219; position, 82; projections, 196-197;

statement, 73
Castille Motors, 107-108
Census data, 50
Chambers of Commerce, 29, 50
Change-oriented process, planning as, 8-12
Collection period, average, 78-79, 219
Columbia Sportswear, 111-112
Commitments, 210-211
Community ambiance, 44
Company mission. *See* Mission statement
Comparative balance sheet, 69; percentages, 71, 72
Comparative financial summaries, 68
Comparative income statements, 70
Comparative percentage summaries, 68-72
Compensation, 92-93, 178; strategy, 195-196
Competence, 210
Competency: distinctive. *See* Distinctive competency; sustainable. *See* Sustainable competency
Competition, 40-43, 57. *See also* Competitive; Distinctive competency; Market; Target market; dynamics of, 36-37; reducing threat of potential, 31
Competitive: advantage, 128-130; edge of small business, 24; position, periodic reassessment of, 9-10; profile analysis, 4-5, 41-43, 58, 202, 207; strength, 136; threats, 40; weakness, 15-17, 103-119, 220
Competitors, key, 41

Confidentiality, 210
Consultants, types of, 208-209
Consulting: nature of, 207-217; process, phases of, 209-217
Consumer orientation, 109
Cooper's Cabinetry, 134, 137-139
Coopers and Lybrand, 208
Copycat manufacturing, 112
Cost containment, 220
County and City Data Book, 50
Courtland Clubs, 104-106, 107
Crisis management, 10-11
Crystal Rug Cleaners, 132-133, 135
Culture, organizational, 219
Current ratios, 75-76, 220
Customer. *See also* Market; Target market
Customer, meeting needs of, 9-12

**D**

Dairy Queen, 168
Data gathering and analyzing, 213-215
Deadlines, 158, 210-211
Debt: strategies, 179, 196; to assets ratio, 79, 220; to equity ratio, 80, 196
Delegating, 11
Demography, 191; changes in, 30-31, 54, 220
Desktop Channel, 130
Detail, in written plan, 186, 198
Developmental growth posture, 133
Discussion questions, 18, 51, 94-95, 115, 140-141, 160, 182, 198-199
Distinctive competency, 15-17, 19, 103-119, 220; and strategic plan-

ning, 112-114, 202; identifying and developing, 107-110, 113-114
Distribution, 89, 194; channel, position in, 123; strategy, 188, 192
Diversification posture, 134-135, 220
Dun and Bradstreet, 67

E

Economic: mission, 127; projections, 31-32
Economy, changes in, 55
Edwards Service Station, 40
Employees. *See also* Human resources: and goal-setting, 146; and mission statement, 122, 125; excellence in, 109-110; lack of expertise, 61-63; strategic plan and, 11; types of, 172
Employment strategy. *See* Human resources strategy
*Entrepreneur*, 50
Environmental: brainstorming, 46-50; opportunities, 103-104
Environmental analysis, 15-17, 23-58, 220; case study, 53-58; defined, 26-27; performing, 44-48; value of, 23-24
Environmental threats and opportunities profile (ETOP), 44-45, 47, 48, 220
Equipment, 100; strategy, 194-195, 206
Equity, 220; funding, 221
Evaluating financial resources, 66-82
Expansive growth posture, 131-133
External information, sources of, 48, 50

F

Facility strategy, 173-174, 221
Failure, reasons for, 178-179
Feedback, 158
Financial: analysis, 66-82; performance, overall, 82; plan, 12, 181. *See also* Financial strategy; Strategic plan; Target action plan; projections, 196-197; ratios, 74-82, 221. *See also* Ratios; resources, evaluating, 66-82, 99; strategy, 81-82, 166, 178-179, 184, 188, 196-197, 206; summaries, comparative, 68
Financing, 178-179, 196-197, 206. *See also* Capital; Debt strategies; other, 181
Finished inventory strategy, 176
Firm analysis. *See* Internal analysis
Flexibility, enhancing, 8, 109
Focused product posture, 128-130
Foresight, importance of for small business owners, 4
Formal direction, 10
Friends and family, 39
Functional-level goals and strategies, 19
Funding sources. *See* Capital; Debt strategies; Financing

G

Gaston Ridge Home Health Care, Inc.: case study of company goals, 161-163; case study of distinctive competencies, 117-116; case study of environmental analysis, 53-58; case study of internal analysis, 97-101; case study of mission and strategic posture, 143-144; case study of unit strategies, 183-184; sample strategic plan, 201-206

Goals: and strategies, relationship between, 166, 189; and writing mission statement, 189-190, 203; characteristics of, 147, 221; conflict among, 148-149; creating, 147-148; horizon. *See* Horizon goals; levels and types, 149-151; mutually exclusive, 148; near-term. *See* Near-term goals; prime, 123; priorities and, 148-149; segmentation process, 152-158; setting of, 17, 19, 112, 145-163; specific, 145-147; statement of, 146-147; target, 151-163. *See also* Target goals; time frames, 149-153

Government procurement programs, 5-6

Gross profit margin, 80-81, 221

Growth: developmental posture, 133; expansive, 131-133; rate, 32, 195; stability strategy, 188; stage, 138-139; uncontrolled, 124

## H

Haagen Dazs, 168
Haberkorn Ace Hardware, 41, 191
*Hardware Age*, 41
Hewitt Associates, 208
High (low) margins, 221
High (low) volume, 221
Hiring, 176-177. *See also* Employees; Human resources
Historical analysis, 46
Horizon goals, 151-163, 166, 203
Human resources. *See also* Employees: evaluating, 92-93, 98-99; strategy, 166, 176-178, 184, 188, 195-196, 205-206

## I

IBM, 112
Image: of business, 88-89, 109; product, 168
Immediate(task)environment, 27, 36-44, 57, 221
*Inc.*, 50
Income statements, comparative, 70, 221
Industry: environment, 27, 32-36; nature of, 32, 56, 201-202
*Industry Norms*, 67
Initial public offering (IPO), 221, 222
Innovation, product, 134, 223
Integrative goal model, 158-159
Interest rates, monitoring, 45
Internal analysis, 59-101, 207, 221. *See also* Internal firm analysis; elements of, 64-66; profile, 65, 101; value of, 60-63
Internal firm analysis, 15-17. *See also* Internal analysis
Internet, 29
Interviews, customer, 49
Intuitive planning, 8
Inventory: control, 90-91; finished strategy, 176; holding period, average, 78-79; turnover, 76-77, 222
Invincibility, attitude of, 50-51

## J

Jacobsen Office Products, 61-63, 64
Joy's Toy Company, 125-126, 193-195
Just-In-Time Inventory, 222

## K

Kangakab, 31
*Key Business Ratios*, 67
Key environmental concerns, 46
Knowledge of markets, 83-84
Kultur International Films, 83-84

## L

Labor relations, 92
Layout, store, 171, 172
Leegin Creative Leather Products, 129
Legal change, 29-30
Leverage ratios, 79, 222
Liabilities, 222
Life cycle, product, 32-36
Liquidity ratios, 74-75, 222
Loans. *See* Capital; Debt strategies; Financing
Location, 14, 84-86, 109, 173-174, 202; expansion of, 131-133
Long term planning, 13-14
Loss leaders, 222
Lunar Productions, Inc., 127

## M

Macro environment, 27-32, 53-54, 222
Make-or-Buy strategy, 175, 188, 194
Manager selection strategy, 176-177
Manufacturing strategy, 175

Margins, 170
Market: development, 222; knowledge of, 83-84; performance, 82-83; research, 49, 194; share, 40, 223
Marketing: plan, writing of, 190-193; postures. *See* Posture; resources, evaluating, 82-89, 97-98; strategy, 166, 167-172, 183-184, 188
Minnetonka, Inc., 25-26
Mission statement, 17-18, 19, 112, 187-189, 203, 223; Ben & Jerry's Ice Cream, 127; Blazing Graphics, 126; Cascade Properties, 127; Gaston Ridge Home Health Care, Inc., 203; Joy's Toy Company, 125-126; Lunar Productions, Inc., 127; parts of, 123-128; value of, 122
Mission, defining firm's, 121-144. *See also* Mission statement
MMO Music Group, 60-61
Morale, 92, 99
Motto, company, 125
Mutually exclusive goals, 148. *See also* Goals

## N

NAFTA, 29
National Retail Hardware Association, 41
Near-term goals, 151-163, 166, 204. *See also* Goals
Neiman-Marcus, 168
New Balance, 34-36
Niche: market, defined, 222; posture, 130-131; specialty, 30-31, 35, 104, 108-109

Non-profit consultants, 209

## O

Objectives, setting, 145-163. *See also* Goals
Operation Quick Strike, 35
Operational resources: defined, 223; evaluating, 89-91
Operations strategy, 166, 172-176, 188, 193, 205-206
Oral presentation, 217
Organizational structure and culture, 91, 99
Osborne Computer Corporation, 63
Outlet stores, 169-170

## P

Partnerships, 39
Peapod, Inc., 25
Percentage summaries, comparative, 68-72
Perception, public, 110
Performance index, 41-43
Personal: aspirations, 136; savings, 39
Personnel. *See* Employees; Human resources
Philosophy of business, 123-125, 203, 222. *See also* Mission; Mission statement
Plan: strategic. *See* Strategic plan; target action. *See* Target Action plan; who to share with, 197; writing the, 185-199
Planning horizon, 223; determining, 13-14
Political policy change, 29-30

Posture: developmental growth, 133; diversification, 134-135; expansive growth, 131-132; focused product, 128-130; niche, 130-131; product innovation, 134; single market, 128-130; strategic, 128-144, 166, 188, 189, 203
Price elasticity, 223
Pricing strategy, 88, 109-110, 169-170, 188, 191-192, 204
Proactive mode, 10, 24-26, 223
Product: development, 211, 223; image, 168; innovation, 134, 223; life cycles, 32-36, 223; line strategy, 86, 123, 188, 191, 203, 204, 223; line, evaluating, 86-87; line, increasing, 31; mission, 127; mix strategy, 170, 223; pricing. *See* Pricing; studying competitors, 49
Production: facilities, 89-90; methods strategy, 193-195
Profile 1.1: Atmosphere Processing, Inc., 12
Profile 2.1: Peapod, Inc., 25
Profile 2.2: Minnetonka, Inc., 26
Profile 2.3: New Balance, 34-36
Profile 2.4;8.2: Haberkorn Ace Hardware, 41, 191
Profile 3.1: MMO Music Group, 60-61
Profile 3.2: Jacobsen Office Products, 61-63, 64
Profile 3.3: Osborne Computer Corporation, 63
Profile 3.4: Kultur International Films, 83-84
Profile 4.1: Courtland Clubs, 104-106, 107

Profile 4.2: Son Won Karate Academy, 106, 107
Profile 4.3: Castille Motors, 107-108
Profile 4.4: Columbia Sportswear, 111-112
Profile 5.1: Leegin Creative Leather Products, 129
Profile 5.2: Desktop Channel, 130
Profile 5.3: Blue Ribbon Car Wash, 131
Profile 5.4: Crystal Rug Cleaners, 132-133, 135
Profile 7.1: Manufacturer's outlets, 169-170
Profile 7.2: Antiques Unlimited, 171-172
Profile 7.3: Business Technology Center, 174
Profile 7.4: Yarn and Hoop Shop, 177-178
Profile 8.1: Reder Electronics, 186
Profile 8.3: Joy's Toy Company, 125-126, 193-195
Profitability ratios, 80-81
Progress, assessing, 139-140
Promotion: from within, 126, 195; strategy, 188, 192, 195, 204-205

## Q

Quality, 91, 109
Quick ratios, 75-76

## R

Rabek Manufacturing, Inc. target action plan, 156
Rapport, client, 209-210
Ratios: accounts receivable turnover, 77-79, 219; acid test, 76, 219; activity, 76-79, 219; asset turnover, 77; average collection, 78-79, 219; current, 75-76; debt to asset, 79; debt to equity, 80; defined, 221; inventory turnover, 76-77; leverage, 79; liquidity, 74-75; profitability, 80-81, 223; quick, 75-76; return on total assets, 80-81
Reactive: management, 224; mode, 24
Real estate firms, 112
Recommendations, client, 215-217
Reder Electronics, 186
References, 18, 51-52, 95, 118, 144, 163, 217
Relevant business opportunities, 103-104, 110-111, 112
Reposition, 224
Reputation, 109
Resources operational, evaluation of, 89-91
Return on total assets ratios, 80-81, 224
Robert Morris Associates, 67
Ross Marketing Services, diversification in, 9-10

## S

Salary. *See* Compensation
*Sales and Marketing Management* magazine, 50
SBA. *See* Small Business Administration
Sears, 112
Service: of product, 87, 109; strategy, 170-171, 188, 192-193

Service Corps of Retired Executives (SCORE), 209
Services provided, 123, 202
Short-term planning, 14
Single market posture, 128-130
Small business: consulting for, 207-217; defined, 5-7; strategic planning in, 1-20
Small Business Administration (SBA), 5, 209; guaranteed loan program, 179
Small Business Development Centers (SBDC), 209
Small Business Institute (SBI): programs, 209; student consultants, 207
Small business magazines, 50. *See also* Trade publications
Social: causes, 111; change, 30-31, 54; mission, 127
Softsoap, 26
Son Won Karate Academy, 106, 107
Special competency. *See* Distinctive competency
Special-purpose planning, 12
Stabilization stage, 138
Standard and Poor's Industry Surveys, 41
Start-up stage, 137-138
Statement: mission. *See* Mission statement; of goals, 146-147; of work, 212-213
Statistical abstract of the United States, 50
Stock: market change, 29; out, 224; sale of, 39
Strategic plan: assessing progress, 139-140; format, 19, 188; sample of, 201-206; writing the, 185-199
Strategic planning: barriers to, 7-8; defined, 12-13; nature of, 1-20; process, 15-18
Strategic posture, 17, 19, 224; choosing, 135-139; defining firm's, 121-144; developing, 128-144; variables affecting, 136-137
Strategic reaction time, 14, 224
Strategy. *See* individual headings, e.g. Financial strategy; Marketing strategy
Strengths and weaknesses, internal analysis of, 64-66
Suppliers: access to, 90; analysis of, 37-38; selection of, 175-176, 194; strategies, 195
Supply and demand, 35-36
Survey of buying power, 41, 50
Sustainable competencies, 111-112, 224

T

Target: customers, 23; goals, 19, 151-163, 166, 188, 197, 206; markets, 23, 37, 83-84, 123, 167-168, 188, 204, 224. *See also* Market; Marketing
Target action plan, 19, 154-163, 166, 188, 197, 206, 224;
Rabek Manufacturing, Inc., 156
Tax law change, 29
Technological change, 28-29, 55, 100
Total asset turnover, 225
Trade: area, 225; association consulting, 209; association reports, 50;

credit, 39; publications, 29, 50, 67, 84
Trends, anticipating, 29-30
Troy, Leo, 67

## U

U.S. Census bureau, 41
Unemployment shifts, monitoring of, 45
Unit goals, 225
Unit strategies, 165-184, 188, 225; in writing plan, 190, 204-206

## V

Variety store, 45
Vendor. *See also* Suppliers: selection of, 175-176
Venture capital, 39, 225
Vertical analysis, 71, 72
Vision, 14-15, 125
Vision statement, Bard optical, 128

## W

Wage strategies, 178, 188
Wal-Mart, 168
*Wall Street Journal*, 29, 50
Waverly Custom Jewelers, 68-82
Woodworking business, 45
Work flow, 90
Writing strategic plan, 18, 185-199
Written report, final, 215-217

## Y

Yarn and Hoop Shop, 177-178